DATE DUE

DEMCO 38-296

Beyond the Rhetorical Presidency

NUMBER ONE:
Presidential Rhetoric Series
Martin J. Medhurst, General Editor

14

R BEYOND •THE Rhetorical PRESIDENCY

Edited by Martin J. Medhurst

Texas A&M University Press
College Station

Library of Congress Cataloging-in-Publication Data

Beyond the rhetorical presidency / edited by Martin J. Medhurst. — 1st ed.
    p.   cm. — (Presidential rhetoric series ; no. 1)
    Papers from a conference held in 1995 at Texas A&M University.
    Includes bibliographical references and index.
    ISBN 0-89096-710-5 (cloth)
    1. United States—Politics and government—1945–1989—Congresses. 2. United
States—Politics and government—1989– —Congresses. 3. Rhetoric—Political aspects—
United States—Congresses. 4. Presidents—United States—Language—Congresses.
    5. Communication in politics—United States—Congresses. I. Medhurst, Martin J.
II. Series.
E839.5.B53   1996
353.03'23—dc20

96-11017
CIP

To

Carroll C. Arnold

Teacher of the field

On the occasion of his 84th birthday

Contents

Acknowledgments

The chapters in this volume were first presented at the 1995 Texas A&M University conference on "The Future of the Rhetorical Presidency," held March 3–5, in College Station, Texas. The conference drew one hundred and thirty-five participants from thirty states and fifty-five institutions of higher learning. As the first of what has now become an annual event, the 1995 conference was marked by excitement, a good deal of scholarly discussion, and an interdisciplinary spirit of inquiry—qualities we strive to retain.

As with most new ventures, many hands had a part in making both the 1995 conference and this volume a reality. The conference planning committee is grateful for a grant from the Texas Committee for the Humanities and the National Endowment for the Humanities. We also extend our thanks to Dr. Woodrow Jones, Jr., dean of the College of Liberal Arts, and to his staff for their ongoing support of the Program in Presidential Rhetoric. The Center for Presidential Studies, under the direction of Dr. George C. Edwards III, and the Department of Speech Communication, under the leadership of Dr. Linda L. Putnam, were major contributors to the success of the conference. Without the assistance of the speech communication graduate students—all thirty of them—the level of logistical support provided to conference participants would not have been possible. To these individuals and groups, we express our sincere thanks.

The twelve scholars represented in this volume comprise only one part of the larger intellectual conversation that characterized the conference. We are especially grateful to those individuals who served as chairs or respondents on panels or who participated in the scholars' or editors' roundtables. Several scholars also participated as facilitators of the doctoral leadership seminars, an opportunity for graduate students to interact informally with leading scholars in presidential rhetoric. We extend special thanks to Dr. David Alsobrook, acting director of the George Bush Presidential Library Materials Project, for his provocative after-dinner talk on presidential libraries as resources for scholarly inquiry.

As this first volume goes to press, we are already planning the second conference, on presidential speech writing. With the continuing support of Texas A&M University Press, we anticipate an ongoing stream of research on various aspects of presidential rhetoric—a subject experienced by many, but understood and appreciated by all too few.

Leroy Dorsey
Martin J. Medhurst
Garth E. Pauley
Tarla Rai Peterson
Enrique D. Rigsby
Kurt Ritter

Introduction

A TALE OF TWO CONSTRUCTS:
The Rhetorical Presidency
Versus Presidential Rhetoric
Martin J. Medhurst

This book is about two constructs, one narrow and theory-dependent, the other broad and practice-dependent; one rooted in the discipline of political science, the other most at home in speech communication; one grounded normatively in the U.S. Constitution, the other grounded, if at all, in the constantly changing dynamics of human persuasion. At first glance these two constructs might seem to be close kin, if not mirror images of one another. But first impressions can be deceiving. The initial task of this essay, therefore, is to clarify the nature, scope, and presumptions of each of these constructs and to examine their actual or potential interrelationships. The second task is to reveal the strengths and weaknesses of the constructs and to speculate how each might benefit from the insights generated by the other. I refer to the constructs known as "the rhetorical presidency" and "presidential rhetoric."

At the most basic level these constructs point to two different objects of study: the presidency in one case and rhetoric in the other. Scholars of the presidency, many of whom find their academic homes in departments of political science or government, have a long intellectual tradition stretching back to Aristotle's *Politics*. Post–World War II scholarship on the U.S. presidency has witnessed an ever-increasing degree of sophistication, from the early work by Corwin, Rossiter, Neustadt, and others, to the more recent scholarship of Cronin, Mansfield, and Skowronek.[1] Scholars of rhetoric, many of whom find their academic homes in departments of speech or communication, also have a long intellectual tradition that reaches back to Aristotle, but to his *Rhetoric* rather than his *Politics*. Postwar rhetorical scholarship has also seen marked improvement, especially since the 1960s when Edwin Black led the charge against what he called neo-Aristotelianism. Presidential rhetoric as a specialized subfield emerged shortly thereafter, dating from the early 1970s.[2]

Scholars often engage in heated debates about when certain trends began, who is to be credited, and what consequences followed from the adoption or rejection of new ideas. But there is no debate about when the interdisciplinary interest in the intersection of the presidency and the practice of rhetoric commenced. "The Rise of the Rhetorical Presidency," written by James W. Ceaser, Glen E. Thurow, Jeffrey K. Tulis, and Joseph M. Bessette was the intellectual precursor to much of the recent interest in presidential rhetoric.[3]

In that seminal essay, Ceaser and his coauthors argued that the rise of the rhetorical presidency constituted "a major institutional development in this century." Their central claim was that "prior to this century, popular leadership through rhetoric was suspect. Presidents rarely spoke directly to the people, preferring communications between the branches of the government." The resort to popular leadership through the medium of rhetorical discourse, primarily speeches directed to the general public, was cause for alarm in the view of these authors. They pointed specifically to three deleterious effects: 1) that words come to replace deeds as the measure of presidential performance, 2) that the office of the presidency becomes weakened by an overreliance on popular rhetoric, and 3) that the public is misled as to the true nature of how the political system works, thus creating a potential credibility gap when performance fails to square with promises.[4]

The basic tenets articulated in this essay were extended in the 1984 book *Rhetoric & American Statesmanship,* edited by Thurow and Jeffrey Wallin, and given formal explication in Jeffrey Tulis's 1987 book, *The Rhetorical Presidency.* In his introduction, Tulis specifically notes that "bound up in the common opinion that presidents should be popular leaders is a larger understanding—of how our whole political system works, of the contemporary problems of governance that we face, and of how the polity ought to function." In short, as these authors noted in their 1981 essay, "the problem is thus not one simply of individual rhetorics, but is rather an institutional dilemma for the modern presidency."[5]

I quote these works at some length to establish one basic point: the primary focus and basic concern of those working within the construct of the rhetorical presidency is largely, if not entirely, institutional. They are most concerned with the nature, scope, and function of the presidency as a constitutional office. It is to the U.S. Constitution and its expressed and implied executive powers that these authors turn for normative guidance.

Tulis even goes so far as to posit the existence of two constitutions. Alongside the original document of 1789, there exists, according to Tulis, a "'second constitution' under whose auspices presidents attempt to govern. Central to this second constitution is a view of statecraft that is in tension with the original Constitution—indeed, is opposed to the founders' understanding of the political system." This second constitution is the rise of the rhetorical presidency—the use of popular speech addressed to mass audiences for the purpose of circumventing or bypassing congressional deliberation. It is the adoption and institutionalization of the strategy of "going public," as Samuel Kernell calls it, in an attempt to impose the presidential will, backed by popular opinion, on the legislative branch of government.[6]

In this volume the chapters by Tulis and Thurow are informed by the construct of the rhetorical presidency. Without going into the specifics of either chapter, I will simply note that the construct and its various explications is not without problems. Five concerns are paramount.

First, the construct, at least as originally formulated, seems to presume that there was once a nonrhetorical presidency (but see Tulis's opening sentence in this volume), and that the rhetorical and nonrhetorical can be easily discriminated by recourse to historical practice and the implied standards for presidential communication found in the U.S. Constitution.

Second, the term *rhetoric,* as used by Tulis and his colleagues, often appears to be rather narrowly drawn, referring primarily to emotional appeals to ignorant audiences. Third, rhetoric is understood as a substitute for, or as a false form of, political action rather than as being, in and of itself, a type of action—symbolic action. Fourth, and closely related, is the presumption that the only form of rhetoric that is meaningful to governance is policy-oriented rhetoric—rhetoric that deals more or less directly with legislative programs or policy stances. Finally, the theoretical understanding of rhetoric as a body of precepts with a 2500-year pedigree seems less than complete. Aristotle may have written the first systematic treatise on rhetoric, but he did not write the last.

These concerns are raised not to pick a fight, but to set forth some of the bases for understanding the differences between those who study the rhetorical presidency and those studying presidential rhetoric. If one conceives the principal subject of investigation to be rhetoric rather than the presidency, then the nature, scope, and presumptions change rather radically. Under this construct the presidency is the particular arena within which one can study the principles and practices of rhetoric, understood as the human capacity to see what is most likely to be persuasive to a given audience on a given occasion. If rhetoric is the principal subject of investigation, then one might well be concerned with the principles of the art and how those principles function to allow the speaker or writer—who might happen to be a U.S. president—to achieve his or her ends by symbolic means.

This perspective would not presume that the speaker or writer has only one end or even one kind of end in mind. Being the complex creatures that they are, humans often have multiple purposes in speaking or writing; some of these purposes may even be in conflict with others. Nor would this perspective presume that rhetoric is limited to the skillful exploitation of the audience's emotions in an effort to secure a rapid, and mostly unthinking, response. Scholars interested in rhetoric would be more likely to begin from the premise that rhetoric is an art that has both practical and productive dimensions—dimensions that point inward to principles of operation as well as outward to the accomplishment of certain goals.

If rhetoric is the subject matter and presidential rhetoric the specific arena of investigation, then the first order of business becomes understanding the theoretical principles from which the practice of rhetoric proceeds.

The most basic principle is that the theory of rhetoric will look different depending on the demands of practice. For example, the theory of how to argue a case in a court of law, which Aristotle labeled forensic oratory, is different than the theory of how one might construct a sermon for an audience of believers. Both are situations that call for rhetorical discourse, but they call for different kinds of discourse, addressed to different kinds of audiences, with different ends in mind. So the most basic principle of rhetorical theory is that the speaker or writer must begin with a thorough understanding of the rhetorical situation.

Lloyd F. Bitzer defines a rhetorical situation as "a complex of persons, events, objects, and relations presenting an actual or potential exigence which can be completely or partially removed if discourse, introduced into the situation, can so constrain human decision or action as to bring about the significant modification of the exigence."[7] Several parts of this definition need to be highlighted.

First, the rhetorical situation is a complex or constellation of relationships, each of which exerts influence on the others. To reduce rhetoric to a linear, one-to-one, cause-effect relation between the message (cause) and audience reaction (effect) is to fundamentally misunderstand the nature of the art.

Second, one or more exigences are always present. The exigence is the engine that drives the rhetorical action—the part of the situation that is in need of remedy or resolution. Bitzer refers to the exigence as "an imperfection marked by urgency . . . a thing which is other than it should be."[8] To understand the exigence or exigences is to know what called the discourse into being in the first place. Bitzer is very clear that not all exigences are rhetorical (some cannot be modified or changed by discourse) and that even those exigences which are rhetorical may not be modified, or may be only partially modified, by the discourse. In short, there are no guarantees of nor formulas for rhetorical success—no assurance that rhetorical discourse, even if artfully performed, will necessarily change the state of affairs which the speaker or writer wishes to change.

Third, all is dependent on "human decision or action." Rhetorical discourse is addressed to one or more audiences, and it is the audience, not the speaker or the speech, that is the final arbiter of persuasion or influence. Rhetorical discourse attempts to constrain human decision making, but it cannot command or determine it. This is why rhetoric must forever and always be an art, not a science.[9] There is no way to predict, with any degree of certainty, how audiences are going to react to attempts to constrain their decision making. The reason for this is clear: the factors that impinge on actors in the rhetorical situation are as complex as the realities of everyday life and, like that life, are constantly changing. There are no constants in any given rhetorical situation; everything is a variable and subject to interpretation.

Fourth, the best that any practitioner of rhetoric can do, be that person the president of the United States or the president of the local Chamber of Commerce, is to attempt to assess the current configuration of forces in the rhetorical situation that presently exists and always to be aware that situations, like humans, are constantly evolving. Then, having made that assessment, the speaker or writer tries to adjust the discourse to the situation as it is believed to exist at the present moment. Since every situation has unique factors present, there can be no common or standard way of proceeding from one situation to the next. What distinguishes the skilled rhetorician from others who attempt to persuade is not the tools or even the outcomes of such attempts, but rather the judgment and powers of interpretation that the speaker displays in assessing the situation and in selecting the appropriate language, arguments, timing, occasion, and audience.

The art of rhetoric lies not in whether persuasion actually happens, but in the intellectual powers displayed by the rhetorician in the selection of what to say, how to say it, to whom, under what conditions, and with what apparent outcome. I say "apparent" outcome, because there is no way to discern with certainty that the selections made by the speaker were the causal factors operative in the behavior manifested by the audience, whether that behavior was in line with the intentions of the speaker or whether it was not.

Given this pervasive indeterminacy, what can be known about rhetoric generally, and presidential rhetoric in particular? In general, we know the places (*topoi* or *loci*) to look for rhetorical potency. There is persuasive potency in the speaker, the message, the audience, the context, and the medium. All of these potencies, taken together, constitute the rhetorical situation.

Aristotle identified three sources of persuasion that every speaker potentially possesses. He called these the appeals from *ethos* (the character of the speaker), *logos* (the apparent reasonableness and rationality of the speaker's arguments), and *pathos* (the speaker's ability to evoke emotions that will make the audience wish to act on the speaker's requests). Aristotle identified the sources of the speaker's appeal from *ethos* as good morals, good sense, and good will toward the audience.

Modern commentators on the presidency have often recognized the importance of the presidential character on performance of duties. *The Presidential Character* by James David Barber and *Personality and Politics* by Fred I. Greenstein are prominent examples, but both are informed more by a psychological understanding of personality development than by a rhetorical understanding of character as a mode of appeal.[10] Likewise, much has been written about the ideas *(logoi)* and policies put forward by various presidents, but again these studies have tended to focus on the content of the policies once they became established rather than upon the advocacy or debate on behalf of those policies or the attempts to create audiences or constituencies for enactment of the policies. Until quite recently, appeals to the emotions or feelings of an audience were regularly condemned but seldom studied, despite the important work of such rhetorical theorists as Kenneth Burke, Richard Weaver, and Chaim Perelman that give value appeals and feeling-states central roles in persuasion.[11]

Messages, too, are central places to look for rhetorical potency. Although many study the content of messages, scholars of rhetoric are more likely to understand content through analysis of the formal dimensions of language. Such dimensions might include forms of argument (enthymemes, examples, maxims, syllogisms), forms of style (literary devices such as metaphor, simile, antithesis, personification), or forms of delivery (facial expression, gesture, motion, and vocalics such as rate, pitch, timbre, and rhythm). By comparing formal dimensions across messages, the analyst of rhetorical discourse can discern the ways in which standard message characteristics function as road maps into the mind of the speaker and as constructs of political culture. To discover how a speaker regularly encodes messages is to reveal patterns of thought and the residues of ideological formations.

Speakers and messages take on significance only in relationship to audiences and purposes. Too often we think of purpose as something possessed only by speakers and writers; audiences, too, have purposes, and it is the process of adjusting the purposes of the speaker to those of the audience that we call rhetoric. Many people, particularly political scientists, sociologists, and business analysts, study audiences in terms of demographics. Were it not for careful demographic analysis the science of public opinion polling, so much a part of presidential politics, would not be possible. But there are other ways to think about audiences.

From a rhetorical point of view, the audience is always a fiction, not a scientifically verifiable, or even a rationally probabilistic construct.[12] This is the case because an audience exists primarily as a construct in the speaker's or writer's mind. It consists of all those people whom the speaker has conceptualized and defined as the audience capable of bringing about change in the exigence. Such an audience may not even exist prior to the delivery of the speech, or it may exist but not recognize itself as an audience until persuaded to be so by the rhetorician. Thus, the speaker may construct the audience even in the process of speaking. People who, prior to listening to the speech, did not consider themselves to be part of an audience now consider themselves to be so. They are constituted as an audience during the rhetorical performance rather than prior to the performance. Part of the rhetorical potency of the audience is its ability to make and remake itself by exposure to rhetorical messages.

To complicate matters even further, speakers often fictionalize one audience (by creating it in their minds and speaking as though they are addressing that fictionalized audience) when they are actually trying to reach a different audience (one that is likely to overhear the address to the fictionalized audience).[13] A proper understanding of audience as a fictionalized construct is necessary before one can understand why there can never be a simple cause-and-effect relationship between rhetorical messages and audience effects, a standard presumption of normal social science.

As if the speaker-message-audience relationship were not complex enough, there is the related matter of context. Since Aristotle, rhetorical theorists have tried to make context a constant. Aristotle tried to do this by making context synonymous with place: the law courts (forensic rhetoric), the political assemblies (deliberative rhetoric), and the public ceremonies (epideictic rhetoric). However, even the great systematizer himself could not make context stand still—as witnessed, for example, by the complete absence of any discussion of ambassadorial speeches, a common genre of the time (and one that does not fit easily into any one of his tripartite divisions). Modern commentators have not done much better, resorting to the notion of genres or distinct types of discourses in an effort to construct boundary conditions for the analysis of political rhetoric. Much work has been done to link specific rhetorical forms to standard political occasions—inaugural addresses, state of the union speeches, veto messages, and the like. The most ambitious effort in this regard has been Karlyn Kohrs Campbell and Kathleen Hall Jamieson's *Deeds Done in Words: Presidential Rhetoric and the Genres of Governance*.[14] Even this path-breaking book has not solved the problem of context, however, for a rhetorical context is more than the formal design of message elements, more than the configuration of historical forces, more than the substantive content of message types, and more than the patterned recurrence of certain kinds of appeals. It is even more than all of these elements combined.

A rhetorical context is the unique array of forces—rhetorical, historical, sociological, psychological, strategic, economic, and personal—that exists at any given moment in time and that impacts the speaker's selection and presentation of topics, the ways in which the message is composed and treated, and the manner in which the audience is invited to experience and understand the discourse. That these factors are everywhere and always different make accurate the descriptor "unique."[15] Clearly there are patterns of argument, standard modes of appeal, and recurring historical configurations. Unfortunately, knowing and recognizing such recurring elements does not assist much in the complex task of understanding any particular rhetorical situation.[16]

Finally, there is the matter of medium. For the better part of 2,500 years, rhetorical theories generally have presumed that the medium under investigation is human language, either spoken or written. Although there was, in the Renaissance, some discussion of the rhetorical dimensions of painting, it has only been the last three centuries that have seen much attention given to rhetorical media other than speech or writing. Starting with broadsides and political cartoons in the eighteenth century, progressing to photography and motion pictures in the nineteenth century, and culminating with radio, television, and computer-mediated communication in the twentieth, the media by which rhetorical messages are conveyed have undergone dramatic change. The change is not simply that of the container, either. Modern media possess unique characteristics of their own—there is a rhetoric of television in addition to the rhetoric *on* television. Aphorist though he was, Marshall McLuhan was largely correct: the medium is the message. It is not all of the message, but it is certainly part of the message, and part of the speaker's ethos, and part of the rhetorical context, and part of the audience's psychology, too. When a president of the United States makes an appearance on cable television's MTV it has implications for the meaning of the message, the form of the message, the ethos conveyed, the audiences affected (including many that never have and never will watch MTV), and the expectations that future audiences will hold for future presidents.

Scholars who study rhetoric in general work within the broad parameters that I have set forth. Some of these scholars apply their knowledge of the art of rhetoric to the study of presidential discourse—speeches, press conferences, debates, campaign advertising, and the like. In the field of speech communication, this tradition of applying general rhetorical precepts to specific presidential utterances goes back to at least 1937, when Professor Robert King published an analysis of Franklin D. Roosevelt's second inaugural address.[17] It was not, however, until the early 1970s that speech communication scholars began to view the study of presidential rhetoric as a specialized subdiscipline. Since that time the study of presidential rhetoric has tended to follow one of four paths. As Theodore Windt notes, "Contemporary studies in presidential rhetoric are primarily *critical* and fall into four categories: criticism of single presidential speeches, criticism of rhetorical movements, development and criticism of genres of presidential speeches, and miscellaneous articles on various ancillary topics." Although Windt penned this description more than a decade ago, it is still generally true, with a few studies of presidential campaign advertising, some full-length rhetorical biographies, and a few general studies of presidential communication having been completed in the interim.[18]

The chapters that comprise this volume draw from both the rhetorical presidency and the presidential rhetoric paradigms. A few of the chapters draw insights from both constructs and one—the concluding chapter by George Edwards—draws from neither. But for the most part authors identify, either implicitly or explicitly, with one school of thought or the other. So, for example, Jeffrey Tulis devotes his opening chapter to a reconsideration, partial modification, and extension of the rhetorical presidency. In doing so, Tulis continues to distinguish between rhetoric that is popular and that which is Constitutional. Tulis is quite clear that he sees popular rhetoric as "a problem, not a panacea." The normative standard is still the U.S. Constitution and its expressed and implied presidential powers and prerogatives. The focus is still on the office of the presidency and how that office has been transformed (extra-constitutionally, in Tulis's view) into a seat of popular leadership, with rhetoric being the main instrument of such leadership. But Tulis also has some new ideas about specific steps that might be taken to "reconstitutionalize" political discourse. He argues that "the president needs to revive a form of discourse in which the president interprets the Constitution as a window on American identity and uses that interpretation to change (and improve) the terms of public debate."

Glen Thurow, another one of the founders of the rhetorical presidency construct, takes a somewhat broader view than Tulis by focusing not on the office per se, but on the character of the person who occupies the office. Grounding his analysis in Washington's first inaugural address, Thurow holds that the founders of American constitutionalism envisioned presidents with "characters preeminent for ability and virtue." He further holds that it was through their speeches and writings that presidents gave form to the virtues and thus modeled those virtues to the public. The role of presidential speech was primarily that of instruction and example—instruction in the great principles of republicanism and example in the actions by which those principles were to be carried out. Together this instruction and example resulted in a character that was worthy, both of trust and emulation. Thurow finds that in modern presidential rhetoric "only common virtues tend to be mentioned" while "praise of virtue in general is replaced by praise of the more sentimental feelings, and admiration of good character has given way to striking personalities." Like Tulis, Thurow finds the rhetorical presidency problematic, even though his diagnosis of the problem is somewhat different.

As scholars of government and political theory, Tulis and Thurow are naturally concerned more with the presidency than with rhetoric per se. Just the opposite is true of Bruce Gronbeck and Thomas Benson. As scholars of rhetoric, they are primarily concerned not with how rhetoric has debased the presidency but with how presidents, in their roles as chief executive, commander-in-chief, party leader, campaigner, and head of state, have attempted to use rhetoric to their advantage as *political* leaders. Here emphasis is placed on politics as the art of the possible and the accumulation of sufficient power to transform the possible into the actual. Rather than start from a normative base, such as the U.S. Constitution or the early inaugural addresses, Gronbeck and Benson start from the existential presidency—the presidency as it has operated in the recent past and as it continues to operate at present. If Tulis and Thurow write from an essentialist stance, Gronbeck and Benson write from a functionalist perspective.

Gronbeck begins his chapter by challenging one of the prevailing assumptions of the rhetorical presidency—that the central explanatory factor in understanding the onset of the rhetorical presidency lies in the rise of "a modern doctrine of presidential leadership."[19] This axiom is crucial to the construct of the rhetorical presidency, for if it is true that political theory or doctrine is the culprit, then a change in doctrine could potentially remedy the situation. But Gronbeck challenges the premise, holding instead that *"the electronic presidency is fundamentally different from the presidency as it has operated and been experienced in any other epoch."*

It is not doctrine or political theory that has resulted in the rise of the rhetorical presidency, Gronbeck argues, but the rise of the modern electronic media. This is a serious challenge to the construct; for if Gronbeck is right, if the defining characteristic of the rhetorical presidency is its reliance on and conspiracy with the mass media, then no amount of theorizing or doctrine shifting is going to return us to the "constitutional" office that Tulis and Thurow envision. Modern media are here to stay; and with each advance of technology the nature, scope, and possibilities of the presidential office have changed and will continue to change. According to Gronbeck, "the veil of mystery, the foundation of political wisdom, and perhaps 'the presidency' itself have been all but destroyed by contemporary televisual journalism."

Rather than long for a constitutional presidency that has long since passed from the scene, Gronbeck calls for an understanding of the powers and possibilities of the electronic presidency. Instead of asking, as Tulis and Thurow might, what has happened to the presidency, Gronbeck asks, "In what sort of *polis* do we live?" Here is the second challenge to the paradigm. Instead of worrying about what has happened to civic republicanism and the federalist form of government, Gronbeck is worried about what has happened to democracy and the ability of the people *(demos)* to make informed decisions in the midst of ongoing political spectacles. "Politics understood as symbolic action," Gronbeck writes, "demands that we analyze systematically the discourses of political ideology and valuation, of political visions and the places citizens occupy in such visions."

Whereas Gronbeck traces the basic structural changes that have resulted in an electronic presidency (wherein the medium becomes the message and the citizen becomes little more than a demographic target), Benson seeks to revitalize the notion of what it means to be a rhetorical audience in the electronic age. Taking McLuhan and Walter Ong one step further, Benson wants to explore the "possibilities for reviving democratic participation." Unlike Tulis and Thurow, who find in presidential rhetoric addressed to the masses a formula for disaster, Benson finds just the opposite: the possibility for a truly democratic politics, perhaps for the first time in our brief history as a nation. Against the construct of the rhetorical presidency, Benson writes of the "importance of direct contact between the people and the presidency," especially on matters of legislative policy and executive decision making.

Benson points to the Internet and the information superhighway as technological points of contact between the presidency and the people. Such technologies hold the potential, Benson seems to suggest in his title, to bring the people *(demos)* into direct public dialogue with the major political actors, including the president. The public sphere may be as close as the computer on one's own desktop. But the very possibility of an expanded public sphere brings more questions than answers. As Benson notes, "We may find ourselves traveling at one bound from a rhetorical presidency that is fragmented into sound bites, and that has adapted itself to such a situation, to a presidency that is all too visibly producing so much text that we cannot read it all in a normal citizen's day—and so, in a new sense, it is still fragmented, still presents itself to us as something other than discourse."

By the end of part I on "Rhetoric and the Presidency," we have moved from a relatively narrow concern with how the rhetorical practices of contemporary presidents fail to square with eighteenth-century constitutional theory, to how presidential speech can embody the virtues of character needed to sustain a republic (and thus model those virtues for the citizenry), to the revolution in presidential rhetoric brought about by the electronic media (both in terms of what counts as rhetoric and how it is structured for mass consumption and partisan political gain), to the liberating possibilities of the Internet and the vision of popular political participation which it seems to offer. In so doing, we have moved from the presidential office, to the presidential character, to the medium of presidential communication, and finally to the audience for such communication. We have also moved from an unabashed defense of Constitutional Republicanism through a functionalist approach to presidential communication, and finally to a vision of participatory democracy.

Part 2 of this volume turns from theoretical and metatheoretical probes to practical criticism. Although the authors' work, for the most part, is within the framework of presidential rhetoric, their findings often have direct implications for our understanding of the rhetorical presidency. Several movements are apparent as one reads through part 2. First, there is a rough chronological movement, starting with Hart and Kendall's chapter on Lyndon Johnson and moving sequentially through Nixon, Reagan, Bush, and concluding with Karlyn Campbell's meditation on the presidency as a two-person career, with special reference to Bill and Hillary Clinton. Second, there is a movement in the basic conceptualization of what constitutes rhetoric. For Hart and Kendall, rhetoric is the metaphorical language found in a private telephone conversation; for Edwin Black, rhetoric seems to be any sort of symbolic action that gives insight into Nixon's psychology; for Goodnight, rhetoric refers primarily to a form of argument and the implications of that form for public memory; for Ivie, rhetoric seems to be a way of knowing, with language structuring our conceptions and guiding/misguiding our actions; for Campbell, it is the synecdochic function of rhetoric that is crucial—how a part, in this case the First Lady, comes to stand for a much larger whole of values, premises, beliefs, attitudes, and ideals. Finally, there is a movement with respect to the goals or objectives of rhetorical criticism. Hart and Kendall seem primarily interested in rhetoric as a barometer of political philosophy; Black examines rhetoric as an index of personal psychology; Goodnight finds in rhetorical discourse a historical consciousness and narrational form that transcends political situations; Ivie seeks nothing less than a reconceptualization of our political culture and its governing representations; and Campbell offers an expanded vision of the rhetorical presidency as a "two-person career."

Each of these critical chapters, in its own way, contributes to our understanding of the multiplex relationships between rhetoric and the presidency. In so doing, these chapters challenge many of our assumptions about the nature, scope, and functions of rhetoric as both theory and practice, as well as our view of the presidency as a rhetorical office. They show us some of the leading rhetorical scholars of the day at work and thus illuminate issues of critical practice, method, scope, and goals. They reveal, at the very least, that rhetorical criticism is not an enterprise for "triflers."[20]

Part 3 of this volume is a critique of both the rhetorical presidency and presidential rhetoric constructs by one of the nation's leading scholars of the presidency, George Edwards. Edwards works within the paradigm of empirical social science. His main areas of research are presidential opinion polling and presidential leadership. Edwards selects some of the major works within the traditions of the rhetorical presidency and presidential rhetoric, and subjects them to critical analysis. It is fair to say that in at least one regard—the ability to make and sustain arguments about the effects of presidential rhetoric—Edwards finds research emanating from both paradigms to be problematic. Is Edwards's critique fair? Has he found the Achilles heel of interpretive research or merely substituted the standards of one kind of social science for those of another? How does Edwards's critique speak, if only by implication, to the chapters in part 2 of this volume? These are some of the questions that will be addressed in the afterword, where the reader, after meditating on parts 1, 2, and 3, can join the volume editor in thinking about what it all means for the future of the rhetorical presidency.

PART I
Rhetoric and the Presidency

CHAPTER I

Revising the Rhetorical Presidency

Jeffrey K. Tulis

In an important sense, all presidents are rhetorical presidents. All presidents exercise their office through the medium of language, written and spoken. Even brute power is expressed in words, through orders, through commands. Our principal access to the legacies of previous administrations is through words. Yet presidents may use words in a variety of ways. They may speak or write, they may follow established traditions and genres, or they may create new ones. They may design their words for one audience or another. In *The Rhetorical Presidency* I tried to show that the American presidency has been marked by settled patterns of presidential rhetoric, that these settled patterns changed near the beginning of this century, that these changes signified and reflected an important transformation of the constitutional order.[1] Rhetoric was my subject, to be sure. But it was a subject chosen to provide access to an even more important one—the changing character of constitutional politics in America.

I tried to show that nearly all presidents in the nineteenth century spoke and wrote differently than nearly all presidents in our century. Nineteenth-century presidents directed their rhetoric principally toward Congress in written messages that framed their partisan preferences in self-consciously constitutional language. By contrast, twentieth-century presidents regularly appeal over the heads of Congress in oral performance designed for popular appeal. It was not this change per se but what the change revealed about the conduct of contemporary American politics that most interested me.

Although I meant the title of the book, and the term "rhetorical presidency," to comprehend both the rhetoric of any president and the newer popular form of rhetoric devised by modern presidents, readers have tended to confine the term to the modern practice. An observation embedded in a larger point has been treated as the discovery of a phenomenon. A term designed with multiple meanings has been confined to one. I was partly responsible for this. In an earlier article that I wrote with James Ceaser, Glen Thurow, and Joseph Bessette, we stressed the advantages of the traditional presidency over a modern rhetorical office.[2] In the book, I did not abandon that thesis, but I did expand it in ways that modified it. The modern rhetorical presidency is not simply good or bad, but rather both. I tried to describe and assess the ambivalence of rhetorical leadership. Direct popular appeals are shown to be indispensable for periodic political needs but problematic when routinized. Thus, popular rhetoric was necessary to contend with the crises of depression, war, and civil strife but problematic in normal times where it traded on images of war and strife inapposite to the politics it sought to effect. I attempted to illustrate these sorts of contemporary prospects and difficulties with brief analyses of Theodore Roosevelt's campaign to regulate the railroads, Woodrow Wilson's League of Nations fight, Lyndon Johnson's War on Poverty, and Ronald Reagan's efforts on behalf of tax reform, the budget of 1981, and "star wars," the Strategic Defense Initiative. These cases served to illustrate both the potential and the limits of modern rhetorical leadership.

Perhaps the most important shift in perspectives from the article to the book is the treatment of the constitutional understandings that undergird and are expressed by alternative rhetorical practices. In the book I suggest that the modern understanding and the modern practices do not simply replace the traditional ones but are rather superimposed upon them. American politics is pictured as a layered text. I locate the problems of contemporary politics in the theoretical spaces between the layers of constitutional understandings. In these spaces, contemporary dilemmas of governance become visible.

All contemporary presidents face these systemic dilemmas of governance: the same power that seems required to effectuate change makes more likely crises of confidence; the same power that promises a more energetic administration makes more likely mutability of law; the same power that brings the decisions of government to the people makes more likely the continued decay of political discourse. These and other persistent dilemmas stem from competing logics of an old Constitution and a relatively new, superimposed, constitutional understanding. President Reagan's leadership well illustrated this ambivalence. In many ways, Reagan best exemplifies what leadership has become for twentieth-century America.[3]

Perhaps because the dilemmas of the hybrid presidency were so manifest in the Reagan era, or because critiques of popular leadership found their way into the political culture, Reagan's successors have attempted to alter presidential practice in order to attenuate the common dilemmas of leadership. These new practices and these new understandings were not publicly articulated. Indeed, it is doubtful whether Presidents Bush or Clinton were (or are) themselves aware of leadership's theoretical difficulties or of the best reasons for their own new practices. Bush and Clinton found new practices, as it were, in the course of business, rather than by careful design. The lack of intellectual attention to the problem, the inability to publicly describe and defend the new practices, and the failure to maintain the practices, may be clues to the deepest problem of each of their administrations. Nevertheless, in these new practices, we can discern the outline of an improved understanding of presidential leadership.

The key to revising the rhetorical presidency is the insight that one can neither return to a nineteenth-century constitutional order nor successfully radicalize or intensify twentieth-century techniques of popular leadership. Somehow one must better conjoin moderate versions of nineteenth- and twentieth-century understandings of leadership. Against the older theory, one must acknowledge that routinely delivered direct rhetoric to the people is an essential feature of governance. But against the present understanding of popular leadership, one must begin to craft a new form of popular rhetoric—a rhetoric that is popular and constitutional at the same time. In the rhetorical innovations of the early Bush and Clinton presidencies, one can glimpse the outlines of a new constitutional discourse.

At the outset of his presidency George Bush tried to abandon the leadership style of Reagan. As one astute commentator noted: "Reagan made the rhetorical presidency the rage in Washington. How else could a president operate effectively, except by going over the head of Congress to the American people? Stirring the nation to action was supposed to be the president's first priority. It's not Bush's. 'This is as unrhetorical a Presidency as you'll get,' says a White House official."[4]

Bush delivered considerably fewer major speeches than Reagan did in his first year. In addition, by leaving much of the task of popular rhetoric to surrogates such as William Bennett and by placing his principal political strategist, Lee Atwater, in charge of the Republican National Committee instead of in the White House, Bush reestablished the important distinction between governing and campaigning.

Thus, in a number of respects Bush resembled the constitutional officer of the first constitution more than the rhetorical president of the second. One must not strain this comparison, however. Like the president of the first constitution, Bush seemed to realize that popular rhetoric is a problem, not a panacea. Unlike the president idealized in that Constitution, however, Bush apparently did not know what to say in place of popular rhetoric or how to say it. The president as constitutional officer needs a principled rhetoric, a form of speech that makes sense of the polity, its constitutive principles, and its political tendencies. Bush did not seem to understand this at the very time his practice seemed to point in this direction.

Consider Bush's first State of the Union Address. The president began the speech like a constitutional officer: "Tonight, I come not to speak about the 'state of the Government'—not to detail every new initiative we plan for the coming year, nor to describe every line item in the budget. I'm here to speak to you and to the American people about the State of the Union— about our world—the changes we've seen, the challenges we face. And what that means for America."[5]

After this promising beginning, Bush proceeded like an inarticulate rhetorical president, reciting a brief catalog of the extraordinary events taking place in Eastern Europe and around the world, with almost no effort to instruct as to their meaning. The bulk of the speech was the sort of laundry list of new legislative and budgetary proposals the president had just promised to avoid. For my purposes here, more important than Bush's failure or incoherence, was his barely noticed (and since forgotten) aspiration—to craft a principled discourse in place of a policy campaign.

At first glance, it seems that President Clinton has responded to the dilemma of the hybrid Constitution quite differently than Bush. Instead of seeking to abandon modern practices only to be coopted by the continued public demand for them, Clinton has embraced the rhetorical presidency, while seeking to modify or reform it and the public's understanding of leadership.

Like Reagan and unlike Bush, Clinton imported the skills and talents of his campaign into the core leadership of his White House. During his first months in office, Clinton experienced firsthand the difficulties of translating the strategies and techniques of campaigning into the processes of governance. Yet his response to these political difficulties was not to abandon the modern conception of leadership, but rather to invite Ronald Reagan's former communications director, David Gergen, to be his own chief strategist. Gergen had worked for Nixon and Bush as well as for Reagan and never before for a Democrat. It is safe to surmise that no political operative was as familiar with the promise and pitfalls of the rhetorical presidency as was David Gergen. Educated in the practices of popular leadership, Clinton's Gergen seemed, when initially appointed, wiser than Reagan's Gergen.

Gergen and Clinton learned that some of the power of the rhetorical presidency may be appropriately harnessed to the tasks of modern governance without many of the common costs of popular leadership if presidents can find a way to avoid utopian visionary speech that overpromises, on the one hand, and detailed policy speeches that seem to preempt and preclude legislative deliberation, on the other. More concretely, Clinton began his tenure with a leadership style that fleshed out Bush's own aspiration for principled discourse. For a short time, this new leadership style had four key attributes:

1. The president personally sets direction and establishes priorities through major speeches which emphasize the principles upon which

the president wants policy constructed rather than concrete rules, regulations, or appropriations that would be the means to realize those principles.

2. The executive branch as a whole is given the task of preparing concrete policies that illustrate and exemplify the president's principles and provide a focus for congressional deliberation.

3. The president and his surrogates reserve for smaller, appropriately chosen audiences arguments regarding the details and technical aspects of specific proposals.

4. Congress is invited to deliberate—to refine, to develop, or even to replace the president's concrete proposals as long as they are consonant with the president's publicly articulated principles.

This leadership style was strikingly evident in the kickoff of the president's campaign for health care reform. Clinton structured his nationally televised address to a joint session of Congress around an articulation, illustration, and defense of five principles that he believed "must embody our efforts to reform America's health care system: security, simplicity, savings, choice, quality, and responsibility."[6] The president explained the meaning of each of these principles, but he did not review the details of his proposal. The speech was neither visionary nor policy-specific. Some news commentators, schooled by the rhetorical presidency, faulted the president on just those grounds. They failed to see that this speech might have come to be regarded as the finest domestic policy speech since World War II if President Clinton had not later abandoned the leadership style that I just outlined. As originally delivered, the speech reset the terms of debate on health care and at the same time left considerable room for legislative deliberation. The president invited Congress to offer its own concrete proposals, as long as they measured up to standards articulated in his speech.

In the early days following the speech, the president and the First Lady, and advisers such as Ira Magaziner, displayed their considerable command of detail as the administration's specific proposal was unfolded for congressional committees and other audiences. In each of these settings the proposals were offered as exemplary of the principles articulated in the major address, not as proposals that need be accepted as is. The president invited deliberation while attempting to structure and lead it.

Of course, we all know now that Clinton's health care plan failed and that its failure is plausibly connected to the realignment signified by the 1994 elections. It is impossible to prove a counterfactual—but I will suggest one that might be at least accepted as plausible. If Clinton had maintained the leadership style that I described, he would have won the battle for health care. To be sure, the bill passed would have been different than the one he proposed, but it probably would have been a better bill than the one he proposed. And had that been the case, the system, not just Clinton, would have won.[7]

At the origin of the health care plan, President Clinton had discovered that it was impossible to return to the first constitution even if one wished to. Instead of attempting such a return as Bush did, only to be carried along willy-nilly by demands born of the second constitution, Clinton's early practice appeared to advance the second constitution by infusing it with principles borrowed from the first. To be sure, the principles could have been better articulated, and more importantly, their constitutional dimensions could have been more prominent and better understood. Nevertheless, these aspirations were implicit in the practices, even if dimly cognized by the president and his audiences.

Although some of President Clinton's speeches and actions reveal the conception of leadership I have just sketched, he never made this conception itself an explicit topic for public instruction. To successfully navigate the dilemmas of the two constitutions, a president must do so. Left uninstructed, political pundits and popular opinion may mark President Clinton as unsuccessful by the lights of the second constitution. With his guidance Americans could come to reinterpret, and thereby reform, the rhetorical presidency.[8]

Before discussing the outlines of a revised rhetorical presidency, I would like to stress that the strategies I suggest for the president are developed principally from the perspective of the system—its needs, tendencies, pathologies. Too many students of the presidency view the system, the polity as a whole, from the perspective of the president, his needs, his partisan objectives, his ability to prevail over other constitutional actors. From a president's perspective, the only salient rhetorical issue is this: will my ability to persuade the people at large advance my ability to secure my policy objectives? But from a systemic perspective, our question is much different: how may a president best contribute to a larger political process? Indeed, from the perspective of the polity it is sometimes a very good thing that the president fails.[9]

Having stressed the point that one should not automatically equate the president's interests within a polity with the interests of the polity as a whole, let me suggest that *in our current political context, the president's own interests and those of the polity as a whole conjoin.* The Republican victory in 1994 has been so massive and the Republicans' ability to interpret that victory so effective that President Clinton finds it increasingly difficult to successfully distinguish his own preferred policies from those of the Republicans.[10] Were he to be an avowed welfare-state liberal, he would lose. If he apes the Republican assault on the welfare state, he loses as well, if not for reelection, then in a more important sense: his place in history would be as a Republican. Familiar partisan strategies are likely to fail to secure Clinton historical authority, in Stephen Skowronek's sense of the term. However, if one turns from the content of the Contract with America to its form, there is considerable political space for presidential interrogation. Traditional Republican concerns to conserve the Constitution are subverted by the manner by which they aim to use and institutionalize power. President Clinton's most potent political vantage point on the Republicans is a view from the Constitution itself. The partisan victory of congressional Republicans makes possible, at least temporarily, a presidency that is, in important respects, above partisanship.

At this political juncture, the president could use the bully pulpit to reinterpret the purposes of presidential leadership and the relation of the president to the Congress. Here is a sketch of the themes such a rhetoric might traverse:

1. The president could explain to the citizenry that the several branches were designed to bring different qualities or capacities to the conduct of government. No one branch has all these capacities. It was traditionally believed that the president was better suited for speed and decisiveness and the Congress better suited for deliberation—not just bargaining but publicly displayed reasoning on the merits of public policy. The president's leadership responsibilities expanded in history in order to better effectuate the Constitution's commitments to energy and deliberation. Thus, for long stretches of American history, congressional action was unlikely lacking the spur of presidential leadership.

2. Today, Congress lacks neither ability nor will to act. Today, the problem is that Congress is too willing to pass legislation without deliberating upon it. It is striking that so many new members (members who have never before constructed national legislation) see their job as requiring them to legislate campaign promises without discussing the legislation. Indeed, many are willing to amend the Constitution without discussing the Constitution. This is liberalism at its worst. Whereas Woodrow Wilson and FDR needed to recraft the American understanding of executive power in order to overcome excessive deliberation, today we need to encourage more deliberation as a corrective to excessive energy. Both the earlier innovation of presidential leadership of policy and today's need for a quite different style of leadership are consistent with the same Constitution. This is not a living Constitution but a living government that seeks to preserve the core commitments of the perpetual Constitution—namely an appropriate balance between energy, steady administration of the law and protection of rights, and deliberation.

3. In the new constitutional order, presidents have new responsibilities.

a. Presidents need not set the policy agenda, if the Congress is capable of doing so. There is no reason why, in a republic, presidents should usually be responsible for the agenda of domestic governance. Of course, presidents will continue to have partisan objectives of their own and partisan objections to legislative initiatives. But the character of this partisanship can change under present conditions. Presidents can shift the public's attention away from presidential responsibility for legislation to presidential responsibility for the integrity of the system.

b. Presidents can highlight their historic responsibility for protecting minorities from the tyranny of overbearing majorities. This will entail vetoes of legislation that violate constitutional rights as well as more carefully crafted veto messages to defend such actions.

c. Presidents can exercise a new form of veto—a conditional veto—to force Congress to further deliberate on legislation that, although it may not violate rights, is too hastily drawn. It is within a president's power to veto a bill and, at the same time, to invite the Congress to resubmit an improved version that he promises to sign if specified conditions are met. The point of this exercise is to invite a simple majority to do a better job without requiring a super majority. Again, a veto message would be the instrument of a new form of deliberative leadership. Presidents would make clear that they are willing to sign legislation that they do not like as long as there is integrity in the deliberative process. One might call this a neo-Whig view of the presidency.

d. Presidents should use their rhetoric to hold the Congress accountable to the standards it sets for itself and to the standards implicit in the Constitution. The State of the Union address would be an especially apt vehicle. Its themes would be the pathologies and performance of Congress (and an assessment of the challenges of foreign affairs) rather than a partisan policy agenda. Presidents should insist that the only official responses to the address be those produced by the congressional deliberative process itself (as they were during George Washington's administration), not by leaders of an opposing party. Of course, the Congress is controlled by the opposing party, but it is important that the respondent speak for the Congress as a whole as the president speaks for the executive. This point is more important than it might first appear. The official response to Clinton's 1995 State of the Union address, a constitutionally mandated piece of rhetoric, was delivered by a state governor and televised from the New Jersey state house. It is hard to restore an informed political discourse when the very form of presentation reveals a perversion of basic constitutional relations: through the use of a Republican governor's state legislature as a movie set, the presidency is reduced to party leader and the function of interbranch deliberation is transformed into a state-based political campaign. That few, if any, of the opinion-making elite seemed offended by this is a mark of the extent of the degradation of constitutional discourse in our time.

e. Presidents should encourage Congress to respond to their own speeches and their own initiatives in formal, written ways. Written texts, especially when they are written texts by political opponents, would provide the president considerable resources in his attempt to make the Congress more constitutionally responsible and accountable. They provide both an occasion for and a constraint upon public deliberation. Making discourse more formal also helps to make government less of a direct extension of talk radio and tabloid television.

4. Presidents need to raise constitutional questions about particular policies and particular lines of policy. By this I do not mean that presidents ought to worry whether the Supreme Court will strike down some proposed law. I mean rather that the president needs to revive a form of discourse in which the president interprets the Constitution as a window on American identity and uses that interpretation to change (and improve) the terms of public debate. Most citizens do not realize that there may be a range of issues that are nonjusticiable but to which the Constitution speaks. Most citizens also do not realize that there is a long and fruitful tradition (now in eclipse) of disagreement among the branches regarding the meaning of the Constitution. Part of the project of reconstituting deliberation would be that of reconstitutionalizing political discourse.

I mentioned that it would benefit the president politically to adopt the kind of rhetorical strategy I sketched. If I am correct about that, it only means that the strategy is politically possible in a way that it was not just a short time ago. The case for the desirability of such a strategy, however, rests not on its advantages for the president but rather on its promise for the polity. Many have worried that Americans have forgotten how to talk about politics. It is the recovery and improvement of democratic discourse rather than need to aid the sitting president that justifies a neo-Whig theory of the presidency.[11]

Can a single man reform a polity? Can a president overcome the opposition of deep structures outside the government itself, such as the technological changes in the mass media and other new forms of communication? One does not know. But whatever change is possible requires a new kind of presidential rhetoric and new civic education. The observations and suggestions I make here are offered as desirable revisions of our present governing practices as well as revisions to my thoughts about governance in *The Rhetorical Presidency*. But with respect to the general need for a new political education and the difficulty of establishing one, I have nothing new to add to the book. Let me close by simply repeating what I said there:

. . . governors and governed need a theoretical compass with which to position themselves to be able to assess appropriate and inappropriate exercises of power. Citizens of a reformed polity, regulated by such a compass, would be able to judge the rhetorical categories in which power is expressed, defended, and understood. Their presidents could responsibly avail themselves of a political tradition that offers rhetorical exemplars of principle, vision, and silence.

One cannot overestimate the difficulties in conceiving and promoting such a polity. Nevertheless, to provide citizens with a new political education, more than to tinker with institutional incentives and disincentives, is the fundamental task facing America today.[12]

CHAPTER 2

Dimensions of Presidential Character

Glen E. Thurow

Why is presidential character important? To this question several answers can be given. It is well known that a president's power depends not only upon his ability to command but also upon his ability to persuade. And, as all students of rhetoric know, one of the primary means of persuasion is character. In fact, in his *Rhetoric,* Aristotle considers the moral character of the speaker, as conveyed through his speech, the most effective means of persuasion.[1] Especially when the matter discussed may be uncertain and doubtful, hearers will be inclined to rely upon the confidence they have in the speaker, which in turn depends upon their perception of his character. If they perceive him to be prudent, virtuous, and to have good will toward them, they will be likely to be convinced. Conversely, if they think him foolish, vicious, or concerned only with his own interest, they will be difficult to persuade even if the speech seems to contain irrefutable logic. Since a president often speaks to others about matters and policies that are debatable and uncertain, the perception of a president's character is a crucial element of his ability to persuade and thus to get others to do what he wishes them to do. To have a good character, or at least to seem to have a good character, is useful to a president.

But it is not only the perception of a good character that is useful to a president; good character itself is needed in order for a president to perform his job well. It is obvious that a president must possess many virtues and abilities if he is to fulfill the duties of the president. In praising the method of presidential election in the Constitution, the *Federalist Papers* laud it for creating a "constant probability" that the office will be filled by "characters preeminent for ability and virtue."[2] These characters are needed both in emergencies, when quick and good decisions are called for from the executive, and in quieter times when foresight and steadiness are required. Good character, Publius suggests, is required in the president in order to turn republican government into good government.

Publius makes clear that not only good character but also great character is required and needs to be encouraged. Presidents under the Constitution's admirable system of election, he notes, will have more than "talents for low intrigue and the little arts of popularity." Virtue is needed not only, indeed not primarily, for the purpose of persuading the people but also for that personal firmness that demonstrates "courage and magnanimity enough to serve the people at the peril of their displeasure," and for those qualities of mind and heart which lead one to undertake "extensive and arduous enterprises for the public benefit."[3] The usefulness of virtue shades into its nobility. We hail Abraham Lincoln because he saved the Union, because he performed a great service for us, but we also give him esteem and lasting fame for what he was. His character seems to deserve the tributes we give to him. He was not only a great public servant, he was a great man. Lincoln provides a model to be emulated. We admire Lincoln's second inaugural not only because it points out a wise path for the country to follow in dealing with the bitter aftermath of civil war, but because of the qualities of mind and character it reveals Lincoln to have possessed—such qualities as equanimity of judgment and generosity of spirit. In Lincoln's greatness we can see our own virtues magnified and perfected. Good character in the president is useful; great character is in addition noble and ennobling.

Character is displayed in both the speech and the deeds of individuals. But since these deeds are by themselves dumb and inexplicable, our access to character is through speech. It is only in the light of people's speech that we can see and assess the character displayed in their deeds. So the access to presidential character is through presidential speech. How presidents and others speak about presidential character may itself affect the possibility of securing good character in presidents. What can be, and is, said in public always reveals what is endorsed by, or at least tolerated by, the ruling opinion in a country. One could not advocate slavery in contemporary America, for example, without suffering severe consequences because we have firmly rejected the view (which once ruled in my state of Texas and in many other states) that slavery is a legitimate institution.

When Woodrow Wilson said that Lincoln made it possible to believe in America, he meant that Lincoln showed that those of the best character could be fostered by, attracted to, and admired by the American democracy. If the excellences of such persons can be both acknowledged and given their due in public speech, then such persons can be said to be embraced by the ruling opinion of a country and can feel a kinship with the political order. But if their virtues can appear in public speech only in a distorted or weakened manner, then they are part of the political order in only an attenuated way, or not at all. If what Aristotle regarded as noble pride, for example, can only be acknowledged in American public speech as a form of insufferable arrogance, those proud of their own excellence are not likely to be chosen for office. Only those willing to humble themselves before the American people will be elected. What cannot be acknowledged in public does not fully belong to the regime.

Thus, character in presidents is important because it is an ingredient in a president's success and power, because it is necessary to enable them to perform well the duties of their office, and because great character ennobles the country. To be able to speak accurately of this character is essential not only in order to see it accurately but also to form and attract people of character to serve our republican government.

In looking at presidential rhetoric since the founding of the country, one can see substantial shifts in the way character and virtue are portrayed. These shifts in part reflect, and in part have helped to bring about, an erosion of our founding republican principles and their replacement by principles less hospitable to the recognition of outstanding virtue. Where once acknowledgement was given to extraordinary virtue, now only common virtues tend to be mentioned in public speech. Praise of qualities chiefly displayed in public affairs has given way to praise only of more domestic virtues. Praise of virtue in general is replaced by praise of the more sentimental feelings, and admiration of good character has given way to admiration of striking personalities. If virtue seems rare in public life today, it may in part be because we find it so difficult to acknowledge and praise virtue in our public speech.

To substantiate these claims I will give a brief account of the major shifts in presidential rhetoric with respect to the portrayal of presidential character, primarily using presidential inaugural addresses to illustrate these shifts. I will seek to bring out how these shifts are related to changes in the understanding of the character of our political order. I will then show what effect these shifts have had upon our understanding of presidential character and the ability of the country to foster and attract men of outstanding character to our highest office.

THE AMERICAN REPUBLIC AND VIRTUE

Washington's first inaugural may be said to contain the most open display of presidential character and virtue of any inaugural address. This was not accidental; rather, the emphasis upon character and virtue was a deliberate choice by Washington. In the address itself, Washington makes clear that he has thought very carefully about what kind of speech he should give.[4] The speech is designed to help strengthen attachment to the new Constitution in the minds of its hearers, and its most notable feature is its careful attention to constitutional forms. He begins the inaugural by calling attention to the official notification of his election transmitted to him by Congress. (Although he had known of his election much earlier, he had made no move to set out for Washington from Mount Vernon until the official notification had been received.) He notes that he considered—but had to reject—the possibility that the inauguration was the proper occasion to fulfill the constitutional mandate of article 2, section 3 that the president recommend to Congress "such measures as he shall judge necessary and expedient." He seems reluctant even to speak, except at the behest of the Constitution. Throughout the speech he is particularly careful to observe the constitutional line between the powers of Congress and those of the president. By indicating his own willingness to subordinate himself to the forms of the Constitution, Washington seeks to transfer the esteem in which he is held to the new Constitution.

Within this clear intention to strengthen the new Constitution by showing the utmost respect for its forms, Washington offers a speech whose central paragraphs praise the virtues of the new senators and representatives, and whose opening and closing paragraphs render homage to the Almighty and express Washington's own emotions and sense of duty upon assuming office. The occasion was not only the first inauguration of a president, but the commencement of a "new and free government." To conciliate the opponents and hearten the lukewarm friends of the Constitution, he recommends action on the proposed Bill of Rights, discourages sectionalism or partisan animosity, encourages and calls attention to the "talents, rectitude, and patriotism" of those who are to lead the government, and offers an appropriate and moving supplication to the "Great Author of every public and private good." He also tries to make himself as good an example as possible for the assembled congressmen and for those who are to follow. He displays his patriotism, his sense of duty, his loyalty to the Constitution, and his freedom from greed or vain ambition throughout the speech. His outstanding qualities provide a model for other politicians and attract the people at large to their government.

Washington's portrayal of his own virtues helps to infuse the Constitution with the proper spirit, but it is not the ground of either his powers or duties. Rather, that ground is the Constitution. There is a subtle interplay between Washington's portrayal of his own character and the authority of the new Constitution in the speech. To see the significance of this interplay, we must be aware of the claim of virtue to rule. If there are people of outstanding virtue, do they not have a right to claim the ruling power, for is it not unjust to subject the virtuous to the less virtuous? Aristotle, who saw this claim very clearly, also saw that such a claim leads to monarchy, not to republican government.[5] Is Washington's praise of virtue in himself and others not fundamentally undemocratic? Washington's virtue is reconciled with republicanism by its not being the grounds of his own authority. His authority, he indicates, rests upon and is derivative of the Constitution. He does not claim the right to rule because of his superior virtue, but he is rightfully president only because he has been constitutionally chosen for office. Yet while Washington scrupulously insists upon his subordination to the Constitution, his own virtue, and the virtue of the assembled senators and representatives, is somehow simultaneously the vindication of the Constitution. Although in form authority flows from the Constitution to Washington, in reality authority also flows from Washington's character to the new Constitution. In the speech Washington is clearly trying to use his own reputation for great virtue, further enhanced by the speech itself, to help establish the authority of the Constitution. The monarchal implications of the full display of his own virtue is blunted by his clear obedience to the Constitution, but only blunted.

This analysis is partially confirmed by subsequent events. Washington felt compelled to remain virtually silent rather than repeat this form of address in his second inaugural. Wishing to dispel the impression of monarchy suggested not only by the speech but also by the general pomp of the first inaugural, Washington contented himself with a two-paragraph speech in which he stressed subservience to the Constitution and promised, in effect, to give his inaugural address on some other occasion.[6] When John Adams attempted to give a speech on the model of Washington's first inaugural, it was unintended parody. Adams's inaugural address contains a ludicrous defense of his own patriotism and a grudging acquiescence in the congressional acclaim of Washington's greatness—all, incidentally, in a single sentence that must be the longest and most convoluted in the history of American political oratory.[7] No subsequent president ever attempted to give a similar address.

It remained for Jefferson, among the founding presidents, to formulate a portrayal of the relationship between presidential virtue and republican government that presidents copied until well into the twentieth century.[8] It must be acknowledged, however, that this portrayal entailed a view of virtue as being less noble than that found in Washington. In his first inaugural, Jefferson, like Washington, praises virtuous persons, the new Congress, and Washington; pays homage to Providence; and indicates his own feelings and duties upon assuming office. But the predominant theme, unlike that of Washington's, is not praise of the virtuous but an exposition of the principles of the Union and its Republican government. This exposition is designed to show, in the wake of the party conflict preceding Jefferson's election, that the difference between the true party of Federalism and the true party of Republicanism is not a difference of principle and that the principles of the American government are shared by all true Republicans and Federalists. Adams, indeed, had spoken of the character of the American government in his address, but he did so in order to argue that it reflected wisdom and virtue and could be approved by disinterested and benevolent persons. The standard of good government was for Adams, as for Washington, the approval of wise and virtuous individuals; the standard for Jefferson is the true principles of republican government. Persons are to be judged by their adherence to these principles.

Consequently, Jefferson praises the virtue of good people because virtue is useful to the end of achieving good republican government, not because it is admirable in itself. He praises the "wisdom," "virtue," and "zeal" of Congress because it will be a "resource" on which he may "rely under all difficulties." Washington is cited for his "preeminent services," not for his outstanding qualities. Indeed, Jefferson goes so far as to suggest that his own wisdom will be a mere effect of his place. "I shall often go wrong through defect of judgment. When right, I shall often be thought wrong by those whose positions will not command a view of the whole ground." This comment not only stands in contrast to the remarks of Adams, who goes to some lengths to establish himself as judge of the Constitution and to portray his loyalty to it to be a result of his own choice, but also to Washington. Washington, like Jefferson, asks indulgence for his errors and weaknesses but makes clear they must be prevented or remedied by his own qualities or the Almighty's beneficence, not his constitutional position. The purpose of presidential oratory, as Jefferson sees it, is to instruct the people in, and fortify their attachment to, true republican political principles. Presidents do not serve the people by means of the lofty example of their wisdom and virtue; Jefferson did not believe in heroes despite having known one and maybe being one. Rather, presidents serve the people by adhering to the Constitution and teaching republican principles.[9] Their virtue is only a means to this end.

Jefferson constitutionalizes virtue. Where virtue in Washington's inaugural is portrayed as an individual characteristic that can be brought to the support of the Constitution, in Jefferson virtue itself seems to be the result of the Constitution and to be noble because it serves the Constitution. Although virtue might seem sullied in this portrayal by its being judged as a means rather than an end, something of the nobility of virtue is maintained because the end it serves is the Constitution and the noble principles of republican government.

CHARACTER IN THE MODERN PRESIDENCY

The understanding of the relationship of character to republican government enunciated by Jefferson is essentially the relationship which is visible in presidential inaugural addresses throughout the nineteenth and early twentieth centuries with two notable exceptions: Lincoln and Theodore Roosevelt. Lincoln's portrayal of virtue and character is a most interesting one, but one which I shall not attempt to elaborate. I will simply note that Lincoln is the only president who ever made the Providence of God the central theme of an inaugural address. Virtue and character, as Lincoln portrays them, would have to be understood in the light of that singular act. Theodore Roosevelt's rhetoric contains simultaneously a harbinger of a new mode of presidential rhetoric and something of a throwback to Washington's praise of virtuous persons. He calls for a return not to the founding principles, as Jefferson might have, but to "the qualities of practical intelligence, of courage, of hardihood, and endurance, and above all the power of devotion to a lofty ideal, which made great the men who founded this Republic in the days of Washington. . . ."[10]

It was Woodrow Wilson who formulated a new conception of the presidency and, with it, a new understanding of presidential character in relationship to republican government. Wilson, as is well known, disliked the American constitutional system and particularly its central feature, the separation of powers. Although he did not bring about the introduction of the parliamentary system in the United States, he did try, as president, to infuse the political order with a new spirit and a new understanding of the role of the president.

In his inaugural address Wilson does not try to relate the policies of the new administration to the true principles of republican government, as had Jefferson, but rather sees his and his party's election as the introduction of a new government, bringing about a new point of view in the nation as a whole.[11] Although this new point of view, Wilson suggests in passing, may be seen as a restoration of old standards, those standards are not to be found in the Constitution, in the work of the founders, or in knowledge of the true principles of republican government, but rather "in our hearts." The standard of our hearts is that of compassion for those who have been trampled in the rush of American life. This compassion is not mere pity but is equivalent to justice because people have suffered unjustly at the hands of the impersonal forces created by our society. Hence passion and justice conspire to give a new direction and a new standard for American life.

Unlike Washington and Adams, Wilson does not look to the difficult virtues of outstanding persons but to a passion, compassion, accessible to all but the most unfortunate and which, by a theory of the causes of misfortune, can be regarded as virtue. We note that this new standard of virtue is both more democratic and more nonpolitical than the previous standards: more democratic because all can feel pity, and less political because compassion can be felt for all and not merely for fellow citizens. Compassion musters not the forces of Americans or those devoted to republican government, but the "forces of humanity." Our principles, Wilson says in his second inaugural, are "the principles of a liberated mankind." Attention to forms of government, in contrast, is attention to "mere" politics.[12]

In Wilson we see a turn away from the Constitution and the principles of republican government. The presidency is not primarily an office of constitutional responsibilities and republican instruction, but an office of popular leadership. His primary duty is to articulate public sentiment, and it is by means of this articulation that a president governs. In another of his speeches, Wilson says:

> A great nation is not led by a man who simply repeats the talk of the street-corners or the opinions of the newspapers. A nation is led by a man who hears more than those things; or who, rather, hearing those things, understands them better, unites them, puts them into a common meaning; speaks, not the rumors of the street, but a new principle for a new age; a man in whose ears the voices of the nation do not sound like the accidental and discordant notes that come from the voice of a mob, but concurrent and concordant like the united voices of a chorus, whose many meanings, spoken by melodious tongues, unite in his understanding in a single meaning and reveal to him a single vision, so that he can speak what no man else knows, the common meaning of the common voice.[13]

A leader, according to Wilson, is preeminently a public speaker. If the true principles of our country are to be found in people's hearts, rather than in an understanding of republican government, then the supreme task of statesmanship is to articulate what people feel. Hearts do not speak, but statesmen do, and they must say what the heart feels but cannot express. Thus the president's ultimate task is to express the unspoken desires of the people, not to instruct or govern them. The skill needed by a president is the rhetorical skill; the virtue needed is compassion. In addition, in Wilson's understanding of the presidency, the president must be able to bring an expertise to bear that is not shared by the people. Although the president may be able to articulate the deep desires of the people, they do not know how to fulfill those desires. Expertise must be added to their desires. The president, as head of the embodiment of expertise, the executive branch, can supply what the people lack. President Carter expressed perfectly the Wilsonian ideal of character in the president when he said in his inaugural address that government should be both "competent and compassionate." Competent and compassionate persons are the ones who should govern. Wilson's view of the presidency, which has dominated the presidency in the twentieth century during both Democratic and Republican administrations, has had many effects on our ability to publicly portray and discuss presidential character.[14]

First, Wilson's view has led to identifying the virtue of the leader with the virtues of the people. Virtue becomes reduced to the lowest common denominator. Consider this passage from a speech by Jimmy Carter: "I promised you a president who is not isolated from the people, who feels your pain and who shares your dreams and who draws his strength and his wisdom from you."[15] Note the quality Carter claims for himself: compassion even to the extent of sharing others' pains and dreams. And those qualities that might seem to be Carter's own, his strength and wisdom, are but drawn from the people at large. Not only are Carter's words the voice of the people, his very being seems to be the people incarnated. This is the theory of representation drawn to a logical and absurd extreme.

But this view is not merely an idiosyncratic view of Jimmy Carter's. In Ronald Reagan's first inaugural, he asked his fellow Americans to "dream heroic dreams."[16] Are we going to be called to difficult and ennobling tasks? No, it turns out "you can see heroes every day going in and out of factory gates. Others, a handful in number, produce enough food to feed all of us and then the world beyond." Even taxpayers, it turns out, are heroes. And then Reagan concludes: "Your dreams, your hopes, your goals are going to be the dreams, the hopes and the goals of this Administration, so help me God. We shall reflect the compassion that is so much a part of your makeup."

There is nothing to look up to in the president because he is identical to the mass of the American people.

The heroic virtues are similarly made easy in George Bush's inaugural. Said Bush, "The old ideas are new again because they're not old, they are timeless: duty, sacrifice, commitment, and a patriotism that finds its expression in taking part and pitching in."[17] The sentence begins to suggest something difficult and noble in referring to duty and sacrifice, but then is undercut by its ending.

A second and related effect of the Wilsonian view is to restrict the ability to admire and seek publicly the qualities needed for statesmanship. This difficulty can be illustrated by one of the striking differences between Washington's and Carter's inaugural addresses. Washington's pride is much more openly displayed than is Carter's. Washington begins his speech by portraying his decision to accept the office as a triumph of his sense of duty over his personal inclinations, established habits, and even the requirements of his own health. Consciousness of his own deficiencies, he adds, increases his reluctance to become president, but his gratitude for the "confidence of my fellow-citizens" as well as his sense of duty lead him to accept the office. Later in the address he indicates he will not accept any "pecuniary compensation" in return for his services.[18] Washington thus portrays himself as preeminently a man who will do his duty, who will not stoop to use public office for private gain, and who, though not insensitive to the honor conferred on him, has the attractive alternative of a private life at Mount Vernon. Washington is able to display both his own dignity—the worth of his life without public office—and the high dignity of public office.

In contrast, Carter's inaugural contains no explicit discussion of his own motives for becoming president. He hides himself by not talking directly about himself. Yet this speech does implicitly portray Carter the man, even in the way in which he hides himself. Washington speaks throughout his speech in the first person singular, distinguishing himself both from the attending dignitaries and from the people at large (whom he refers to in the third person plural). Carter speaks throughout of "we," identifying himself with the people, again hiding his particular characteristics. Only in the introduction does he use "I." The speech begins, "For myself and for our nation, I want to thank my predecessor for all he has done to heal our land," thus emphasizing both the personal character of his gratitude and his right to speak for the nation (perhaps not an entirely gracious thing to emphasize in thanking a defeated predecessor). He also uses the personal pronoun in quoting the favorite cliché of, and thus honoring, one of his high school teachers. Finally, he uses it to indicate that he has taken the oath of office on a Bible given to him by his mother (in preference to, or at least in equal honor with, one on the podium that had been used by George Washington): "Here before me is the Bible used in the inauguration of our first President in 1789, and I have just taken the oath of office on the Bible my mother gave me just a few years ago, opened to a timeless admonition from the ancient prophet Micah. . . ."[19]

Both Washington and Carter take pride in having been elected to the presidency. Yet there is a great difference in their expression of this pride. Washington's is more manly and less boyish than Carter's. Washington's pride is that of a man for whom public office is but one choice among others, who can claim at least the intention of unusual virtue and who can make visible his lack of greed in rejecting the presidential salary. Historians may debate whether Washington equalled this self-portrait, but it is significant that Washington could publicly claim such a space for himself. On the other hand, there is something furtive about Carter's display of his pride. Carter's is disguised in the dutiful stance of the schoolboy made good, attributing his success to his mother, schoolmarm, and piety, while obviously basking in his own success. To a degree much greater than Washington, Carter has difficulty in displaying the basis of his own pride. Washington claims that high office is properly the reward of talents, virtue, and patriotism, and can at least claim some share of these attributes. But Carter cannot claim such a thing without implying his superiority to others and to the American people. But that claim would be inappropriate because of his and others' understanding of the character of the presidential office.

A third effect of the Wilsonian view is not only to make it difficult to take due credit oneself but also to narrow the understanding of the qualities needed in government. Again, this can be seen by comparing Washington's and Carter's inaugurals. As mentioned, Washington praises the virtues of the assembled members of Congress, revealing virtues Washington would like to see in these people, as well as virtues they actually possess. He praises their talents, rectitude, and patriotism. In praising their talents, he particularly mentions a "comprehensive and equal eye, which ought to watch over this great assemblage of communities and interests." The representatives ought to be free of local and party prejudices, a virtue not only always needed but also particularly needed in the circumstances in which Washington spoke. The analogous virtue praised by Carter is competence: "Our government must at the same time be both competent and compassionate."[20] It is clear that Carter is speaking to the opinion that the federal bureaucracy is composed of incompetents, but it is nonetheless interesting that this is the highest virtue he can find to praise.

Competence is a virtue one expects the average employee of a large organization to possess. One does not expect more because one does not expect large numbers of people to have unusual virtues. There is something very democratic about Carter's virtue, which does not ask too much, in contrast with the "comprehensive and equal eye" of Washington, which requires one to forego one's particular interests and natural attachments to be an attentive and intelligent overseer. Competence can be displayed in even minor activities; a comprehensive and equal eye can show what it can do only if it has a large and complex scene to contemplate.

A fourth effect of the Wilsonian view is to lead to a confusion of the public and private spheres. Washington wishes that "the foundation of our national policy will be laid in the pure and immutable principles of private morality and the preeminence of free government be exemplified by all the attributes which can win the affections of its citizens and command the respect of the world." Patriotism applauds this morality because "there is no truth more thoroughly established than that there exists in the economy and course of nature an indissoluble union between virtue and happiness; between duty and advantage; between the genuine maxims of an honest and magnanimous policy and the solid rewards of public prosperity and felicity."[21] But Washington also makes clear that there is a tension between his private good and his public duty. His age and inclination would lead him to a wonderful retirement at Mount Vernon; his duty compels him to become president. Carter's inaugural seems to be similar to Washington's, echoing his sentiments by saying that we have a special obligation "to take on those moral duties which, when assumed, seem invariably to be in our own best interests."[22] Yet his speech, compared to Washington's, hides the degree to which morality may be contrary to our interests in their more immediately practical meaning. Although Washington emphasizes the sacrifices he has had to make to become president, Carter implies that there is nothing he would rather do than be another's servant and mouthpiece. Washington suggests that we ought to be grateful to God for He might desert us, but Carter suggests He dwells among us through the sacramental character of the inaugural ceremony. As I have already noted, Carter replaces the Bible from Washington with that given to him by his mother.

This replacement of the public sphere by the domestic one is characteristic of recent inaugurals. George Bush went so far as to portray the grand facade of the Capitol as a backwoods front porch: "We meet on democracy's front porch, a good place to talk as neighbors and as friends."[23] The organizing image of the entire address is that of the nation as a sentimentalized family sitting on the front porch, wafted by gentle breezes, bemusedly looking out upon a world which will surely not make too great demands upon them.

Finally, the modern view of the relationship between character and republican government leads to a denigration of character altogether. Indeed, contemporary presidents tend to see their highest function not to be loyal to political or moral principle, but to have a vision or a dream. If one does not have one's own dream, then one must get one somewhere. "I have no new dream to set forth today, but rather urge a fresh faith in the old dream," said Carter.[24] A dream is not only that human conscious state in which the intellect is least active, it is also the most private of human conscious states. The "vision thing," as George Bush called it, is a replacement for principles. Instead of pointing towards character, judging a president by his vision suggests judging him by a creative, individual act. It leads to the conclusion expressed by President Clinton in his inaugural, "This ceremony is held in the depth of winter, but by the words we speak, and the faces we show the world, we force the spring. A spring reborn in the world's oldest democracy that brings forth the vision and courage to reinvent America."[25] The image of forcing even the course of nature out of its accustomed path, and that of not restoring or improving but reinventing America, suggests the degree to which politics becomes simply a matter of the will when guided by neither character nor principle.

The loss of the tie between virtue and the principles of the political order means that character tends to be reduced to personality. A person's character points towards those qualities which are admired in people generally; a personality is something idiosyncratic. One of the most well-known modern studies of presidential character is James Barber's *The Presidential*

Character. A more accurate title would be *The Presidential Personality.* Barber is in the Wilsonian line of political science, arguing that political power is the power to persuade.[26] Barber seeks the character most suitable for successfully persuading others. But he reduces persuasion to style. Presidential rhetoric is not measured by its success in addressing the problems facing the country at a particular time but as a component of the style of a president. Although he argues in places that style is distinct from character, whose primary component is self-esteem or the lack of self-esteem, both are parts of personality.[27] Self-esteem is a virtue only if the self involved is worthy of esteem. Self-esteem without this element becomes merely another form for the assertion of the will. Both self-esteem and style, as understood by Barber, are divorced from a concern for virtue.

Prior to Wilson, American presidents tended to view the presidential office through the Constitution. In contrast, modern inaugurals seldom make reference to the Constitution or to its principles. The office and its tasks are defined not by reference to the Constitution but by the president's extraconstitutional relationship to the American people. The president is the mouthpiece of the people and shares their character: "You have given me a great responsibility—to stay close to you, to be worthy of you, and to exemplify what you are. Let us create together a new national spirit of unity and trust. Your strength can compensate for my weakness, and your wisdom can help to minimize my mistakes," prays the modern president.

The traditional view, as we have said, allows for a display of justified pride without being undemocratic. For all have a duty to the Constitution, and some may be better than others at fulfilling its injunctions without thereby implying that the people do not properly have the ultimate say. For their ultimate say is the Constitution, and they may choose to select for its offices persons who have talents and virtues that they may admire and find useful without possessing them themselves. The Constitution, among other things, is a means for making room for uncommon people in a democratic regime, without undermining democracy. Replacing the Constitution by a direct relationship between the president and the people has been intended to perhaps superficially strengthen the presidential office. In fact, however, it has undermined it by undermining the basis of the strength it may gain by being occupied by independent and talented people, who can openly and publicly display their talents and virtues and receive credit for them.

CHAPTER 3

The Presidency in the Age of Secondary Orality

Bruce E. Gronbeck

What Jeffrey Tulis has designated "the rhetorical presidency"[1] has been in fact a change in kind in the executive branch of government brought about by the electronic revolution. We live in an era where access to the presidency—and, for the president, to his various constituencies—is controlled and conditioned by electronic channels. Franklin Delano Roosevelt's success in making himself and his office into powerful presences among the electorate depended upon radio. His campaign manager and confidant, James Farley, noted in 1938 that reelection in 1936 for Roosevelt "might conceivably have been an impossible job" without radio. Joy Hayes has argued that Americans' very conception of citizenship and of their collective political identity was grounded in their experience with political broadcasting in the 1930s.[2]

Electronic political life, it must be remembered, did not begin with television. The wired age of American politics did not start with the baby boomers; our collective experience with an electronic presidency runs back over seventy years to the campaign of 1924. Furthermore, although we are probably most conscious of the roles that radio, television, film, and the computer play in our politics during election time, in fact those media frame and fill our political visions day after day, congress after congress, presidential term after presidential term. The ubiquitousness and unavoidability of electronic political communications force us to deal with a question even more profound than that which guided Tulis's charting of the growth of the rhetorical presidency. That question is this: how have electronics changed the essential nature of the presidency? Such a question suggests that electronic communication media are more than conduits carrying the detritus of political activity through the system; they are more than our windows on the political world, more than the machines that accelerate political reckoning, more than hookups that bring the coasts together in time-zone bending political simulcasts. All of these observations are true, but more signficantly, it can and will be argued that *the electronic presidency is fundamentally different from the presidency as it has operated and been experienced in any other epoch.*

That argument can be developed in three movements: first, through a brief review of the electrification of the twentieth-century presidency, then through an examination of some of the present-day characteristics of the presidency that can be considered the forces of metamorphosis, and third, some thoughts about the reconceptualization of political rhetoric that follow from viewing political leadership through an orthicon tube.

ELECTRONIC POLITICS
IN THE UNITED STATES

Many have traced pieces of the history of electronic politics in the United States.[3] This chapter will not report on all that work, but, rather, limit itself to a brief overview. Most of the events mentioned deserve much more attention than they have received from scholars interested in the mass mediation of American politics, but I will return to some of these events at the conclusion of this chapter.

The beginning of the electric presidency is usually set at 1924, for in that year radio broadcast gavel-to-gavel coverage of the party conventions. The Democrats provided the histrionics needed to entice a great audience—a seventeen-day marathon featuring 103 ballots as Al Smith, champion of the Turks or anti-Klan forces, took on Gibbs McAdoo and the Klucks, the pro-Klan army.[4] In that same year, faced with the prospect of trying to convince the electorate that Calvin Coolidge had enough manliness to lead the nation, the GOP hired William Fox to make a film depicting him not only as a family patriarch but as a leader virile enough to protect the women and children of the country.

Yet, despite his reputation as "Silent Cal," Coolidge in fact was a media personality; his New England twang had acoustic characteristics well-suited to the qualities of radio electronics of his time, and thus his presidential performance was enhanced. The first real stars of political radio, however, were Franklin Roosevelt and the social reformers of the 1930s. Roosevelt's first fireside chat of March 12, 1933, launched his famous Hundred Days campaign for New Deal legislation; he was able to create both a sense of intimacy and the heroic role of citizen for his listeners, as can be seen in the letters that flowed into the White House following his performances. Hot political radio, however, was promoted by the social reformers of the right and the left: Huey Long's Share-Our-Wealth Society was envisioned during 1934 and 1935 in his radio broadcasts, as were other proposals for social security and American self-identities in the populist radio programs of Father Charles Coughlin, Francis Townsend, and Gerald L. K. Smith. As some of these groups attempted to join forces under the banner of Coughlin's National Union for Social Justice and behind the presidential candidacy of William Lemke in 1936, their Union Party managed to draw over 16.6 million votes in that election—surely a tribute to radio's political reach.[5]

The 1940s was the transitional decade. Radio was a dominating medium of political communication. Roosevelt's December 8, 1941, address to the joint session of Congress for a declaration of war against Japan forged a unity of national resolve that would have been impossible in this country prior to radio. Following the war, Churchill's iron curtain speech in Fulton, Missouri, on March 5, 1946, the president's articulation of the Truman Doctrine before a joint session of Congress in 1947, as well as George C. Marshall's plan for European recovery later that year, and Senator Arthur H. Vandenberg's resolution favoring a collective security pact with Western hemisphere nations (i.e., NATO) all depended on radio's reach for their political force—for pulling the U.S., for better or worse, onto the plains of international politics. Yet, before the end of this wrenching decade, a new era was born: President Harry S. Truman delivered an address to the American people in front of television cameras on October 5, 1947, appealing for help with the world food crisis.

In 1952 television became a significant force, with convention coverage that popularized the concept of the television commentator; Walter Cronkite sat to the side of the camera aimed at the podium, allowing him to both report and interpret the goings-on through an engaging live remote. As well, ads appeared on the round screen when Dwight Eisenhower spent between $800,000 and $1.5 million on TV spots, somewhere between ten and twenty times the $77,000 spent by Adlai Stevenson. With music by Irving Berlin, animation by Walt Disney, and words crafted by Ben Duffy of Batten, Barton, Durstine, and Osborn, the Eisenhower election demonstrated that television would become the giant on the electoral beach. Nixon confirmed that as well, saving his place on the GOP ticket through the earnest performance of his Checkers speech. In 1956 Cronkite bestirred our imaginations again with his use of MIT's behemoth Univac computer to call the election. The next election demonstrated that candidates could put the binary data-cruncher to their own uses, as the Kennedys built many of their campaign strategies, themes, and locations around 1960 census data.

Outside the presidential arena, General Douglas MacArthur's presentation of his "Don't Scuttle the Pacific" address to a joint session of Congress in 1951 was such a powerful political event that it contributed to Truman's decision not to run again for the presidency in 1952.[6] Televisual political drama came of age in the televised Army-McCarthy hearings of 1954, even as another televised political event—Edward R. Murrow's interview of Senator Joseph McCarthy on his *See It Now* program—hastened the senator's downfall.

It was in the 1960s, however, that America found out that politics and television had been alloyed into new material. Not only did 1960 see the first thoroughly televised presidential campaign, but soon our comprehension of political spectacle was also taken to new levels. Live remotes from multiple sites were used in 1963 to cover both the March on Washington and the Kennedy assassination. The sunlit, high-contrast videotapes surviving from the Kennedy Rotunda ceremonies and the horse-drawn catafalque parading from the Capitol to the National Cathedral, with almost no journalistic commentary, strike even contemporary college students with an eerie power that is unmatched in the history of political television.

As the technology improved, so did television's role in politics expand. The colored gore of Vietnam coverage during suppertime news not only turned a lot of stomachs but also helped to turn public opinion and to drive a president out of office. The assassinations of Martin Luther King, Jr., and Robert Kennedy in 1968—again, with extended live coverage of funerals—led the country through mourning, while the inside-the-hotel/outside-the-hotel dialogue at the Democratic national convention that same year broke down barriers between citizens' political and social worlds.

Nothing has been said yet about political film. The crude, silent, candidate film of Silent Cal has taken many forms since 1924, some more successful than others: Goldwater offered an embarrassing moral lecture in 1964; the tributes to John Kennedy in 1964 and Robert Kennedy in 1968 demonstrated that heightened emotions could be triggered by combining politics and melodrama; Ronald Reagan's 1984 *A New Beginning* became the gold standard in convention film making with its episodic alteration of Reagan's accomplishments and his private feelings for America; and Bill Clinton in 1992 offered the slickest celluloid myth, one strong enough to reframe a drifting campaign thanks to Linda Bloodworth-Thomason and Harry Thomason, a sitcom production team able to infuse the biographical film with divine prescience and breast-heaving sentimentality.[7]

Other aspects of film's political history are better known. Pare Lorenz's documentaries made for Roosevelt during the 1930s—*The River* and *The Plow That Broke The Plains*—helped sell the Tennessee Valley Authority and rural recovery projects to the electorate expected to pay for them. Francis Capra's *Why We Fight* series during World War II was pro-war propaganda at its best. CBS's *Harvest of Shame* (1960) is a powerful indictment of America's social and political treatment of its migrant workers, and its *The Selling of the Pentagon* (1971) represents the acme of anti-institutional attack by a network.

And the list of political media events goes on: live coverage of Nixon opening China; the drama of Watergate speeches, hearings, and resignations; the Begin-Sadat peace accords; the Iranian hostage crisis and the nightly humiliation that brought down another president; the almost-live coverage of the attempted assassination of Ronald Reagan; the Challenger disaster; the destruction of the Berlin Wall and Moscow's White House with live and near-continuous CNN coverage. The color guns of our television sets have burned these political images deep into our visual memories.[8]

For some, American politics is whatever the *New York Times* or *New Republic* reports and comments on. But for most citizens, American politics is whatever appears on the TV news, the public television talk shows, NPR's *All Things Considered, Larry King Live,* and C-Span's call-in discussions of Washington.

REMAKING AMERICAN POLITICS ELECTRONICALLY

Walter Ong has characterized this era as the age of secondary orality. As with McLuhan's earlier metaphor of the global village, the notion of secondary orality suggests that our electronic public sphere has restored some of the characteristics of ancient oral culture. We are not talking about actual oral transactions, of course, but virtual intimacy, a verbal-visual-acoustic construction of a sense of conversation, what Horton and Wohl have termed para-social interaction.[9] Ong's metaphor of secondary orality usefully captures what has happened to the American presidency; although not actually oral in the sense of face-to-face communication, our political conversations have the feel of face-to-faceness, and our televised political spectacles are constructed to give the electorate a virtual presence—a ticket to what looks like a front-row seat to the political history of our times. The computer has been the digital servant to both the spectacle and the talk, to both the show and the tell.

More specifically, the electrification of American politics has altered its dynamics determinatively: computerized representations of public opinion have recast relationships between the presidency and its constituencies; film and video have enlarged the role of spectacle in politics; and the new technologies have all but destroyed the traditional distance that has existed between leaders and the led. Consider these ideas:

PUBLIC OPINION. Eighteenth-century Anglo-American politics worked on a notion of virtual representation, on the notion that the public's opinion was registered through the votes of its parliamentary or legislative representatives. By late nineteenth-century America, a clientelistic understanding of public opinion was in place, as party bosses and their precinct captains delivered specific services to those precincts in exchange for the power *to be* their opinion within the political system.[10] We live in a different time. Public opinion is electronically constituted on a daily basis.

So, the *Des Moines Register*, at least weekly, statistically traces the opinion of Iowans on everything from abortion to motorcycle helmets for its state and national representatives. During the last month of the 1988 campaign, the *New York Times* ran twenty presidential campaign-related poll stories on its front page, while the *Washington Post* ran twenty-four.[11] Between them, they represented public opinion to the Bush and Dukakis campaigns about one-and-a-half times a day. The public opinion poll has fully saturated political culture.

This sort of representation offers public advice to political mavens. When polls chart public opinion with but 5 percent error on a daily basis, they create a virtual conversation between leaders and constituencies. Carville and Matalin's recent chronicling of their joint lives through the 1992 campaign illustrates the hysteria that hit both the Bush and Clinton campaigns when the polls moved a notch or two this day or that, causing tears of joy or despair, and reinforcements or realignments of campaign strategy.[12]

As well, the computerized charting of voters not only allows the president to count support but even to select appeals to the uncommitted. The Bush advisers soon discovered from the polls that the public was uncomfortable with the idea of going into the Persian Gulf to protect American oil interests. That appeal dropped out of Bush's public talk after August, 1990, as he focused on the much more popular positive appeals to the vague New World Order and brotherhood of nations, and the negative appeals to a new Hitler who was gobbling up territory via the same tactics and presumably with the same motives as had the old Hitler.

The statistical, computerized representation of public opinion, in other words, has introduced a rhetoric of action and reaction based on virtual relationships. That is, the public becomes constituted, not as the little old lady from Dubuque or the kindly black man from Tupelo—not synecdochically, but in an oddly metonymic frame, as a demographic matrix sorted by a gender-race-socioeconomic status-educational level-party preference-strongly agree or disagree system that permits political segmentation and targeting. An action is taken, the matrix is checked to see which squares show signs of strong positive or negative reaction, the action is revised, the matrix checked again, and so it goes until the president and his party win or lose a key vote. Abraham Lincoln worked with no such virtual relationships when he instituted the draft during the Civil War. Bill

Clinton did, however, when he pushed on the gays-in-the-military issue in 1993. Lincoln bulled his way through draft riots and threats of impeachment; Clinton was able to temper, tune, and alter his policy statements throughout the legislative and then executive order processes, adjusting his linguistic and argumentative acts in the face of public reactions. He had miscalculated his opposition, but, with the help of poll data, could cut his losses and yet act presidentially. Clinton lives in a revolutionary political world.

SPECTACLE. Certainly politics has always been saturated by spectacle. Homer hymned visions of war councils and treaty negotiations. The Roman triumph was nothing if not a visible parade of slaves, booty, and political prisoners attesting to the might of Rome and the superiority of its civilization—a visual encomium. Elizabeth I, as illegitimate daughter of Henry VIII, upon coronation undertook a tour of England so that her royal personage and queenly radiance could be seen by the little people, establishing, as Geertz has argued, her charisma.[13] In doing so, she firmly established herself as the shining legitimate center of power in a century when demonstrations of rights to power were regularly demanded. Daniel O'Connell, the Irish-Catholic rights patriot, chose another form of demonstration; he staged so-called monster meetings, drawing together a quarter of a million screaming Irish Catholics who struck fear or at least concern even in that temperant British prime minister, Robert Peel.[14]

With photographic reproduction, editing, enrichment of pictures through sound and graphics, narrative, and intercut images from a thousand sources, spectacle in our time has become the North Pole of politics. Spectacle provides our polaris to the political; it is central to the process, as Murray Edelman argued in 1988: "The spectacle constituted by news reporting continuously constructs and reconstructs social problems, crises, enemies, and leaders and so creates a succession of threats and reassurances. These constructed problems and personalities furnish the content of political journalism and the data for historical and analytic political studies. They also play a central role in winning support and opposition for political causes and policies."[15]

Edelman brilliantly builds the case that our definition of political problems and their solutions is the product of visualization. One could suggest as well that the very outline of our political environment—of the symbolic universe within which we do politics—is constructed through spectacle, and that the voters' so-called subject positioning, that is, the voters' gaze upon the political process, is likewise a product of electronic media.

In the classic epigram that television does not tell us what to think but rather what to think about, we have one articulation of a defensible position. We must move beyond the idea of mass media as agenda setting to the proposition that not only are issues defined and ordered but even our sense of what *is* an issue is set spectacularly. The "unseeing eye"[16] becomes our eye; seeing is believing and not seeing is not knowing. During the Gulf War of 1991, attention was focused among other things on the Iraqi's damage to the environment, as the image of an oil-drenched cormorant standing on a pier was shown again and again, synecdochically condensing all of the anti-Hussein arguments about environmental destruction into a single image. Never were we shown Allied harm to the environment. It was an idea without articulation; it fell outside the symbolic environment and hence was not a part of the conversation of the culture. Seeing the sites with on-location shots is an essential part of what gives TV its power to direct and influence public decision making.

The idea of subject positioning or specularity relies upon a psychoanalytic understanding that makes some commentators uncomfortable, though the thrust of the concept is provocative.[17] In arguing that film makes us into voyeurs, controlling both what and how we gaze upon objects, Laura Mulvey asserts that we who view films are positioned in particular ways as subjects; our subjectivities are constructed by what we watch. Fiske tries to generalize Mulvey's argument to all mass media experience through the idea of specularity; spectacle not only provides us with something to watch but with the way of watching it, again, controlling our subjectivities. To Fiske, we are interpellated or hailed by images not simply to a way of seeing but even a way of being. Politically, the notion of interpellation suggests that we are called to public action via images of citizenship, to positions or roles in public proceedings.

To extend these ideas specifically to presidential politics, one could argue that political spectacle positions us, interpellates us, to the role of citizen in particular ways. Seeing the fireworks of the Army-McCarthy hearings in 1954 day in and day out not only provided viewers with breathtaking drama but also positioned them as viewers who had to choose between the Commie-baiting demagoguery of a hysterical senator and the law-and-order, due process work of a congressional committee. We were more than witnesses to those hearings; we became concurring judges through our voyeuristic journey into that site. Spectacle must be understood in terms of both what is seen and who it is who is doing the seeing.

POLITICAL DISTANCE. Politics always has involved a separation of the ruler and the ruled; psychosocial distance has been important to all societies, whether between the shaman's backstage and his front stage performances or between the scaling of the political hierarchy on one's way to office and the embodying of power in the inaugural ceremony and surrounding events. Secrecy that becomes mystification, knowledge that is transformed into wisdom and insight, and a mere person who becomes the president—all such transformations are distancing. Effective politics has traditionally been managed across a symbolic gulf.

The veil of mystery, the foundation of political wisdom, and perhaps the presidency itself have been all but destroyed by contemporary televisual journalism. Joshua Meyrowitz in his marvelous book *No Sense of Place* (1985) argues that the commentator-style of journalism popularized by Cronkite, Huntley and Brinkley, and their successors has destroyed the traditional distinction between political front stage and backstage. Citizens are neither mere spectators located on the front side of political events nor in-the-know insiders located on the back side of those happenings. Rather, we are on the side stage, allowed to witness the event yet subjected to continual analysis and interpretation of the item to the point that the interpretation can become more important than the event. The number of words devoted by journalists during the 1994 bielection period to Clinton's leadership skills or lack thereof allowed us, even encouraged us, to focus on those skills rather than his positions and arguments.

In carrying political dramas directly to us through the reproductive electronic technologies of radio and television, especially, those media may well be destroying the symbolic distance between the leader and the led.[18] The leader's actions are analyzed to death in terms of backgrounds and consequences, political uptake and popular support, and their representativeness of good or bad leadership. And as President Clinton was followed to McDonald's, his vacation spots, his mother's funeral, and whatever other environs he could be found, he became humanized—he became again one of us. And so his political power was weakened.

Political power exercised too closely to a citizenry is either feared or discredited. This is not the place to discuss the symbolic and ritualized aspects of political power, though it has been a subject of speculation at least since Yahweh of the Old Testament tested Adam and Eve's allegiance by forbidding the eating of the fruit of the Tree of Knowledge. The metaphor of the Tree of Knowledge captures not only the sort of deference citizens must pay central authority, but, of course, also stands as tribute to the role of mystification and public dramaturgy in the exercise of power. Knowledge can destroy relationships between leaders and the led by shrinking the gulf between the executive and the people. Discovering the mundaneness of the Wizard destroyed his ability to govern Oz.[19]

Today, the mundaneness of politicians is emphasized in myriad ways. Franklin Roosevelt's physical condition was noticed but not subjected to political commentary; even Dwight Eisenhower's heart attack—which could have precipitated a crisis had the public known of its severity—was depicted within a business-as-usual style of reporting. Not so today. Lyndon Johnson's hemorrhoids, Richard Nixon's phlebitis, and Ronald Reagan's polyps filled headlines and newscasts. Reagan's fondness for jelly beans, Bush's dislike of broccoli, and Clinton's weakness for burgers and fries were public knowledge and vehicles for constructing them as ordinary.

Today presidents have not only advisers but also spin doctors, thus surrendering their meaning-making powers to bureaucrats. During the 1992 campaign "President Bush" gave way to the moniker "George Herbert Walker Bush" by those attacking him, emphasizing his eastern ancestry rather than his office. The constant pop psychoanalysis of Jimmy Carter and his "malaise"—together, perhaps, with his accent and his sweaters—did nothing but blunt his power to act whether on energy or his reelection campaign. Thus, in the elevation by the electronic media of the popular and their corresponding delegitimation of the powerful, they have degraded political office and destroyed significant symbolic resources. Electronic journalism has taken its toll.

If, in sum, the electronic opinion poll has made the president's relationship with his constituencies into a quasi-interactive process, if the spectacle not only shows us what but also tells us who to be, and if the chasm between presidents and their constituencies has been all but breached, where are we? In the age of secondary orality, where literateness is deemphasized, interactiveness is emphasized, and phantasms frame both politicians and constituents, in what sort of *polis* do we live? The term *polis* must be understood not only as a *polity* or mode of collectivization but also as a *policy* or typology of actions taken by political actors and as *politics* itself or the strategies used by competing individuals and groups to gain resources.[20] How have we remade the American *polis* since 1924?

THE ELECTRONIC PRESIDENCY

Let us enlarge our vision somewhat by examining four markers that define the electronic presidency in our time:

(1) the comparative importance of a multimediated rhetoric,
(2) the acceleration of rhetorical process,
(3) the centrality of *ethos* to presidential success, and
(4) the diffusion of what counts as presidential rhetoric.

MULTIMEDIATED RHETORIC. As has been suggested, rhetoricians have written too little about the visualization of power and politics. Stephen Houlgate goes so far as to posit the "hegemony of vision," an ocularcentrism that has governed western thought and actions perhaps since Plato and certainly since Descartes; it is the complicity with which we yield to seeing that so infuriated Jacques Ellul in his book *The Humiliation of the Word,*[21] and that complicity is more deeply engrained in our psyches than ever.

While characterizing political rhetoric in the age of secondary orality as ocularcentric, we must remember that it also is verbocentric and phonocentric. So, a cuddly moment in the 1992 Republican national convention was the showing of a kind of music video, with Louis Armstrong singing "What a Wonderful World" over variegated images of bigendered, multiracial, multiaged Americans, with big smiles or sentimental, doe-eyed countenances. The film was visual, to be sure, but the music of a sacred black American jazzman opened the GOP's ties to something other than the generally conservative country music community, and the lyrics depicting the colors of the rainbow metaphorically argued that the GOP is an all-inclusive party.

The rhetorical force of that convention film comes from meanings created across the ocular, verbal, and phonic codes. The proposition that the GOP now is a broad-based political party was not directly articulated, yet the proposition was unmistakably present. Political rhetoric in our time is multimediated in that all three codes contain signs that, when taken together or agglutinated, become the political meanings upon which we act. Unstated propositions—but propositions nonetheless—riddle our political environment. Meaning making is a multichannel activity.

The implications of this fact are enormous. Depiction rather than word smithing is now the main task of the president's key aides.[22] A president needs the right words, but he also needs to be well-positioned, well-timed, well-tuned, and well-framed visually. Bill Clinton worked hard to be at the right place at the right time, to turn on his sincere, reedy voice, and then to switch over to his sincere, concerned, hoarse voice. The ability of leaders to control all three channels in today's mediated world is absolutely essential to political survival.

Presidential rhetorical acts thus have virtual dimensions we cannot ignore. The president not only acts but in the act of acting is also making political statements. That is, presidential rhetoric is discursive, a saying, but also symbolically meaningful as an act of saying. So, in 1976 Jimmy Carter promised a government as good as its people and then acted out the role of man of the people, carrying his own suitcase and being photographed washing his socks in hotel bathrooms. His earliest large-scale campaign poster had him in denim jeans, leaning on a fence and saying "I'm Jimmy Carter and I'm running for President." Not only did his populism scream at his audiences across the ocular, verbal, and phonic media but also his modes of acting resonated with the post-Watergate era. No president can succeed without multimedia skills.

ACCELERATION. Second, the instantaneousness of electronic communication media necessarily speeds up politics. We must study closely and systematically the impact of computerization on political process. Richard Wirthlin was fond of wiring a group of citizens watching a Ronald Reagan speech with response meters on which they would register their positive and negative reactions with twists of the dials. Wirthlin then would have computers monitor the sites so that he would have a continuous readout of audience reaction; overlaying the aggregated responses on the speech text gave him an analysis of every sentence of the speech.

On a larger scale, in the face of daily opinion polls, radio-television journalists—those on roundup shows, especially—with too much time to fill, and the Rush Limbaughs of our talk-show democracy, political decisions not made today will be talked out and interpreted; the president will be criticized, a hundred alternatives will be offered, and those listening in on these political conversations likely will come away unsure. In the electrified public sphere, dozens of experts appear on dozens of programs; each expert, armed with facts and opinions, self-assured and with an airtight analysis of some problem area, is granted a kind of legitimacy by his or her very appearance on a respectable TV program. Especially when television has much time to fill—as with the Gulf War in 1991 or the O. J. Simpson trial in 1995—so much data and opinion of contrary sorts are presented that the public loses its ability to comprehend political decision points.

And, the longer it takes the president to act, the greater the doubt. Surely the great medical reform political circus of 1994 deserves our attention. The number of players was legion. The arenas of talk were everywhere. The lobbyists outnumbered the good guys. The more President Clinton's team tried to slow us down, to talk reasonably (it thought) through the issue, the worse matters got. In contrast to NAFTA, where he took a stand, called in some chips, and pushed Congress to make as quick a decision as it could, Clinton let himself get beaten on medical reform at least in part through delay and overexposure.

The computer has allowed images to be edited faster, information to be crunched more quickly, opinion to be generated and assessed more regularly. The political process has taken on a sense of urgency in the age of secondary orality. The legislative process, especially, has become an exercise in frenzy, in part because of the increased legislative load, but also in part because the electronic connections between the players who perform politics in front of an electronically accessed electorate have sent our political engines down the track at a reckless speed.

THE CENTRALITY OF ETHOS. The American electorate exists in the paradoxical state of drowning in political information even as it is starving for political knowledge. Voters dwell in a technoculture that has expanded their knowledge of their own neighborhoods even as the new technologies have brought everyone else's neighborhoods, from all around the world, into their direct experience. This situation has produced multiple political crises. We have too much information about our own problems, our state's problems, our country's problems, and the world's problems to make sense out of any of them. We surfeit with information and yet lack the practical, ideological, and moral wherewithal to use the information to solve the problems. The gridlock that we believe characterizes our times comes not only from the pigheadedness of political parties playing zero-sum games but also from the multiplication of centers of information and expertise that in turn feed their analyses and solutions into the public sphere via the mass media. Faced with too many reasonable analyses of ugly problems and unable to comprehend the interlocks that tie local banks to multinational finance, citizens throw up their hands, curse the darkness, and rate politicians somewhere near the bottom of occupational scales.

In such an environment, it is little wonder that moral issues—abortion, the death penalty, gun control—dominate even campaigns for local office. People may not know what's what, but at the least they know what's right. The baffling success of Dan Quayle probably was related to his ability to articulate a moral response to a family-value issue and a patriotic response to the Gulf War. Condensing problems and their solutions to moral and patriotic—which is to say, to valuative—principles has the virtue of making it possible to unlock the grid. Moral and patriotic principles are reducible to a binary decision point—either something is good or bad, just or unjust, right or wrong. The cacophony of voices is thus organized into a two-sided argument, where a vote can be taken and a principled decision made. Vice President Quayle worked two-valued issues very well.

And thus, much of American politics has been telescoped down to the moral and patriotic—to a question of *ethos.* The word *ethos* itself, standing for both community as well as individual character, perfectly captures the primary criterion for presidential success in the age of secondary orality. If the electorate cannot comprehend the multiple facets of issues, it has little choice but to select leaders on the basis of character. *Logos* has been disempowered by the complexities of the information age. *Pathos* has always been distrusted as a basis for political decision. *Ethos* is the one element of the classic trilogy left. Character can mediate between thought and feeling, tempering self-interest and providing criteria—Aristotle's good sense, good will, and good morals—for cutting through the mountains of information to find the *krisis,* or point of decision, that allows action to occur.

To Aristotle, *ethos* was more than reputation. It was a performance of one's good sense, good will, and good morals. The performative dimensions of the presidency are almost beyond cataloging. Once the barrier between the personal and the public was traduced and once the electronic media brought the electorate words, sounds, and sights, presidential *ethos* would be assessed in hundreds of ways. Ask Bill Clinton. Voters saw him playing his sax, taking his daughter to basketball games, jogging in goofy outfits, waving from good seats in Lincoln Center, riding in a bus, visiting schools and hospitals, holding hands with his wife, bailing water in Des Moines during the flood of 1993, burying his mother, laying wreaths for warriors in the cemeteries of Europe and America, wearing his commander-in-chief clothes on a ship or at a base, taking on all comers on call-in television shows, and hunting ducks back home in Arkansas.

The public access to the president—not only in campaigns but even during off years—is enormous. It is direct, as when the president appears for the photo opportunities and news conferences, and it is indirect, as when the electronic journalists edit him into stories and subject him to interpretive commentary. The process of building and maintaining a political *ethos* is continuous, complicated, and absolutely compelling. Ronald Reagan was amazingly good at it, Bill Clinton struggled with it, and George Bush was both made and then broken on this symbolic process. Bush constructed an incredibly powerful character during the Gulf War, only to be broken on the issue of character a year later when struggling with the domestic agenda.

RHETORICAL DISCOURSE. Underlying much of what has been argued is a fourth proposition: in the age of secondary orality, what we are to understand as political rhetoric must be monumentally expanded. The *Public Papers* will never again contain the rhetorical discourse of a president. Videotape, compilations of polls, and content analyses of the Vanderbilt news records will be required to circumscribe a president's rhetorical arts.[23] The idea of discourse, if understood as acts granted political meaningfulness, has exploded. Inside the Beltway, the entrails are read daily: exercise and fast food habits, marital relationships, presence or absence of politicians at key prayer breakfasts, talk-show performances, overnight polls and the responses they draw. And even attendance at basketball games: the fact that President Clinton took daughter Chelsea to a George Washington University basketball game and then stayed for part of the following women's game as well was seen as a significant political act.

What are the outer limits of that which we can define as political rhetoric? If political rhetoric includes those signs, icons, behaviors, and multicoded discourses out of which audiences construct political meaning—and perhaps more particularly those signs, icons, behaviors, and multicoded discourses used in the service of power—then we are dealing with an elastic concept. Such a definition as yet must be taken as provisional. It at least has the virtue of putting on the table of rhetorical analysts something more than speeches, thereby allowing us, even forcing us, to study more categories of acts and events. As we listen to metapolitical talk on the *NewsHour with Jim Lehrer* or a CNN face-off specifically to notice what sorts of acts and events are granted status as political signs, we ought to be able over time to refine that definition, all the while reflecting what functions rhetorically in the political arena.

CONCLUSIONS

This chapter is a hesitant step in a journey many have been taking in refashioning our understanding of political rhetoric generally, and the symbolic operations of the presidency more particularly. The task is complicated because the changes in the operations of especially American and European politics in the age of secondary orality are morally and ideologically charged. Critics from the right express grave concern in the electronic age for the loss of stability, the loss of centeredness, and the overriding of some of the key systemic controls in our country. They fear the loss of rationality that they believe inevitably accompanies the de-emphasis of the verbal in political process. Critics from the left often take two routes into this topic: those with a taste for the French postmodern decry the emptiness of the political sign, even the ineffectuality of political life in the simulacra, but those with a stronger Marxist commitment see in our surrender to the visual and the performative dimensions of politics grounds for even greater concern for political hegemony and the "mystification of social relations."[24]

In many ways, both ends of the political spectrum are grounded in political truths. Political systems and political offices without centers are indeed dangerous. And yet, it nonetheless seems odd to ground a critique of American political drift on a critique of television. Society's use of it, after all, is culturally conditioned; the remaking of American politics has not been caused by the new technologies but rather by how we have used them politically. They can be used in other ways, as with Iranian television, for example. For that matter, as Dayan and Katz have argued, television—especially the live broadcasting of such special events as the Sadat-Begin peace accords—actually works to center or stabilize political systems.[25] Similarly, although critics must be ever watchful for the merely ideological that potentially can perpetuate hegemonies that imprison a citizenry, to drag up images of Orwell's Big Brother or Foucault's Panoptican is to rely on ghosts rather than careful analysis.

So yes, we must recognize that political systems have undergone redefinition and remanufacturing throughout time. Were that not a fact, we would be treated to trials by combat between bare-chested Bill Clinton and Newt Gingrich in a deadly political version of all-star wrestling. And, we must recognize that political issues—more especially still, the moral bases of political argumentation and resolution—have always been matters for rhetorical contestation. Social mores are seldom stable for very long periods of time; democracies, especially, regularly redefine their domestic and international agenda and the valuative bases upon which those agenda rest.[26]

Critique is called for, but the wringing of one's hands in despair when contemplating the operation particularly of the presidency in the age of secondary orality is counterproductive. The age of radio, television, film, and computers is here to stay, and it matters not one whit whether we scorn it. Cursing the darkness only leaves us hoarse. The electronic presidency can operate in grand or lowly ways; it can produce moments of thrill and embarrassment; it can bring us to tears of joy when we are intimate witness to the highlights of history or tears of shame when we are forced to watch inept fools and charlatans fritter away our time, money, and resources of power.

The system can always stand reform, and the presidency itself simply must find better ways to handle the bureaucracy, to manage public time, and to triangulate relationships with its varied constituencies. Richard Neustadt's understanding of the power of the president being the power to persuade still stands as a hallmark of the office, though the kinds of bureaucratic negotiations he described are now done publicly in most ways, and hence we must find ways to reframe the president's negotiation processes.[27]

Talk of reform of the operations of the presidency we can leave to others with more experience in such matters. Yet, all teachers of government, sociology, journalism, politics, and the various communication studies should move the electronic presidency onto their syllabi. To ignore the presidency in the age of secondary orality is to fail to arm students with the means of verbally and visually deconstructing it. To ignore the moral uptake of political process is to let atrocities go unexamined. To allow the

Revolving Door and Willie Horton ads to go unanalyzed is to permit them to take their civic tolls.

To the army of scholars who live off of presidential studies, the challenges of secondary orality are especially vexing. Political scientists have studied the presidency's relationships to other institutions; historians have combed public and private papers in search of the essences of political leaders; rhetorical critics have dissected their speech texts; and policy analysts have explored the relationships between political doctrine and political action. Few, however, have taken the public faces of the presidents—their public appearances, their public behavior—seriously enough. Relationships between the political campaign films of the 1920s and attempts to frame public policy with mass-distributed films in the 1930s have not been explored. Roosevelt's presidency was mediated successfully by radio, and we need to know more about that mediation; his radio addresses as responses to other reformers need special attention. Was the Truman administration as aware of the potential of television as it was of filmed newsreel pictures of his family to improve his popularity? The distinction between a private and a secret life seemed to disappear in the trial and 1953 execution of Julius and Ethel Rosenberg.[28] To what degree were they victimized by the voyeuristic aspects of newsreel film and television? What happens to our understanding of the *Missiles of October* if we interpret the Kennedy administration's actions as telespectacle? What happens if we interpret the Nixon administration's opening of relationships with the People's Republic of China through the same lens? Carter's energy initiatives in 1977 and 1979 provide us with contrasting public-performative styles that deserve more attention than they have received.

This list can be expanded almost indefinitely—and it should be. As Murray Edelman has argued, "To understand either stability or change, it is necessary to look at the social situations people experience, anticipate, or fantasize." To Edelman, and to me, "political life is hyperreal,"[29] which is to say, discursively constructed, maintained, altered, or destroyed. Material reality can be processed by human beings only via discourse about it, and hence political discourse—verbal, visual, acoustic, behavioral—is inevitably hyperreal. This is not, of course, to trivialize or relativize life anymore than it already is, nor is it to argue that all political constructions of the world are equally useful or accurate.

Rather, it is to argue that politics understood as symbolic action demands that we analyze systematically the discourses of political ideology and valuation, of political visions and the places citizens occupy in such visions, of the means by which self-interests are converted into communal interests—and into public policies. It is to argue, as well, that discursiveness itself must be reexamined. If we limit our understanding of discursiveness to the merely verbal, we overly narrow our understanding of both politicking (the process of doing politics) and politicization (the reinterpretation of some aspects of life as political).[30] The doing of politics—acting, attaching political values to aspects of the world—is executed via multiple symbol systems, each of which demands careful attention in particular situations.

And, of course, the presidency itself must be comprehended in symbolic terms. Indeed, *the presidency* is a deliberate reifaction—a condensed term capable of blending an individual and his actions into an institutional web of meanings. To call the presidency an institution is not simply to locate it on a civic organizational chart. It is to recognize that even a reified concept has rhetorical significance, that even *the presidency* works ideologically as a discursive concept attended by the accoutrements of power.

Finally, then, to argue that the electronic presidency is fundamentally different from the presidency as it has operated and been experienced in other epochs is to recognize that today presidents seek to influence and guide such public political activities as elections and policy making in new ways. Radio, television, and film have not simply amplified their voices and mass-distributed their faces. Rather, they represent new arenas of discourse within which the presidency takes shape and gains force. In other words, the age of secondary orality both refashions presidential rhetoric and refabricates the presidency itself.

Precisely how both actions occur remains to be studied systematically. That is our challenge: to understand the presidency's use of and construction by the instruments of secondary orality.[31]

CHAPTER 4

Desktop Demos:

NEW COMMUNICATION TECHNOLOGIES
AND THE FUTURE OF THE
RHETORICAL PRESIDENCY
Thomas W. Benson

The rapid growth of computer-mediated communication (CMC) technologies and practices in the 1980s and 1990s has led to a variety of experiments with the political uses of electronic networks, often marked by a utopian sense of the possibilities of the medium for reviving democratic participation. This chapter combines a theoretical discussion grounding predictions about political uses of computer-mediated communication with a description and analysis of some actual practices, with special reference to the Clinton administration.

This report is motivated in part by a question central to rhetorical theory and criticism: Is politics possible? Such a question might seem absurd at a time when we are bombarded not only with political messages but with the overwhelming insistence by the media that politics is unavoidable. Why, then, should we ask whether politics is possible? If by politics we mean an activity that takes place in a universally available public sphere built upon the context of an actively civic society, implying citizens who recognize and enact their public obligations both locally and nationally, and discursive practices that are by some measure rational, accessible, and reciprocal, then there are many reasons to entertain doubts about the vitality of our politics. And so my inquiry is motivated by the curiosity as to how, if at all, the Internet as a medium of communication is contributing or might contribute to the public sphere and civil society.[1]

The rapid expansion of what is sometimes called the Global Information Infrastructure has led to competing utopian and dystopian predictions about the influence of changing communications technologies on the human prospect. In this context, the presidency of Bill Clinton has begun to employ computer networking to alter the rhetorical accessibility of the presidency itself. Any person with access to the Internet—a complex of networks connecting millions of personal and mainframe computers in homes, schools, and workplaces around the world—can send electronic mail to the White House and can gain access to speeches, press conferences, and other public documents issued by the White House.

Use of the Internet by the presidency and citizens offers a prospect of enhancing democracy by reshaping the rhetorical tools and contexts of presidential leadership, altering the conditions of vertical and horizontal political participation by citizens, providing access to immediately relevant rhetorical texts and government documents, and recovering the arts of historical memory that are essential to the practice of democracy. These prospects interweave the themes of leadership, participation, access, and memory as key elements in the future of the rhetorical presidency.

A significant theme in the White House development of Internet access is the importance of direct contact between the people and the presidency. Presidents have long complained of the pernicious interference of the press in their attempts to make their case to the people, and have adopted a variety of institutional means to manipulate or supersede the press. Reinforcing these White House complaints, a large body of scholarly and critical literature laments the destructive effects of the mass media on political discourse and participation.[2]

Presidents and candidates have always struggled for the means to communicate effectively in the context of opponents and recalcitrant media systems. The swing around the circle, the fireside chat, the whistle-stop campaign, the television address to the nation, and the Saturday morning radio address are all attempts both to speak over the heads of the press and to create a story for the press, while incidentally dramatizing the president's persona as a unique national figure.

The development of press secretaries and formal staffs of speech writers has institutionalized the role of president as communicator. In 1968, the Nixon administration created yet another institution, the White House Office of Communications, which has increasingly been the site for presidential adaptations to the media. John Anthony Maltese has documented the Office of Communications from its origins in Richard Nixon's antagonism toward the media. According to Maltese's account, the Nixon presidential campaign of 1968 "shielded him from reporters" and created the television illusion of direct public access to the candidate speaking to the people.[3] The strategy of control employed in the campaign was formalized in the White House Office of Communications, wherein an attempt to manage or speak over the heads of the Washington press was presented as a gesture of creating greater direct access to the presidency. Nixon increased the number of television speeches to the nation at the same time that he "all but phased out news conferences."[4]

Richard Nixon's hostility to the press set in place the structure and the terms of presidential communication management that continues to this day and that in part contextualizes the computer-mediated public access project of the Clinton White House.

It is probably accurate to characterize much of the activity of the White House Office of Communications as spin control. And yet it might not be unreasonable to turn just that charge back upon the press. Virtually any examination of press coverage of a presidential speech reveals an account not of the primary themes and arguments of the speech but rather of the motives and strategies hidden by the speech but revealed by the reporter. Hence, citizens not only do not have access to the text of the speech itself, but they are also told over and over again about conflict, strategy, motive, and personality. Under conditions in which the president's words are filtered through television and newspapers, those presidential words are reduced to a symptom or an event; their function as argument (if the words should happen to contain any arguments, which is not always the case) is radically obscured.

The experimental use of electronic networks to distribute Bill Clinton's speeches in the 1992 presidential campaign seemed to yield a glimpse of a completely different mode of apprehending national politics, one in which candidates were attempting to set forth connected arguments instead of merely producing sound bites. The 1992 campaign and the subsequent development of a presidential presence on the Internet has raised hopes that access to computer networking technology can provide not only a national audience for reasoned political discourse but a mechanism, through various computer bulletin board and mailing list systems, for citizens to correspond with one another about politics.

TECHNOLOGY AND DEMOCRACY

It is not unusual to read claims that increasingly widespread access to computer technology will enhance democracy and build community.[5] Such claims often appear to predict "nothing less than a new organization of society—a state of things in which every individual, however secluded, will have at call every other individual in the community, to the saving of no end of social and business complications, of needless goings to and fro, of disappointments, delays, and a countless host of those great and little evils and annoyances which go so far under present conditions to make life laborious and unsatisfactory."[6]

This prediction, which might have come from any number of recent White House reports extolling the economic and social benefits of computer networking, in fact was discovered by Carolyn Marvin in a discussion of the telephone that appeared in *Scientific American* in 1880. In her book on the introduction of electrical technologies in the nineteenth century, Marvin describes a series of debates that closely parallel current discussions of computer networking. On the one hand, some commentators foresaw "the building of better, usually construed to mean more open and democratically accessible, communities."[7] On the other hand, there were predictions of social disorder, distortions of settled zones of public and private, and the rise of new hierarchies based on commercial power or technological expertise.

Cultural debates such as those Marvin discovered in the late nineteenth century have been repeated, with variations, with the introduction and development of other communication technologies, including the printing press, the electric light, the large circulation daily newspaper, the telegraph, radio, documentary film, television, and now the computer, as well as with the introduction of new modes of transportation, such as canals, railroads, and paved highways.[8]

Countless observers in education, journalism, and government have celebrated the introduction of computer-mediated communication as an opportunity to renew endangered forms of participatory democracy in education, the workplace, and the public sphere.

The Internet traces its history to the establishment by the United States Department of Defense of the ARPANET in 1969. The ARPANET was conceived as a means of connecting university research scientists with the defense establishment, for the exchanging of computer programs and working files. But a mostly unplanned and spontaneous parasite soon emerged. Those with access to the ARPANET—a rapidly expanding group—developed a practice of exchanging electronic mail that may or may not be strictly work-related. In 1979, computer scientists at the University of North Carolina and Duke University collaborated to establish USENET, a system of computer bulletin boards. The Internet, which has evolved out of ARPANET and other public and commercial networks, now hosts more than five thousand USENET bulletin boards. In turn, these bulletin boards have become a model for those available on some of the commercial networks, such as CompuServe, Prodigy, and America Online. Computer networks also make possible the automatic distribution of electronic mail to groups of subscribers, frequently through the Listserv program. There are now thousands of Listserv lists on the Internet.

The technical features of electronic mail, USENET, and Listserv were first exploited in an on-line cultural context that emphasized a strongly consensual spirit of anarchy, participation, and democracy. Resistance to censorship in any form occasionally allowed episodes of information overload, harassment, personal abuse (called "flaming" in the jargon of the networks), widespread propagation of computer viruses, and what some have objected to as obscenity and pornography. But the freedom of the networks also led many to celebrate it as a model in which widespread information access and ungoverned communities of discourse could herald a new spirit of active and participatory self-governance in education, workplace, and public sphere.

Computer-mediated communication enables users, once they have achieved access to the Internet—an accomplishment that is by no means trivial in terms of money or learning—to communicate with an unprecedented combination of speed, convenience, and scope to a worldwide community of other users, exchanging written and other data asynchronously—that is, in an environment where sender and receiver do not need to be logged on at the same moment but where, because transmission is so rapid, complex interactions can extend to many turns in a short period of time.

Computer-mediated communication is modeled on two capacities that sometimes operate together, sometimes separately. First, CMC can allow for an unprecedented new power to store, distribute, and access enormous quantities of useful information. Second, CMC can amplify and in many ways has altered the power of humans to interact communicatively with one another. In commenting on both of these dimensions, scholars and advocates have often written of their effects in political terms, repeatedly celebrating the ways in which computers have altered the politics of everyday life. Users have expanded access to knowledge and the means to influence others, thereby building collaborative communities of work and learning. Increasingly, government and politics in the literal sense have been finding a role on computer networks.

THE PRESIDENCY AND THE INTERNET
The American presidency came to the Internet in 1992, when the Clinton campaign began sending out transcripts of the candidate's speeches, along with other campaign materials, to USENET and various Listserv groups. At the same time, arising from a number of positions of grass roots leadership, discussion lists and bulletin boards were started on the Internet, BITNET, and some of the commercial networks. The organizer of the Clinton campaign e-mail effort was Jonathan Gill, who after the 1992 election joined the Clinton White House as director of a project to put the White House on the Internet.[9] Vice President Al Gore, who since his days in the United States Senate has been a strong advocate of measures to expand telecommunications infrastructure, has been a strong force in prompting the administration along this path.

Although the electronic distribution of campaign documents in 1992 can hardly be said to be more than a demonstration of potential, rather than a major force in the campaign, the experience of those who were able to participate was reportedly one of renewed belief that American politics at the national level could go beyond the sound bite and the thirty-second spot. Viewing the campaign by reading speech after lengthy speech, one had an entirely different sense of the campaign than that conveyed by commercial television news. In the speeches, slogans were of course embedded for the sound bites of the nightly news, but one also read actual arguments, chains of reasoning, and evidence that altered the tone and substance of the campaign as a rhetorical experience.

Once he joined the White House staff, Gill began to put into effect the promise made by Bill Clinton and Al Gore to provide electronic access to the White House and to the executive branch generally. Since the Clinton inauguration, every presidential speech, proclamation, executive order, and letter to Congress, as well as media interviews with the president and press conferences with the president, the press secretary, and a variety of senior administration officials have been made available in electronic text over the Internet, usually within twenty-four hours of the event. It has been possible to subscribe to these materials for delivery by electronic mail, with the choice of receiving all documents of whatever sort or filtering them so as to choose only specific types (such as speeches or press conferences) or on specific topics (such as the economy, health, foreign affairs, and so on). It is also possible for individual computer users to gain access to these documents by retrieval from various large computer data banks maintained by the federal government, by various universities, or by commercial computer networks. Various indexes and catalogs and other retrieval mechanisms have been developed, as well as a daily summary of White House documents published electronically by the extension service of the Department of Agriculture.

It quickly became possible to address electronic mail to the White House, addressing either President@WhiteHouse.Gov or Vice.President@WhiteHouse.Gov. Correspondents were asked to include their regular postal addresses so that replies could be sent to them on paper. A few members of Congress also announced e-mail addresses, though with concerns that they might be the target of electronic mail from nonconstituents. At the opening of the 104th Congress in 1995, some forty members of the House of Representatives listed e-mail addresses.[10]

The sheer volume of material available on-line seems revolutionary. In its first two years in office, the Clinton White House alone sent approximately three thousand separate documents to various Internet subscribers. All of them are available for remote search and retrieval. This enormous mass of documents would always, in principle, be available to anyone with the resources to locate a depository library and consult the *Weekly Compilation of Presidential Documents* and the annual compilation in *Public Papers of the Presidents*. Not all citizens, of course, are within easy reach of such documents, though the same could be said at this point about electronic access. It is estimated that perhaps ten to thirty million users had access to the Internet in 1994, with access growing as rapidly as 15 percent a month.[11] Even for researchers with local access to a university library containing *Public Papers of the Presidents,* the ability to access these documents remotely and in electronic form not only makes research more convenient but alters the kinds of research that are feasible.

More recently, the White House has gained access to the rapidly developing World Wide Web, an Internet service that offers hypertext access to text, sound, and images. Those with very fast modems or direct access to high-speed fiber optic connections may employ such software as Mosaic and Netscape to work their way by pointing and clicking with a mouse or similar input device through nested screens of text and icons; a click on an icon or highlighted bit of text takes the user to another screen, often at a remote site, where he or she can read or download various documents. For example, in a recent issue of the on-line journal *Postmodern Culture,* published by Oxford University Press, an article appears by film critic Robert Kolker of the University of Maryland. A reader browsing Kolker's written text may click on embedded icons that download full-motion video clips from the films he is explicating.[12]

The White House address on the World Wide Web is stated in the form: http://www.whitehouse.gov.

Upon accessing the White House web page, the user is presented with a color photograph of the White House that is surrounded with a number of icons, which may be used to gain access to materials on various subjects, including the same White House speeches and press releases available by Gopher, FTP, and electronic mail, and also some materials prepared especially for the web, including brief sound tracks from the president and vice president welcoming the user to the White House web page; several pictures of Socks, the White House cat, as well as other Clinton family pictures; a tour of the White House, the Executive Office Building, and the White House gardens; and a tourist map of Washington. Because of these additional materials, the White House web page is very different in tone from the Gopher resources. Using the Gopher, one can obtain the official texts of White House documents that were brought into existence and communicated to press and public with no reference to the Internet, which acts merely as a storage and retrieval device. To be sure, to call the text-retrieval devices merely storage and retrieval devices is a bit misleading. When it was introduced soon after the 1992 campaign, the wide availability of the full text of presidential speeches was welcomed as another indication of the way the Internet was going to extend democracy, modeling a system in which the presidency was not filtered down to sound bites and the cynicism of the press. At the same time, there was a sort of dignity and austerity in the essentially text-only systems in that citizens were not being directly and specifically addressed through the system by which they were retrieving presidential texts.

On the White House web page, however, though there is the same state of high expectation about the contribution that access to presidential texts can make to representative democracy, the addition of direct address from the president and family photo album pictures of the First Family turns the service slightly in the direction of a White House tour. One might use the service as a gateway to presidential or other executive branch documents or as a slide show directed at armchair tourists. There is bound to be some experimentation as the White House tries to discover the appropriate mode of address and the appropriate content for its newly emerging electronic direct access. In any case, when a system resembling the World Wide Web becomes accessible to electorally significant numbers of Americans, it is likely to exert pressures on both the production and distribution of White House rhetoric and journalism's coverage of the presidency. There are any number of examples of such effects in our history, perhaps most recently in the interactive effects of television and politics. When television first offered gavel-to-gavel coverage of presidential nominating conventions, the event was hailed as a uniquely democratizing window on politics. But as conventions adapted to being covered by television, the television networks altered their own coverage, substituting interviews, commentary, and other material for podium coverage. More devastating has been the interaction of campaigns and television. National and statewide campaigns now exist primarily as television spectacles. So much money must be raised to campaign on television that politicians are cut loose from party discipline—substituting instead the discipline required to generate huge amounts of money to pay for individual, especially incumbent, campaigns. Such interactive effects will surely occur with widespread access to the Internet and its successors, though it is now difficult to predict what those effects will be.

What would it mean for presidential e-mail to succeed? Should its success be measured by its ability to answer mail or distribute speech texts electronically? Would rapid and universal distribution of presidential speech texts be the realization of the evolving rhetorical presidency? Under such conditions, is it reasonable to expect that the president would continue to travel widely and speak frequently, as he now does, but with the present scarcity of access to his words turned into abundance? Would we then wish for presidential discourse to maintain its present forms—speeches, interviews, press conferences—and change only the level of general access? In a sense, such conditions might seem at first to realize what we sometimes take to have been the ideal of nineteenth-century eloquence, an ideal never realized or perhaps even idealized in the nineteenth century, in which public oratory was eloquent, rational, deliberative, unique, abundant, and accessible. But if we were now to adopt this cluster of attributes as our own ideals for the rhetoric of the presidency, how would we go about it? Would we expect all other conditions governing the rhetorical scene to remain stable, changing only in such a way as to enhance the president's direct access to a national audience?

What would be the government's role in rendering the president's discourse widely accessible? Would we want a government or public space reserved by law on the Internet? We have already decided, in the United States, not to have government broadcasting or a system of predominantly public broadcasting, in favor of commercial broadcasting with a small semipublic network. The Internet seems likely to become entirely privatized in the United States; would we want the government to insure free and universal access to presidential rhetoric, or would access to it be on the same commercial terms charged by the carriers of the rest of the information?

Roderick Hart has pointed out how frequently the president speaks—too frequently, in his opinion.[13] And yet, for all that frequency, it may be said that presidential speaking is a scarce commodity, since it has been so difficult to gain access to the full text of the president's public speeches. The scarcity of access would appear to govern the logic of the rhetoric's production and use. For example, though the president speaks in public several times a week, his addresses to a variety of immediate audiences take on a dramatic meaning in addition to their manifest textual meaning. The president can more or less repeat himself—a sign not that he has exhausted rhetorical invention but that he is spreading the word. The news media, if they report these speeches at all, convey their own boredom with the repetition and their familiar stories about the game of politics, but they also play their part in telling the story of the president's reaching out to the people, getting out of Washington, sticking to the message. And when the president wants to make a major statement, he can, on special occasions, stage a speech to the nation, asking for and getting prime television time on the major networks. Universal access to the president's messages would pose a challenge to these settled practices, especially when we consider that within a very short time it will be possible for the White House to send us not only the transcript of a speech but also full audio and video coverage. Already it is possible to download from the White House, over the Internet, digital audio code of the president's Saturday radio addresses to the nation. Why, if the public had access to every presidential speech, would some speeches merit the exceptional treatment of being carried over network television? How, if we had access to all the president's speeches, would we know that some were more important than others? Why, if the public had full access to every presidential speech, would the president need to travel at all? Clearly it is important to the present drama of the presidency that the president should travel outside of Washington to meet citizens; those meetings are marked by the delivery of speeches. But if all had free and full access, would not the fiction of such travel begin to seem thin? Would the travel not seem, even more than now, merely staged? On the other hand, to stay in Washington and deliver frequent speeches to us from there would both overexpose and isolate the president. Would universal access make frequent speaking seem absurd? Would universal access make it seem peculiar that the president's messages were spoken rather than merely written? But if they were merely written, what would happen to the persona of the presidency? When the president delivers a speech written with the aid of ghostwriters, his giving voice to it enacts the fiction of his authorship; the writers fade into the background. Written messages from the president to the public are much more likely to seem to have been written by committee.

In what sense is the text of a presidential speech made accessible on the Internet—particularly when such access is, in principle, free and universal? In important ways, it is not merely the text that is thus made accessible but the text as the record of an event. We who read it, instead of hearing it as direct address, are witnessing it at one remove. And once we do have such access, we may experience not simply a great calling into the public sphere but a paradoxical recoil. We may find ourselves traveling at one bound from a rhetorical presidency that is fragmented into sound bites, and that has adapted itself to such a situation, to a presidency that is now all too visibly producing so much text that we cannot read it all in a normal citizen's day. And so, in a new sense, it is still fragmented, still presents itself to us as something other than discourse. The shock, the sense of repulsion, absurdity, and misdirected effort that Hart experienced when he calculated just how much presidents talk in public is an experience that has been denied to most citizens, who simply did not have access to all that talk. What happens when we do have such access? Will we recapitulate Hart's experience, or will we be redeemed as citizens of a newly discursive republic? Whether such a situation constitutes a renewed civic space, or merely induces a useful illusion of the public sphere, or, on the contrary, throws the constantly talking president into absurdity is unclear. Presidential emulation of a discursive public sphere on the Internet may become visible as merely a gesture, a simulacrum, reinforcing, in the context of the image world we all inhabit, a disorienting sense of our condition as decentered postmodern subjects rather than as citizens of the public cybersphere.[14]

It is also unclear, I think, whether such a series of changes would enhance or diminish the rhetorical potency of the presidency. It is not obvious that widespread distribution of presidential speeches would occur while all other features of the rhetorical situation remain stable, nor that such access would strengthen the rhetorical power of the presidency.

But the White House has always adapted to changes in the country's information infrastructure, from the postal service to television. Motion pictures were used in campaigns at least as early as those of Woodrow Wilson. FDR used radio for direct address to the people in his fireside chats and in what we might call indirect address, when radio broadcast political conventions and special addresses to Congress. Dwight Eisenhower made effective use of direct address over television in speeches to the nation from the Oval Office as well as indirect address in press conferences and other occasions. For the time being, the White House has used the Internet fairly conservatively. Part of its model is that of mail. The presidency receives a great deal of mail, but, unlike the Congress, the presidency does not send blanket mailings to constituents. Another part of its model emulates functions of the Government Printing Office and libraries, providing access to public documents. So far, little use has been made of the models of television and radio to use the Internet for direct address to the nation. This may change as the penetration of the Internet reaches the levels of radio during Roosevelt's presidency or television during Eisenhower's. By the time such levels of penetration occur, the Internet itself will have changed, perhaps into patterns of ownership, access, and mode of presentation that are very unlike what is now state of the art, as telephone, television, and computer networks converge.

In these speculations I am attempting to illustrate how imagining a different mode of presidential rhetoric throws our present modes into visibility, making them seem in many ways arbitrary and peculiar, elaborately maintained group fictions dependent on a complicated set of circumstances. I am also attempting to illustrate how the realization of what may now seem to be the suppressed potentials of democratic rhetoric could have paradoxical effects.

Because our consideration of the future is speculative, it is easy to turn it in optimistic or pessimistic directions. The future, of course, will have a way of taking care of itself and will create contexts that will become normal to those who inhabit them.

As of the beginning of 1995, the World Wide Web is a state-of-the-art mode of information storage, search, and retrieval on the Internet. But even the brief picture of it that I have presented here is highly idealized. Access to the Internet is by no means trivial for the average user in terms of money, equipment, and training. Connections to World Wide Web are often arcane and even unworkable. Even when it does work, retrieval is sometimes so slow that it hardly seems worth the effort. But the delays and frustrations of the World Wide Web will probably diminish quickly as hardware and software begin to catch up with its demands and as the medium is absorbed into the everyday world of millions of users.

Public documents from the entire federal government have become vastly more accessible since 1993. Partly at the urging of the Clinton administration, the United States Congress has also been working since 1993 to develop a useful presence on the Internet. In October, 1993, Democratic congressman Charlie Rose, chair of the Committee on House Administration, announced that as of that month the full text of all bills introduced in the United States House of Representatives would be made available for retrieval from the House Information Systems data center. The daily version of the *Congressional Record* for both the House and the Senate is available for search and retrieval, starting from the 103rd Congress of 1993–94. Early in 1995, with the beginning of the 104th Congress, the Congressional Record and other congressional documents were made available on the World Wide Web.[15] In announcing Web access to the 104th Congress, newly elected Speaker Newt Gingrich, who was quickly becoming recognized as another technological futurist, claimed that such access would "change the balance of power" so that the public could gain access to its representatives "untainted by the media's cynicism."[16]

Internet communication between citizens and the legislative and executive branches in Washington is two-way, but it is not reciprocal. It is possible for citizens to send electronic mail to the president and vice president, and to about forty members of Congress. White House instructions for such mail tell users:

> As we work to reinvent government and streamline our processes, this electronic mail project will help put us on the leading edge of progress. Please remember, though, this project is still very much under construction. The Office of Correspondence is currently working on defining what this system will do, as well as addressing equipment and staffing needs.
>
> When you send a message to the White House you will receive an immediate acknowledgment that your message has been received. THIS IS THE ONLY ELECTRONIC RESPONSE YOU WILL RECEIVE FROM WHITEHOUSE.GOV. If you include your street address in your message, you may receive a response by U.S. mail. Please be assured that every electronic mail message received is read and analyzed by staff. Your concerns and your ideas are carefully recorded and reported to the president and vice president weekly.[17]

As an illustration of the White House electronic mail service, I sent a note to president@whitehouse.gov on a Sunday morning, January 15, 1995, supporting continued funding of public television and national public radio. Within a minute the autoresponder at the White House sent an acknowledgment of my message along with the latest information on citizen access to government on the Internet, and with the information that since June, 1993, more than 400,000 electronic mail messages had been sent to the White House.[18]

The evolving House of Representatives electronic mail system displays some of the ways in which the politics of the Internet contrasts with traditional Constitutional practices. The Internet is experienced in some ways as a space in which thousands of others are exchanging messages. This space, sometimes called "cyberspace," does not usually—although it could—represent or respect political or topographical boundaries. Nicholas Negroponte, founding director of the MIT Media Lab, argues that the growth of the Internet is creating a "seamless digital workplace," which will spatially decentralize commerce and industry around the globe. He continues:

> The nation-state itself is subject to tremendous change and globalization. . . .
>
> . . . . While politicians struggle with the baggage of history, a new generation is emerging from the digital landscape free of many of the old prejudices. These kids are released from the limitation of geographic proximity as the sole basis of friendship, collaboration, play, and neighborhood. Digital technology can be a natural force drawing people into greater world harmony.[19]-

To send an electronic mail message to an on-line member of Congress is to experience a challenge to traditional geographic/constitutional assumptions. Members of Congress work in a national legislature, talk to lobbyists from international corporations, and accept money from special-interest public action committees (PACs) outside their districts. It is especially anomalous, using a decentralized medium like the Internet, to send electronic mail to a member of Congress who then insists on his localism. For example, an electronic mail message to Robert Walker of Pennsylvania, described by *Time* magazine as Newt Gingrich's "oldest ally and closest friend in the House," elicited an automatic response saying in part:

> Thank you for contacting me through the House of Representatives' Constituent Electronic Mail System (CEMS). I am pleased to be a part of this

effort to offer citizens a quick and efficient way to communicate with their representatives in Congress.

As the ability of Congress to communicate and share information over the Internet is expanded, I expect that program enhancements will be announced and additional members will choose to participate. Your patience during these early stages of the CEMS is greatly appreciated. You can learn more about the CEMS through the Internet address CONGRESS@HR.HOUSE.GOV.

If you live in my Congressional District, please be assured that any message you send me over the Internet will be brought to my attention.

Be sure to include your mailing address in your Internet message. Thank you again for your interest.[20]

Congressman Walker is certainly entitled, indeed he may be obliged, to discourage mail from ordinary citizens who are not his constituents, but the decentralized culture of the Internet, as it has developed into the middle 1990s, makes his letter seem a rhetorical gesture from another age. This example of the way cyberspace reframes and recontextualizes Congressman Walker's attempt to retain localism on the Internet suggests how difficult it may be to step into the deep and unruly torrent and attempt to stand still.

Services for sending electronic mail messages to the White House are a supplement to the Office of Correspondence already in place for decades. For a practiced computer user, sending an electronic mail message is considerably faster and more convenient than creating and mailing a letter on paper. The White House very long ago reached the point where incoming mail from citizens had to be aggregated into clusters representing some measure of public opinion, and so in a sense incoming electronic mail presents a shift in scale rather than a difference in kind, despite the considerable problems of dealing with such a huge volume of mail and responding to all of it in some manner. From the point of view of resource allocation, then, the White House has committed itself to providing sufficient staff to deal with a volume of mail that is huge even in these early days of the Internet and that may well expand by orders of magnitude. It is not so clear yet whether the electronic mail service from citizens to the White House actually provides the White House with usable information, influential in White House decision making, that would otherwise not be available. Nor is it clear whether the people who write electronic mail to the president are the same sorts of people who are likely to write letters on paper. It appears that the White House is assuming that the very act of sending mail to the president, even if it is acknowledged only by a clearly labeled generic autoresponse and even if it is read only as a unit of opinion aggregated into gross pro and con categories, encourages citizens to believe their government is paying attention to them and rehearses citizens in a performative act of civic engagement.

As a rhetorical matter, it takes a certain willing suspension of disbelief to send a paper letter to the White House and then receive a signed letter from the president. All of us who have done this realize that the president does not read all his mail. A signed letter from the president is usually adapted by a very junior staff assistant, intern, or volunteer from a computer data base of generic responses on various issues, and then signed by a machine. But even knowing that there is a sort of fiction involved, we seem to feel that there is also a sort of decorum, just as we can listen to a presidential speech and bracket out the knowledge that it was largely or perhaps entirely ghostwritten, since, after all, the president is saying it and would have written it if he had the time. We seem, as a public, to have put aside any insistence on absolute literalness in the production and performance of the rhetoric of our national leaders, and though it may be the job of academic critics to deconstruct the appearances for analytical purposes, it is also our job to catch the ways those appearances are produced, maintained, and interpreted as part of taken-for-granted reality.

Should the White House develop its electronic mail system in such a way as to simulate direct electronic replies to those who write to the White House by electronic means? Should the White House develop large bodies of informational material, either policy-oriented or ceremonial in nature, that are directed solely at Internet users, either over the president's signature or on his behalf by spokespersons or surrogates? Whatever may be our enthusiasm for the way electronic networking has provided access to the discourse of the presidency, the answers to these questions are not obvious.

Jeffrey Tulis, Roderick Hart, and other scholars have shown us that the presidency is a rhetorical office, but the rhetoric of the presidency is very peculiar. The president is expected to act, in Woodrow Wilson's phrase, as the chief legislator, and as the chief advocate of American policy, foreign and domestic. But because he is a president and not a prime minister, he is not part of the legislature and does not engage in direct, public discourse with it. He may address it and it may address him, but the two will not engage in mutual debate. Part of the power of the presidency resides in this uniqueness and in the evolution of a mode of presidential discourse that advocates without debating. As Tulis has pointed out, a paradox of the rhetorical power of the presidency seems to be that it may impede rather than promote deliberation, since the president never speaks from a position that welcomes debate, and, therefore, by implication typically treats public matters as somehow beyond debate.[21] When a president does treat public issues as debatable, as has sometimes happened in the Clinton administration, he may be denigrated by the press for not being sufficiently forceful, for not knowing his own mind.[22]

Hence, it seems unlikely that the president will step directly and continuously into the open debate of the Internet community, though there are likely to be some experiments emulating an on-line town hall or call-in talk-show format, as there were during the 1992 presidential campaign. The Internet community embraces significant numbers of elite and participating citizens, whose allegiance is worth cultivating. But despite its rapid growth the Internet does not have the reach of radio in 1940 or television in 1955. For this reason direct address to the Internet audience reaches a constituency but not the constituency, not the nation—though that will change, perhaps within five years. It is too early to use the Internet as the exclusive site of messages directed at the nation, but it is not too early to experiment with clearly delimited direct address, surrogate address, and widespread indirect address. Every step needs to be considered not only in its informational but in its dramatic and rhetorical dimensions, and with the understanding that the Internet is a rich and rapidly changing context, and not merely a delivery medium. No single presidential message or practice will be able to define the medium as a whole. For example, even as the White House considers merely shifting its occasional replies to citizen e-mail from paper to electronic form, care will have to be taken to preserve the persona of the presidency.

As for developing a full array of on-line advocacy for the president's proposals, that, too, could have its dangers. At present, what is available is in most cases already available, albeit less conveniently, in other media. Information services of various kinds are a major business of the federal government, producing speeches, press releases, informational materials, film, and television. But some forms of government rhetoric have provoked backlash from the Congress, as when it killed the New Deal's documentary film unit.[23] The White House is necessarily partisan, speaking for all the people but in the voice of the party that won the last election. When any new medium of communication opens to the presidency, some balancing needs to take place between the communicative access of the ins and the outs, both in the interests of democracy and, more narrowly, to create at least the appearance of fairness. But when government funds are used directly by incumbents to establish a medium of communication with the public that is available to the opposition only through the expenditure of its own private funds, we must be very cautious about the sorts of precedents we are setting.

There is another sense in which the Clinton administration's entry into the Internet is rhetorical. Entirely apart from the specific content of any of the speeches and press conferences, the whole apparatus of electronic access to the White House functions as itself a rhetorical sign—a sign of the future realized in terms of a new technology, embracing the futurism of the information superhighway and the traditional populism of open and accessible government. Such signs may be, but are not necessarily, trivial, since we do attach ourselves to each other primarily by agreed upon semiotic conventions.

But if the president is a sign, so are we. Those of us who do participate in on-line politics experience the powerful sensation of being involved in a democratic community. But we are likely to efface from our own self-awareness that part of the appeal of our reflected selves in this medium is that we seem part of an elite, part of a future, part of a small class of privileged observers with special knowledge. At present, our own democratic enthusiasms for on-line politics may be subtly sweetened by our not-so-democratic position as elite participants. Whether it will be possible to attain universal access, thereby stripping away the privilege, and scale up by orders of magnitude the style and substance of democratic participation that present developments hint at, we simply do not know. It is also not clear whether we can scale *down* from the level of the presidency, using computer-mediated communication to foster the civic society at the level of region, state, town, and neighborhood.[24]

Let me turn briefly to the subject of memory. Of course, part of the president's responsibility as the nation's chief orator is to cultivate in his speaking a usable sense of public memory. In another sense, his speeches and papers, once uttered or printed, themselves become part of the national memory. It is significant that private citizens and information elites in universities and the press now have on-line access to the public papers of the presidency. It is possible to search through the texts of presidential speeches and press conferences by keyword and subject, tracing the president's advocacy in such areas as crime, the economy, foreign policy, and education, holding him accountable by an exercise of memory that the day-to-day press coverage of the presidency mostly ignores.

There is another form of memory that the Internet makes possible, and a book on the rhetorical presidency should spend a moment at least in emphasizing how important it would be to scholarship and citizenship to have available on-line not only the public papers of the presidency but the vast collection of documentation that, after a presidency, finds its way into a presidential library. There is simply no reason why all the papers available to scholars in our presidential libraries should not be scanned and made available both as facsimile images and as machine-readable texts. The cost would be considerable, of course. Perhaps, for the time being, the costs would be prohibitive. The results, in our historical understanding of an institution that belongs to the people of the country, could be significant. Not only for the sake of scholars but also for the sake of the country, the task of digitizing presidential library materials should be adopted as a high priority, as should plans to make such materials available for remote searching and downloading. For some purposes, of course, extended visits to the on-site library to examine the actual paper files will be necessary. For many research purposes, however, remote searching of digitized documents would be completely satisfactory from the point of view of authenticity. Such access would not merely free scholars from some of their pilgrimages but would also immediately alter the terms on which documents could be searched and compared. The presidential libraries exist as something more than monuments and museums; they are repositories of the people's memory.[25]

In *Lenin's Tomb,* a brilliant account of the collapse of the Soviet Union, David Remnick assigns a key role to the rediscovery of historical memory. As first Khrushchev and later Gorbachev gave speeches hinting at a revised version of Stalinist history, and later as Soviet archives opened to scholars and as those scholars were able to speak and publish, it became possible to regain a sense of history as the property of the people and a sense of a renewed historical memory as the necessary condition of a hope for freedom. Here in the United States we are perhaps likely to take our own freedoms for granted, but at a time when our major cultural institutions do not encourage much in the way of historical memory or a vivid sense of participation in the public sphere, it would be a shame not to employ the tools of our new information technologies to civic ends. Insuring the widespread availability of major presidential and congressional documents would be a small but significant step in the right direction.

I have concentrated in this chapter on the presidential use of the Internet. But it is important to recall that users of such presidential materials are working in a larger context. As presidential activity on the Internet becomes more vigorous and more visible, it will necessarily develop in the context of the rest of the Internet. If we are to understand the influence and prospects for use of the computer networks as a medium for presidential rhetoric, we must take some notice of its relation to other political activities on the Internet, a vast, dynamic writing space. Full exploration of that larger context is beyond the scope of this discussion, but it is especially important for us to insist that however valuable it may be for democratic legitimacy, the ability to send electronic mail to the White House and to download speeches is no substitute for the concurrent development of institutions whereby citizens may participate actively in discussion and resolution of public matters. Access to information is only part of the story, which would be thin indeed unless supplemented with the story of citizens interacting with one another, discussing and debating politics, struggling to define a mutually agreeable civil society.

It is certainly the case that no single article or book could provide a comprehensive and stable description of political activity on the Internet. For our purposes as historians, that is a significant constraint, but it need not be paralyzing. As students of communication, we may rather use the vast size, the diffusion, and the dynamism of the Internet as themselves important dimensions of the single user's experience. No single Internet user, no matter how dedicated, could hope to read all the political information currently passing through the Internet each day. Even to keep up with small corners of the activity is beyond most users—there is simply too much material.

Presidential documents are circulated in a medium that also makes extensive use of the capacity of computers to serve as the host for ongoing, interactive discussions on bulletin board systems, both on commercial networks such as CompuServe, America Online, and Prodigy, and on the USENET/Netnews bulletin boards typically associated with educational, research, and corporate entities attached directly to the Internet.

In terms of sheer volume, presidential texts occupy a fairly small space on such interactive bulletin board systems. Let us take the example of USENET. The amount of open discussion and other material on USENET is staggering. On the system as a whole, more than a million messages are propagated in any two-week period.

A small part of the content of some of the political newsgroups comes directly from the Clinton White House. In July, 1994, for example, the news.lists newsgroup listed the top 25 submitters of messages to all newsgroups on the USENET/Netnews system in a two-week period. The top poster was a network source of weather data, which posted over 9,000 messages. All but 1 of the other top 25 were posting large multimedia files of pictures and sounds, which by their nature are big files. The only poster of text files listed in the top 25 was the White House, which ranked 19th of the top 25 posters with 316 messages carrying 5468.5 kilobytes of data, representing 0.3 percent of the traffic on the network for the two-week period ending July 25, 1994. The White House messages were posted from the address publications-admin@whitehouse.gov (the White House) and were evenly divided among 6 newsgroups to each of which, apparently, all the messages were sent:

16 percent	alt.news.media
16 percent	alt.politics.clinton
16 percent	alt.politics.org.misc
16 percent	alt.politics.reform
16 percent	alt.politics.usa.misc
16 percent	talk.politics.misc

Even if we discount for the possible cross-posting, assuming that the White House sent the same messages to each group, the White House sent out 53 messages to each group in a two-week period.[26]

Despite White House contributions of official documents to the USENET newsgroups it considers most relevant, such documents constitute a small percentage of the number of messages on those newsgroups.

For the most part, the political newsgroups consist of freewheeling political debate from ordinary users.

If we approach the USENET political newsgroups from the perspective of an inquiry into the Clinton administration's contribution of presidential documents to those groups, we are impelled to ask whether those documents appear to set the agenda for other contributors. If this is the test for the efficacy of the distribution of presidential documents over the Internet, the answer must be that the president's words are almost never quoted or referred to in the ongoing newsgroups discussions. Rather, the agenda for the discussions is set by general users, who in turn seem to choose their topics either from a list of perennial issues (gun control, abortion, welfare) or from what the news media have established as current events.

A glance at the alt.politics.clinton newsgroup on January 26, 1995, gives a fairly typical picture of the political lists. On that day, there were 1,434 messages on the newsgroup, most from January 17 or later (each night the computer purges most messages that have been on the computer for a set period, usually a week, 10 days, or 2 weeks). Of those 1,434 messages, 17 were White House documents. Several others were also documents of various sorts: 7 were numbers of the *Federalist Papers* posted by one user with a scanner; some were newspaper articles on various topics. Virtually all the rest were fairly brief messages from dozens of users debating various political issues with one another.

One impression emerges clearly. If the Clinton presidency is setting the agenda of these discussions, which in part it is, the agenda setting is occurring not from the direct posting of presidential messages to the lists but from a multistep process in which the presidency contributes to the national political agenda through the medium of the press or in interaction with the Congress, which is in turn reported by the media. Such a finding does not mark the presidential e-mail project as a failure but indicates, on the one hand, the continuing power of the national media to stimulate our consciousness of what counts as political and, on the other hand, shows the enormous attraction of the participatory quality of Internet bulletin boards and discussion lists.

If my impression is correct, we are still making use of presidential rhetoric in secondary and tertiary ways, and this finding applies even to most of those citizens who have access to full texts of presidential speeches. At the same time, the political discussions on the Internet indicate a tremendous eagerness to engage in political discourse in which presidential texts may eventually come to play a larger and more direct role. And so we find ourselves in the curious situation of urging continued and increasing access to the texts of presidential rhetoric, as a right of all citizens and as a call to responsible participation in the public sphere, but without, as yet, clear empirical or theoretical indications as to the precise role such access will play in the contestation between public sphere and image-driven postmodern dislocation. We cannot know, perhaps will never be able to resolve except for our preference for one story over another, whether on-line politics is a tool for the reconstruction of participatory democracy or a simulacrum, a form of voodoo politics speaking to our fascination with the absence of the referent, the presence of our own illusionary mystification, that mode of construction of the real not just through symbols but perhaps only in simulacra. "Today," writes Jean Baudrillard, "abstraction is no longer that of the map, the double, the mirror, or the concept. Simulation is no longer that of a territory, a referential being, or a substance. It is the generation of models of a real without origin or reality: a hyperreal."[27] Perhaps it is the task of both citizens and rhetorical scholars to collaborate in acknowledging the hyperreality of our politics without forgetting the simultaneous materiality of its practices and consequences. Richard Lanham urges us to consider, as rhetorical theorists, that rhetoric is the fundamentally centripetal social practice that balances the oscillation between style and substance, acceptance of reality and manipulation (or demystification) of illusion, and that the rhetorical paideia exists in precisely that balance. Lanham argues that

> the great works of classical rhetoric, the scriptures of the paideia, are fundamentally self-contradictory. Their training and doctrine is built on a social self and a dramatistic society but their value judgments are all made, finally, in reference to a central self and an externally sanctioned, nondramatic social reality which is really out there and full of real events and good old-fashioned, back-to-basics historical fact. . . . The entire rhetorical tradition is deeply self-contradictory in this way, beginning with Aristotle. Rhetorical education regularly invokes two opposite kinds of reality, a self that is first social and then central, a society that is first dramatic and then externally sanctioned, a physical reality that is both "deco-

rous," that is to say created by the discourse which describes it, and at the same time "out there" and independent of the language describing it. The tradition includes . . . both deconstruction . . . and . . . reconstruction . . . held in perpetual oscillation.[28]

The Clinton administration has chosen a path of active engagement in the policies and practices of rhetoric in the newly emerging electronic sphere. At the very least, in the coming years it will be interesting to observe the oscillation of forces that govern American rhetoric and politics in the information spaces of the future and that will inevitably extend the contestation between a return to localism and the obliteration of boundaries, between community and isolation, between self-government and computerized hegemony, between the electronic commonwealth and cyberDisneyism.

PART 2
Case Studies in Presidential Rhetoric

CHAPTER 5

Lyndon Johnson
and the Problem of Politics:

A STUDY IN CONVERSATION
Roderick P. Hart and Kathleen E. Kendall

On June 3, 1963, Lyndon Johnson had a conversation—
an unsurprising fact. Lyndon Johnson, then the vice president of the United
States, was a man of constant conversation. But the forty-five minute conversation he had with presidential adviser Theodore Sorensen on June 3
was a special conversation. It was not special because of the medium he
used—the telephone—for Lyndon Johnson was born to cradle an earpiece.[1]
Nor was it special because of his interlocutor—another politician—for
Lyndon Johnson spent virtually all of his waking moments with politicians. And it was not really special because of his topic—civil rights—for
Lyndon Johnson addressed himself to that issue constantly, in part because
the politics of the South was so often a politics of race and in part because
issues of social justice—poverty, joblessness, and illiteracy, primarily—were
issues that bedeviled his rural Texas neighbors when he grew up among

them in the 1920s and 1930s. Mr. Johnson's conversation of June 3, 1963, was also not important because of its eloquence or its intellectual novelty. With Ted Sorensen speaking only three hundred words during the entire conversation, the event was more a monologue than an exchange, a far cry from the ideal sort of dialectic that thinkers from Plato to Rawls had envisioned for political affairs. But perhaps the most important feature of Mr. Johnson's conversation is this: In wandering through the thicket of civil rights politics as he did, Lyndon Johnson reminds us of certain central and unsettling aspects of political life. In an era in which concepts of the political are finding their ways into discussions of medical ethics, multicultural relationships, and literary criticism, Lyndon Johnson's conversation begs us to reexamine the politics of politics. We shall attempt just such an examination here.

BACKGROUND

On the day Sorensen called Johnson, the Kennedy administration's civil rights policy was, at best, ambiguous. Civil rights activities in the United States, however, were hardly ambiguous. They were incendiary. Two months before the conversation, massive protests were staged by blacks in Birmingham, Alabama, protests which quickly led to the arrest of some four hundred demonstrators (including Martin Luther King, Jr. and Ralph D. Abernathy). Two weeks later, a crowd of two thousand blacks demonstrated, some hurling rocks at the police, who clubbed them in return. Fourteen days later, a month before the Johnson-Sorensen talk, the infamous Eugene (Bull) Connor, a legally deposed but nonetheless functioning commissioner of public safety, led white resistance to the sit-ins, boycotts, and public demonstrations then spreading in Birmingham (as well as in Greenville, South Carolina; Savannah, Georgia; Durham, North Carolina; and numerous other cities in the Old South). Protests led by such personages as comedian Dick Gregory were met with high-pressure water hoses on some occasions, taunts, jeers, and general incivility on all occasions. Nine days later, President John F. Kennedy dispatched federal troops to Birmingham to quell the disturbances, and nine days after that Governor George Wallace of Alabama interposed himself between two black, would-be students and the registration hall at the University of Alabama. Shortly thereafter, Attorney General Robert Kennedy met in New York with several prominent blacks, including author James Baldwin and entertainer Harry Belafonte, and pledged renewed federal action in behalf of civil rights. Events such as these, according to psychologist Kenneth Clark, helped to transform the issue of civil rights in the minds of the Kennedy administration from "a special problem of a particular group" to a national problem.[2] The tangible results of this change in attitude came on June 19, 1963, one week after NAACP field secretary Medgar Evers was shot to death in Jackson, Mississippi, when President Kennedy sent to Congress his draft Civil Rights Act of 1963.

It was in preparation for this piece of legislation that Sorensen had called LBJ to learn something about the realities of power on Capitol Hill. For many observers, Kennedy's sudden interest in civil rights legislation was too little too late. *Time* magazine reported considerable black disappointment with "the President's failure to rally the great moral and political force that his office and prestige can command" and noted on another occasion that "only under the occasional stress of crisis did the Kennedy Administration move vigorously [on civil rights]."[3] Some observers argued that Kennedy's recalcitrance was borne more from political than attitudinal factors and that the president, although determined to move ahead on civil rights was obliged to consider the fate of his overall legislative program and, as a result, moved cautiously. As Roy Wilkins observed, there was also the matter of political skill to consider: "John Fitzgerald Kennedy had a complete comprehension and an identity with the goals of the civil rights movement. Intellectually he was for it . . . [but] he just did not know how to manipulate government to bring it about."[4]

If he knew anything, Lyndon Johnson knew how to manipulate government. In some ways he knew little else. To his way of thinking, there was little else to know. Perhaps that is why he responded so effervescently when receiving Sorensen's call at 12:20 P.M. on June 3. As vice president, Lyndon Johnson had been underutilized up to this point, perhaps because his acknowledged political skill with Congress was seen by the Kennedys as a double-edged sword. To his credit, though, Lyndon Johnson kept his own counsel when serving as vice president.[5] Thus, several ironies were operating when Sorensen called Johnson. One was that, in the conversation, Johnson described the precise strategies he would use one year later to guide the first comprehensive piece of civil rights legislation through the U.S. Congress. Another irony was Johnson's own civil rights record. According to his oftentimes nemesis, Joseph Rauh (long-time head of the

Americans for Democratic Action), Johnson was his greatest opponent of the 1950s on civil rights. Theodore White buttresses this claim when he says: "in his early years in Congress as a representative and senator, Johnson voted as a white southerner thirty-nine times on matters of civil rights. Among these votes were: six times against proposals to abolish the poll tax; six times against efforts to eliminate discrimination in federal programs; twice against bills to prohibit and punish lynching; once against the FEPC (Fair Employment Practices Commission); and once to maintain segregation in Washington, D.C."[6] To Johnson's apologists, the stark contrast between his sorry personal history on civil rights and his remarkable record as president could be credited to the changed constituency (national, not regional) he came to serve. Others argue that his private dispositions always favored integration and that he was more active on civil rights than any member of the Kennedy administration when it met behind closed doors. Still other commentators fix Johnson's change of heart in psycho-anthropological terms: "there is something in the folklore of Negro life that a reconstructed southerner is really far more liberal than a liberal yankee."[7] In any event, on June 3, 1963, the Democratic Party was in political trouble on civil rights, the Kennedy administration was clearly inexperienced in dealing with Congress, the nation's cities were threatening to boil over, and Lyndon Johnson was on the phone.

THE CONVERSATION

To Lyndon Johnson, June of 1963 must have seemed a month given by the gods. During those thirty days, he had four conferences directly with President Kennedy (including a one-hour meeting with former President Dwight Eisenhower), two phone calls from the chief executive, was included in the president's meetings with various civil rights groups, had three telephone conversations with Ted Sorensen and one with Attorney General Robert Kennedy, and talked by phone more often, and more substantively, with leaders of Congress than was usual for him. This hyperactivity stood in marked contrast to his pursuits in April and May of that same year when he devoted himself to purely ceremonial and personal matters. Somehow, for reasons not completely clear to him, Lyndon Johnson was let off his leash halfway through 1963.[8]

One of the most striking changes in Mr. Johnson's schedule was the call he got from Sorensen. Heretofore buried in the archives of the Lyndon

Baines Johnson Presidential Library, the Johnson-Sorensen conversation has been referred to in passing as "a message from an expert to a bumbling amateur" by one commentator,[9] but it has not yet been seriously analyzed in the scholarly community. That any such conversation has been preserved is a remarkable stroke of good fortune since it provides at once a cameo portrait of great decisions being made as well as the human pettiness that accompanies their making. Johnson's theme in the conversation, if we may impose theme on what is really a blizzard of ideas, arguments, and character sketches, is that political legislation passes when its proponents' and opponents' most human needs are met. Legislation does not happen when those needs are unmet; in fact, nothing happens when they are unmet.

That these were Johnson's themes in the conversation should not be surprising to experienced LBJ-watchers. As James David Barber has observed: "the details about men remained relevant as long as the men did, so [Johnson] filed them more permanently. . . . Men were his books; knowledge was a tool to control men."[10] It should also not be surprising to learn that LBJ implicitly urged Sorensen not to let matters of principle guide the president's thinking on civil rights since principle so often obscures political vision and is so often used to explain political failure. According to Johnson biographer Doris Kearns, "Johnson saw preoccupation with principle and procedure as a sign of impotence. Such men were 'troublemakers,' more concerned with appearing forceful than in exercising the real strengths that led to tangible achievement."[11] Although he did not say so directly, Johnson unquestionably thought that the Kennedy staffers were politically naive about civil rights as well as unclear about exactly what ideological posture they wished to assume on the matter. As a result, he used his forty-five minutes to critique the rather bloated, liberal rhetoric of the day and to focus Sorensen's thinking on the people who stood between the Kennedy administration and enlightened civil rights policy. Johnson's tumult of ideas left Sorensen gasping for air: "Well, I think that's a good idea," "There's a lot in what you say," "I'd like to see a copy of your report," "No doubt about it. I'll pass that on. . . ."[12] There is little of the vaunted Sorensenian eloquence here. Indeed, there is little of the vaunted Sorensen; LBJ interrupted almost one-third of his thirty-two feeble turns-of-speech.

The content of the Johnson-Sorensen conversation presages much of the Kennedy administration's civil rights strategy that summer. In the conversation, Johnson offered Sorensen a five-point strategy for passing a civil rights bill: "I'd say Republicans, one. Public sentiment, two. The South, three. Legislators, four, individually. Negro leaders, five." History records that Mr. Johnson's advice was heeded, a fact amply demonstrated in Table 1.

Table 1.
STRATEGIC ADVICE OFFERED AND TAKEN
IN THE JOHNSON-SORENSEN CONVERSATION

Johnson's Strategic Advice	Kennedy's Political Actions
June 3, 1963	*June–July, 1963*
Talk to Republican leaders	*June 11:* Meets with House and Senate leaders Halleck, Arends, Dirksen, and Kuchel *June 12:* Meets with former President Dwight Eisenhower and Senator Barry Goldwater *July:* Holds five legislative leadership breakfasts
Go on national television immediately	*June 11:* Gives national presidential address
Get the support of the clergy	*June 17:* Meets with 243 Catholic, Protestant, and Jewish clergymen on civil rights
Go to the South	*Early June:* Commences Southwestern speaking tour; takes LBJ with him
Go to Texas; stop at a space research center	*June 5:* Goes to El Paso; has Governor Connally on platform with him; goes to space project in New Mexico
Curry favor with Senator Richard Russell of Georgia	*Early June:* Takes Russell on speaking trip with him
Work on Democratic legislators, especially Senators Smathers and Mansfield	*June–July:* Increases number of private meetings and phone calls with Smathers and Mansfield
Enlist assistance of entire presidential cabinet	*June 20–26:* Departments of Defense, Justice, and Urban Renewal declare need for civil rights progress

| Begin a more earnest dialogue with black leaders | *June 15:* Sends envoy to Medgar Evers's funeral; called on Jackson, Mississippi mayor; praises forthcoming March on Washington |
| Make a moral commitment to black leaders | *June 22:* Meets with thirty civil rights leaders; meets privately with Martin Luther King, Jr., and Roy Wilkins |

While no direct, causal connection can be established between Johnson's advice and Kennedy's subsequent behavior, the circumstantial evidence seems overwhelming. Admittedly, some of Kennedy's actions in the summer of 1963 may have originated in his own staff, but his best strategic moves seem to have been Johnson's, a conclusion that seems especially plausible when we compare LBJ's advice on phrasings and language to Kennedy's historic speech on civil rights of June 11, 1963, the details of which are presented in Table 2.

Table 2.

RHETORICAL SUGGESTIONS OFFERED AND ACCEPTED
IN THE JOHNSON-SORENSEN CONVERSATION

Johnson's Suggested Phrasings	Kennedy's Actual Remarks
June 3, 1963	*June 11, 1963*
"When I order men into battle, I order a man without regard to color."	"When Americans are sent to Vietnam or West Berlin, we do not ask for whites only."
"We all know that golden rule, uh, you got to do unto others than have 'em do unto you."	"[The issue] is as old as the Scriptures and is as clear as the American Constitution. The heart of the question is . . . whether we are going to treat our fellow Americans as we wish to be treated."
"He [Kennedy] should state the moral issue and should do it without equivocation."	"We are confronted primarily with a moral issue. . . . We face, therefore, a moral crisis as a country and as a people."
"And I don't think you want these people to go the unemployment road—Detroit and Los Angeles.	"Today there are Negroes unemployed, two or three times as many compared to whites . . .

Johnson's Suggested Phrasings (cont.)	**Kennedy's Actual Remarks** (cont.)
Heck, they ought to be trained here at home so they can earn a job like your children."	moving into the larger cities, unable to find work, young people, particularly, out of work."
"So the only big problem is saying to the Baldwins and the Kings . . . You're not going to have to do it in the streets. You can do it in the courthouses and the Congress."	"We have a right to expect that the Negro community will be responsible, will uphold the law."

Upon hearing the president's speech of June 11, Washington pundits reported the emergence of a "new Kennedy." James Reston of the *New York Times* noticed the dramatic shift in the president's tone and tenor, observing that Mr. Kennedy no longer saw civil rights as the problem of a particular group but "as an American problem now. That is the change." The *Times* also praised the president's bipartisan efforts with congressional leaders and commented on the sudden flurry of talks in the White House on civil rights matters. *Time* magazine also paid attention to the sudden shifts in the Kennedy administration when it opined that "at long last" the president had chosen "to appear on national television with a declaration of his own views about the moral issues involved." Finally, Anthony Lewis commented on Kennedy's attempt to shift the civil rights discussion from a political to a moral plane. "In effect," said Lewis, he [Kennedy] asked the whites in his audience to imagine themselves with a different color of skin."[13]

There seems little doubt, then, that Lyndon Johnson's unheralded and highly personal phone conversation with Ted Sorensen influenced the course of the Kennedy administration's civil rights policies, a connection between Johnson and Kennedy that historians have not yet explored in detail. But there are other reasons to reexamine Johnson's conversation. After all, John Kennedy did not need Lyndon Johnson to tell him how to be a politician in the main. In the main, no, but Lyndon Johnson was a man of specifics, and it is the specifics of his conversation with Sorensen that are most instructive.[14] The Johnson-Sorensen conversation (more accurately, the Johnson monologue) is important primarily because of its philosophical texture. It asks questions that the great political theorists have long asked: What is political and what is not? Which social conditions make politics possible or impossible? What distinguishes the political mind? What do people gain and lose when entering a voluntary political relationship? The Johnson conversation also asks unnervingly current questions: Do a society's means of production constrain its options for governance? What is the individual's fate in a polity influenced primarily by pressure groups? Can a politics of change exist apart from a symbolism of change? Is politics assisted or undone by its inevitable aporia and discontinuities? On June 3, 1963, Lyndon Johnson had no intention of asking such questions. Indeed, he would have thought them silly. But he answered them—pellucidly—and his answers provide questions aplenty.

POLITICS AND THE MODERN MIND

To understand most contemporary American politicians, especially Lyndon Johnson, one must reckon with modernism. Modernism was born in the cradle of feudalism which, as Carl Schorske argues, was an attempt to replace aristocratic absolutism with a constitutional monarchy, aristocratic federalism with parliamentary centralism, and religion with science. These innovations, says David Harvey, promised an entirely new world, including "freedom from scarcity, want, and the arbitrariness of natural calamity. The development of rational forms of social organization and rational modes of thought promised liberation from the irrationalities of myth, religion, superstition, release from the arbitrary use of power as well as from the dark side of our own human natures. Only through such a project [it was believed] could the universal, eternal, and the immutable qualities of all of humanity be revealed."[15]

Modernism had its detractors from its inception. Numbered among them, quite naturally, were the monarchal and religious authorities it sought to replace, but also included were agrarians, aesthetes, theologians, and communalists clinging to premodern sensibilities. But despite its opponents, despite its capacity to be "culturally and morally injurious," and despite its "festering ambiguities," says Albert Borgmann, modernism remained powerful "as long as the economy was productive and consumption was moderate."[16]

This was no less true in the United States. Whether Dixiecrats or Free-Soilers, whether Republicans or Democrats, American politicians have long been modernists. If Tocqueville is to be believed, even the earliest of Americans embraced the possibility of human advancement, the bounties of science and technology, appreciation of corporate efficiencies and, to a lesser extent, bureaucratic systems of governance. This was surely less true in the seventeenth century than the eighteenth, but it became a life-style for Americans in the nineteenth century and a mandate for those in the twentieth century. All four generations complained, often bitterly, about modernism's depredations, but they never foreswore them, not entirely.

Lyndon Johnson was no different. His very first job—educating dirt-poor children in Cotulla, Texas—and his first major political activity—electrifying rural Texas—imprinted modernism on his soul. There was much of the premodern cowboy in Lyndon Johnson, to be sure, but he had seen firsthand how cruel unbridled nature could be to his neighbors, and so he went to Washington to capture its bounties, bring them home, and thus change his beloved Hill Country forever.

It should not be surprising that modernism became imprinted on his rhetoric as well. In Marxian terminology, the means of production—capitalism—left certain overdetermined markers on Johnson's discourse and, in so doing, determined both its energy and its social consequence. For a person like Lyndon Johnson, modernism was not an additive but an interstitial necessity, the first and only measure of both rhetorical force and philosophical worth. Accomplishment—clear, empirical accomplishment—was the sine qua non of his politics. And so his ultimate complaint about Kennedy, his boss, was this: "I think he's got to have his bill. And he, uh, he, he's sitting over there. We've got six months; we haven't passed anything. I'm thinking he ought to make them pass on this stuff [other legislation] before he moves this thing [the civil rights bill] up." In other words, politics only becomes politics when it takes on material form. Ideas, arguments, needs, passions, relationships—the effluvia of politics—mean little if they lead to unpassed legislation. And so he can urge the passage of a finance bill over a morality bill and do so without blinking: "I think there are a good *deal* of things you can do. You ought to get your tax bill passed, instead of *killed*. This Kennedy program oughtn't go down the *drain*. And I'm afraid that's what's going to happen if you send this *thing* up there [prematurely]." [emphasis ours]

Politics as a bargain? Legislation as inert matter? As effluent? Civil rights as merchandise? These are the metaphors of modernism and they were Lyndon Johnson's favorites. Tables 3 and 4 catalog the 173 identifiable

Table 3.

METAPHORICAL CLUSTERS IN THE
JOHNSON-SORENSEN CONVERSATION

Ocular:

(6) With an image of anti-Negro
(10) exchange some viewpoints
(27) this aura [of the president]
(35) looking at them straight in the face
(97) [the president] looks them in the eye
(104) the Negroes share one point of view
(198) I want to make it clear
(262) I looked them right in the eye
(337) he ought to . . . look them in the eye
(340) with an image of his own choosing
(354) without any reflection on anyone
(497) it'd be good . . . to appear at Lockheed
(502) you've been the beacon light

Thermal/Tactile:

(75) the risk of touching off . . . debate
(76) debate would . . . inflame the country
(83) any institution that can prick the conscience of the nation
(364) they'll be picking at this thing
(366) I'd let them pick at it
(534) this thing is going to boil

Corporeal:

(45) in the heart of the Southland
(70) get you off my back
(136) make them stand up and vote
(147) let them chew on it
(220) his program would be hurt
(255) people that got a wounded air
(322) get them off their back

(344) what I know is in his heart
(402) they're going to cut his outfit off
(432) standing on their own feet
(494) the loudest language a president can speak
(508) he stood right up to them
(527) the only person that's hurt by this
(606) right from the shoulder
(652) they want to know . . . really at heart
(749) this is a far-reaching decision

Sedentary:

(78) the legislative approach ought to be abandoned
(124) he's sitting over there
(129) they're sitting back
(145) I can't sit idly by
(152) I wouldn't be stopped
(209) sat in on . . . the conferences
(229) the Negroes are tired
(229) this patient stuff
(290) endure half-slave and half-free
(333) you've got to sit down with them
(369) have Dick Russell sit down
(384) we were prostrate
(400) they're going to sit quietly
(741) sit on your fanny

Theological:

(15) we all know that Golden Rule
(28) this halo around the president
(92) not as a demon trying to punish
(219) he'd be a sacrificial lamb
(386) let Mr. Javits go straight to hell
(590) put you on the country circuit

Domestic:

(8) we've got to do our homework

(36) lecturing . . . as a father
(90) talk frankly . . . and maybe fatherly
(144) do it in either the streets
(153) they messed around here
(196) program oughtn't go down the drain
(230) this piecemeal stuff
(268) they called it corn pone
(315) that legislation ought to be screened
(350) you haven't done your homework
(355) I don't know who drafted it
(402) put it in their pocket
(404) move my children . . . through the line
(405) get them down the storm cellar
(405) get it locked and keyed
(454) a hundred and fifty were screened
(484) hope they'll take them in
(625) you may have it sweep all over
(746) he ought to adopt [my proposal]

Naturalistic:
(4) have a bunch of Democrats
(27) run . . . right in the hole
(53) I think that would seep in
(63) with a bunch of Congressmen
(77) wind up with a mouse
(322) right from the horse's mouth
(330) he's like Bob Taylor's goat
(787) we're going to have a storm on it

Mechanical:
(79) specific proposals ought to be weighed
(98) if he . . . pushes the Christian issue
(130) Javits gets Humphrey souped up
(253) the moment that message hits
(700) I'd turn . . . loose on it

Structural/Hierarchical:
(149) I got a good solid program

(199) I'm . . . strong for his program
(232) he's behind them
(233) if he'd make [the speech] down in Jackson
(258) a high, lofty appeal
(325) talk to Republican leaders from Eisenhower on down
(657) I would get them some support
(758) he'd be in worse shape
(759) Dillon is strong for it
(760) Budget and McNamara are weak [for it]
(763) name one man to be the czar

Financial:
(9) spend some time on the message
(93) [It] might cost us the South
(119) they're not going to pay much attention
(139) [make the Republicans] buy my program
(286) the contributions that they have made
(316) legislation . . . added to or taken from
(428) those twenty-six [jobs] will cost us
(603) the poor president's just been misled
(706) there's the same amount of jealousy
(797) I don't want to spend this week

Recreational/Competitive:
(81) lining up on this play
(82) going around right end
(103) they're on the losing side
(105) on the side of the Negroes
(116) we are on their side
(135) I wouldn't let them call my signals
(139) put Republicans on the spot
(166) I'm on the team
(186) good deal of thought
(304) [a crowd] like a football stadium

(327) get his own team and line them up

(338) wrestling with Wallace

(374) make them show every card

(428) [we'll lose] in the long run

(460) we've got training programs

(504) ought to have a chance to do it

(529) played right into the Republicans' hands

(558) when I got ready to swing

(627) many voters on his side

(652) the president's . . . on their side

(698) he's made a book against you

Martial/Lethal:

(76) that would kill his program

(86) get in a tussle with him

(109) until that's laid to rest

(133) and blow up the bridge

(133) cut off from the South

(153) shoot from the hip

(195) get your tax bill passed instead of killed

(218) he'd be cut to pieces

(220) program would be hurt . . . if it's not killed

(341) pulverize a good many of them

(379) killed all the other programs

(382) we divided our forces

(382) [we] split them to pieces

(383) killed everything else we had

(395) I would've . . . pulverized the South

(406) and then I'd make my attack

(518) they'll knock the damn bigot down

(539) he's going to lay it on us

(558) I would go in for the kill

(569) we got a little pop-gun

(570) I want to pull out the cannon

(593) the president ought to get all of his troops

(603) Lyndon Johnson, the traitor

(626) if he pulverizes away

(682) if this is not warfare

Actional/Directional:

(59) every person has to sign that manifesto

(93) those states might be lost anyway

(116) make them all act like Americans

(120) they're gonna approach it with skepticism

(151) when I'd moved

(163) we're at that stage now

(194) get your tax bill passed

(245) go the unemployment road

(313) he'll have that behind him

(361) Russell just ran him off . . . the balcony

(363) they just slipped it in on me

(367) Do you follow me?

(398) they're going to come running out there

(540) take a position between the Negro and the South

(541) we couldn't get in that position

(638) as soon as you do it, go ahead

(664) I haven't explored that

(681) we are in on the landing

(681) we are not on the takeoff

NOTE: Parenthetical numbers refer to transcript lines.

metaphors Mr. Johnson used in his conversation, roughly one metaphor every 15 seconds, a rate which surely qualifies him as one of the nation's most colorful politicians—not to mention the most masculine. Recreational and competitive metaphors were among his most used, and his competition of choice was full-contact, no-pads football: "lining up on

Table 4.

Metaphorical Type	Total	Percentage
Sensory	(35)	(20.2)
Ocular	13	7.5
Thermal/Tactile	6	3.5
Corporeal	16	9.2
Familiar	(47)	(27.2)
Sedentary	14	8.1
Theological	6	3.5
Domestic	19	11.0
Naturalistic	8	4.6
Antiseptic	(27)	(15.6)
Mechanical	5	2.9
Structural/Hierarchical	12	6.9
Financial	10	5.8
Aggressive	(64)	(37.0)
Recreational/Competitive	21	12.1
Martial/Lethal	25	14.5
Actional/Directional	18	10.4
Total	**173**	**100.0**

this play," "going around right end," "get his own team and line them up."
For Johnson, all of politics could be reduced to "sidedness," and such binary thinking infused every political decision he made.[17]

Because modernism, like most "isms," is often interpreted as a struggle
for ultimacy, it is hardly surprising to find that LBJ's most preferred metaphors were martial/lethal, a logical extension of his recreational/competi-
tive metaphors. For Johnson, this made politics a game turned serious.
Images of the Revolutionary War ("Lyndon Johnson, the traitor"), the old
West ("shoot from the hip"), and the Civil War ("cut off from the South")
are woven seamlessly into his speech, so seamlessly that it is often hard to
remember that his ostensible topic—civil rights legislation—was a manifestly gentle one: legislation that allowed all children to learn their ABCs,
elderly women to ride in the fronts of buses, and teenagers to have a ham-

burger where they pleased. But when the modernist mandate is held for safekeeping by Lyndon Johnson, it is defended with a "cannon," not a "pop-gun," and its attackers are "cut to pieces," "pulverized," "blown up," and then "laid to rest." The fact that such competitive and lethal metaphors frequently occur in close proximity in Johnson's speech—and that they often eventuate in mixed metaphors (e.g., "they'd cut off the South from him. . . . If I were Kennedy I wouldn't let them call my signals")— suggests how rapacious the modernist mandate can be and how rapacious Lyndon Johnson could become when fighting for something he dearly wanted.

Modernism and capitalism are not the same thing, but they are not uncomfortable with one another. Johnson's structural, mechanical, and financial metaphors together suggest a massive political edifice under construction, coolly overseen by talented social engineers and confidently financed by a gaggle of corporate wizards. Such images give to modernist rhetoric a confident air, with quid pro quo bargains being struck early and often. Thus, speaking as if he were John Kennedy, Lyndon Johnson could effortlessly offer the following advice: "I'd go into the South a time or two myself. While I was doing that I'd put the Republicans on the spot by making them buy my programs. . . . I would try to, uh, call in my Southern leaders that got Lockheeds around over the country and others and say 'Now we got to do this in the streets or the courts. And they're doing it in the streets. I can't sit idly by. What do you recommend, Senator?'" For Lyndon Johnson, at least, social justice is something to be *purchased:* butter for guns or, in this case, equal rights for Lockheed bases. Although politicians normally trade a *quid* for a *quo* a bit less starkly, Mr. Johnson nevertheless makes clear the main codicils of the modernist contract: Social improvement is assured because it is tangible; because it is tangible, it can be purchased.

When phrased in such ways, modernism is not pretty. Democratic rhetoric makes it more attractive. This is why Lyndon Johnson's conversation with Ted Sorensen is especially interesting. In a rather unattractive way, Johnson evidences the irresistible processes of commodification that attend modernism. Note, for example, how Johnson gives ordinary realities what the economists call "use value" and thereby makes them politically functional:

RELATIONSHIPS: "I've been into North Carolina this year, in Jefferson, and I've been into Florida. Neither place would they allow Negroes to come. And I said, 'I'm going to come and I'm going to talk about their constitutional rights; I want them on the platform with me. And if you don't let them, I'm not coming, period.'"

THE PRESIDENCY: "This aura, thus, uh, uh, this thing, this halo around the president, everybody wants to believe in the president, the commander in chief, and I think he'd make the Barnetts and the Wallaces look silly. Uh, the good people, the church people, I think, have to come around to him."

TIME: "And he's got plenty of time to propose [legislation]. We can propose right up to September. You ain't even going to get even started discussing it until September anyway. . . . I don't think [right now], uh, I think this is a Republican time to send it up. . . ."

NATIONHOOD: "[I'd make] maybe a fifteen-minute stop at a research, space, uh, medical center. And talk maybe two minutes on that, maybe seven minutes on, uh, America . . . and then a man's put in a position almost where he's a bigot to be against the president."

BLACKS: "I told the president at that time that Rockefeller was going to try to out-Negro our administration, just like he out-Negroed, uh, Averell Harriman."

BLACKS AND HISPANICS: "I took the United Nations down there [to San Antonio], and they said they didn't believe that this was the South because they saw fifty high school bands with Negroes and Mexicans and whites all marching down the street and they saw five hundred thousand people—like a football stadium. . . . And I think television ought to see that."

RELIGION: "Every preacher [should start] preaching about it. And we ought to recognize that and get them busy. Why? Because Dean Sayre spoke up at my meeting the other day—how derelict they've been and what all he wants to do about it. And I said 'Why, I'll just put you on the country circuit right now and you can head South.'"

If power corrupts, and if ultimate power corrupts absolutely, modernist rhetoric corrupts with élan. No entity—neither God nor humankind—can fully resist its grasp. And there is no self-consciousness on Johnson's part here, no gainsaying, no second-thinking. He uses whatever resources he has. If that turns ideas into slogans and people into functionaries, then so be it.[18] His mind moves quickly as he sizes up the available options, and at one point he commodifies region, religion and relationships all at once: "I know these risks are great. Might cost us the South but, uh, those states might be lost anyway. But the difference is that if a president just enforces court decrees, the South will feel it's yielding to force. But if he goes after them, looks them in the eye, states that moral issue and, uh, pushes the Christian issue, and he does it face-to-face, these Southerners will at least respect his courage and they'll feel that, uh, they're on the losing side of an issue of conscience."

Modernism is both restless and relentless. Mr. Johnson's actional/directional metaphors contrast sharply with his sedentary metaphors and occur with roughly equal frequency. Such metaphors are clearly foils for one another, with Mr. Johnson typically generating the action ("I wouldn't be stopped," "I can't sit idly by," "I haven't explored that yet," "Do you follow me?") and virtually everyone else—the legislature, the president, the Republicans—doing too little too slowly. For Lyndon Johnson, modernism means movement. So, for example, unemployment becomes a "road" that can be traversed, not a rut to be settled into. He warns the president not to get himself into "positions" that limit his mobility but, instead (and in the favored imagery of the scientific 1960s), to be in on the "takeoff" of all things political. Above all, he warns, the modernist must eschew the static castes ("take a position between the Negro and the South"), static conceptions of time ("we're at that stage now"), and static forms of patriarchy ("every person has to sign that manifesto") characteristic of preindustrial society.

Our discussions of martial metaphors, commodification, and unbridled action make modernism seem just as masculine as the monarchal and militaristic systems it was meant to replace. And surely one finds virility in Lyndon Johnson's rhetoric (at one point in the conversation he warns Sorensen that the House Appropriations Committee "is going to cut [Mr. Kennedy's], uh, outfit off and put it in their pocket and never mention civil rights"). But above all, modernism is meant to be efficient. From a structuralist perspective, male tribalism was hardly efficient. Its doctrine of old wars in old lands produced uncertain employment, antiquated technologies, and oppressive social systems. And so modernism domesticated tribalism, introducing an unmistakably female (which is not to say feminist) dimension into the public sphere. As a result, even at the height of industrialization the Western world began to see child labor laws, embryonic welfare systems, public hospitalization, compulsory education, and more enlightened marriage contracts. Although it is not normally credited with such, modernism represented a turn to the feminine in political and corporate affairs, no matter how cynical its motivations for doing so might have been at times.

Not only does anecdotal evidence of the feminization, or better, humanization, of Johnson's rhetoric lie in his heavy use of domestic and corporeal metaphors (table 3), but his discourse also evidences the feminine in two additional ways. First, he constantly calls attention to what Erving Goffman would call the "facework" of political relationships.[19] He does so functionalistically, to be sure, but that he does so at all seems a clear attempt to emphasize politics' human scale. When Mr. Johnson notes that "the president's got to go in there without cussing anybody or fussing with anybody," he acknowledges that nobody profits when politics becomes a blood feud. Second, Johnson was sensitive to the dangers of hierarchicalization, noting at one point that the president "should state the moral issue, and should do so . . . not as a demon trying to punish a child" but more multilaterally; at another point, he urges the president to look "them straight in the face, not lecturing them as a father" but as an equal. Throughout his conversation, Johnson makes the obvious, which is to say utilitarian, point that when an Everett Dirksen feels "he hadn't been consulted" or when a George Wallace feels personally "confronted," the chances of fashioning enlightened public policy are doomed. "Go to the South," Johnson tells Kennedy through Sorensen, and tell its residents that they have been "a beacon light for the nation" before you upbraid them for tasks left undone. For Johnson, because politics is a human enterprise (that is, both human and an enterprise), it is potential incarnate. "Work the people," says Johnson, and all things are possible: "I slept on this couch I'm looking at for thirty-seven nights, but I produced quorums at two o'clock and four o'clock and that's what you've got to be prepared to do, and you might as well notify these wives that you're going to have some unpopularity because they cussed me all the time."

In many ways, modernism was as much a collectivist response as was Marxism. Both systems strived to cope with the facts of community, with the needs to maximize resources and minimize costs for a network of constituencies. Capitalism placed its faith in consumer-based industries, communism placed its faith in agricultural cooperatives. But both systems sought to reduce tensions between the personal and the communal. Nobody, perhaps, was more sensitive to such tensions than Lyndon Johnson. Politics for him was a sociogram, a map of political habitats: northern Blacks versus southern blacks, the "church people" in the South versus the rednecks, the House Judiciary Committee versus the Senate's Interstate Commerce Committee, Western Republicans versus Southern Democrats, the NAACP versus the Student Nonviolent Coordinating Committee.[20] For Johnson, politics could be reduced to bloc management (a thoroughly modernist notion—this idea that people can be managed), and so his conversation became a cybernetic of political clusters: "And I think I have spoken from, uh, Milwaukee to Chicago to New York to Los Angeles to Illinois last night. And Gettysburg. And Dallas. And Johnson City, Texas, and, uh, I think I know one thing and that's the Negroes are tired of this patient stuff and tired of this piecemeal stuff, and what they want more than anything is not an executive order or legislation. They want a moral commitment that [the president's] behind them."

Lyndon Johnson concerned himself with matters of facework because personal animosities can undermine group possibilities. His three key words in politics were constituency, constituency, and constituency. For him, the personal-communal distinction was fundamental, and so even his literary quotations became opportunistic: "And, uh, uh, see, this fellow, uh, Baldwin, he says, uh, 'I don't want to marry your daughter. I just want to get you off of my back.' And that's what these Negroes want, uh. They want that moral commitment." In reducing James Baldwin to a tag line, modernism does little for literature. But modernism was only incidentally a literary and an architectural movement. More powerfully, it was a social, scientific, economic, and, hence, political movement. It was a movement designed to tame what Hannah Arendt might call the brute facts of natality.[21] It inspired political compromise in the name of efficiency; it inspired economic competition in the name of creativity; and it commodified people and their ideas in the name of patriotism. Lyndon Baines Johnson was thoroughly implicated in all of this. He saw politics as a way of helping people adjust to life in a corporate culture, as a way of grinding down the sharp edges of modernity. Political rhetoric was most often his millstone of choice. Let us examine why.

POLITICS AND THE RHETORICAL MIND

Lyndon Johnson was diffident about rhetoric. That his mind operated rhetorically, that he was fascinated, perhaps overfascinated, by the strategic use of language, cannot be questioned. Behaviorally, though, he was often uncomfortable with it. The more formal the speaking occasion the more uncomfortable he became. Television, especially, unnerved him.[22] Still, every breath he took was a rhetorical breath—deciding whom to talk to and when, examining why strategy A worked better than strategy B, discovering a new group whose egos needed stroking. The fabled "Johnson treatment," whereby LBJ loomed over an unsuspecting interlocutor and showered him with flattery and spittle, is a favorite Washington story. Less well known is that Mr. Johnson could be coolly cerebral about rhetoric. In the best modernist tradition, he planned his spontaneity as well as Shakespeare's Iago. His conversation with Ted Sorensen documents that.

One seemingly incidental, but telling, fact about Mr. Johnson's conversation is his heavy use of ocular metaphors (see tables 3 and 4). It is as if politics were a completely projective art for Johnson, a phenomenon without phenomenal depth. "Images," "viewpoints," "appearances," and "reflections" abound in his talk. These visual metaphors greatly outnumber his thermal/tactile metaphors, implying that there was more shadow than substance in Lyndon Johnson's *polis*. No doubt, Mr. Johnson would argue that perception and reality are phenomenally interlocked in politics, that virtue cannot triumph nor perfidy be expunged unless both are *seen* as such. Rhetoric was thus a tool of vision for Johnson, a way of making reifications useful.[23] We must "make them act like Americans" where civil rights is concerned, declares Mr. Johnson; "we must make them act like Americans no matter what their real feelings," implies Mr. Johnson. Similarly, when he says "I think the presidency can get it [civil rights legislation] for him," Johnson treats the highest office in the land as more a locus of perceptions than a locus of law. In like manner, he sees "reason" as something co-created, not as something inherent. "You've got to sit down with them, help them have a reason" to vote for your bill, he says, demonstrating that congressional leadership is often a matter of rhetorical coaching, of helping one's colleagues discover an articulate way of endorsing a touchy piece of legislation. To call Lyndon Johnson an intersubjectivist is to understate the case.

As Kenneth Burke has observed, rhetoric is a dramatistic art, a way of making ideas come alive for persons who have not confronted those ideas via firsthand experience.[24] Lyndon Johnson understood the truth of Burke's observations. He knew that politics was often little more than a colloca- tion of symbolic acts that constrained people in particular ways. Politics was power and money, too, of course, but it was always power and money for a reason. Rhetoric dramatizes such reasons: "I'd go to San Antonio. I'd get a Mexican congressman, and I'd just show them there's not anything terrible about this business [of race]. That here, right in the heart of the Southland, you've got a fellow whose father and mother were born out of this country and he's in Congress. I'd let him introduce him with that white suit on and every television in America [would take notice]." Here, and elsewhere, Johnson showed a keen eye for the symbolic. "The first time that George Smathers has ever had dinner with [blacks] in Saint Au- gustine" happened because Lyndon Johnson made it happen during one of his staged speaking events. Scenery is important, too, says Johnson, since a presidential speech on civil rights made "down in Jackson, Missis- sippi . . . would be worth a hell of a lot more than it would in Harlem." In an electronic age, Johnson claims, the mass media can never be ignored, so central have they become to political drama. "Went out there [to Los An- geles] and spoke to them," complained Mr. Johnson, "but I can't get in the paper." When the vice president of the United States presides at a minority training program's graduation ceremony, argues Johnson, the media should be automatically interested, especially since he had taken such pains to set the scene: "Uh, uh, had every, every aerospace manufacturer in California present with a hundred graduates. And they're semiskilled people; they all got jobs when they come out of this technical school that they graduate from. Dan Kimble of Lockheed, president of North American, every one of them. And that's what got to be done all over this country."

As J. L. Austin has observed, symbolic events often have performative aspects to them—speech *does* as well as *says*.[25] When he went to Los Ange- les, for example, Mr. Johnson knew full well that the fact of his speaking there counted for a great deal, no matter what words he actually spoke. And so he advised President Kennedy to follow his lead and to go to the South. He also wrote him a script carefully adapted to Southerners: "'You people, uh, you people don't believe in starving your fellow man. You think a man that wants to work ought to have a chance to do it, so, uh, see that these unions let them in, see that these employers let them work.' Uh, uh, and I'll tell you those Negroes will be whispering to each other, 'He walked right in there, and he stood right up to them, and he told them the facts.'" For Johnson, speaking events like these were the overt markers of leadership because they were so tangible. His theory of governance was thus a theory of rhetoric: "Unless it's stated dramatically, convincingly," warned Johnson, "they're not going to pay much attention. . . . They're gonna approach it with skepticism." And so whenever Lyndon Johnson envisioned political triumph, he conjured a rhetorical vision. When he envisioned political disaster, he also imagined people in dialogue: "And, uh, while you get your [civil rights] message off tomorrow, my friend, uh, probably Everett Dirksen and Dick Russell'll be sitting around next Sunday over a mint julep with an understanding that they're going to do a good deal more, Dirksen is, than you've asked, and that, uh, he hadn't been consulted. . . . Then he'll go along with Russell. And he's made a book against you. Now, I'd make a book with him instead of Russell making a book with him."

Dramatic scenery is one thing, words are another. Mr. Johnson knew both. He knew about such ancient notions as genre ["(I'd speak) not in a lecture form but in kind of an information form"], and he also knew what the ancients called "commonplaces," stock sources of argumentation preserved in a culture's history—stories, myths, and modes of reasoning that persuade with special power because they so faithfully capture essential values and experiences. During his conversation with Ted Sorensen, Mr. Johnson tapped several of these commonplaces. At one point, for example, he reached deep inside the nation's emotional center for an argument: "And I think the South, uh, I don't know much about it, but I think it'll respect [the president] because here's a man, uh, with conscience. They think that, uh, they don't believe in anything that the Pope believes in. You know that. But they believe this man is a sincere man, and he's a Catholic because he believes that's what he ought to be." With this as his premise, Mr. Johnson proceeds immediately to his conclusion, displaying rhetorical, as well as metarhetorical, understanding of the political possibilities when doing so:

> And when you tell them the one about the, uh, Joe Kennedy and that Baptist boy of Fort Worth going down in the same plane, uh, they, they'll knock the damn bigot down who questions his religion. And, uh, they'll do the same thing here [with civil rights]. . . . Let him reach over there and

point and say, 'I have to order these boys into battle, into foxholes, with, carrying the flag. And I don't ask them what their name is, whether it's Gomez or Smith or . . . what color they got, what religion. And if I can order them into battle, I've got to make it possible for them to eat and sleep in this country.'[26]

Anyone with as rich a rhetorical imagination as Lyndon Johnson tends to conflate essences and surfaces to produce a kind of postmodern mélange. Prejudice, for example, is thought not to inhere in the individual but to reside almost completely in semantic space: "[The president] ought to make it almost, uh, uh, make a bigot out of anybody that's against him." Political commitments, too, are dynamic, not static, and therefore an endless source of political possibilities: "I don't know where Smathers is; I don't know where Mansfield is. But I'd find out where they are." Even the tangible aspects of physical space can be transformed by rhetoric into a kind of hyperspace: "The president could do this in North Carolina or someplace . . . in, uh, Mississippi or Texas or Louisiana and just have a few, uh, honor guard there with a few Negroes in it."[27]

A rhetorical world is a fluid world, a world without traditional boundaries. Thus Mr. Johnson can—in one breath—recommend that the president give a speech in, say, New Orleans about, say, the space program, even though the purpose of the speech is to better position civil rights legislation so that, say, Hale Boggs will not be discomfited since, say, he "will have already voted for his tax bill and he'll have that behind him." The Johnson-Sorensen conversation is often just such a dizzying dash between the moral and the quotidian. Both are parts, arguably equal parts, of Lyndon Johnson's political cosmos. And so right in the middle of his vote counting, Mr. Johnson can segue into an ethical observation and then out of it, and then back again, without missing a beat:

> But if he pulverizes away, why he'll have as many voters on his side as these legislators got on theirs, if he tells them the truth. *Because he's right, Ted.* Uh, but, uh, you think we have exploited that personality and that office and that man, uh, and bled him for everything he's got to give this leadership movement? I don't think we've done any of it. [emphasis ours]
>
> You ain't going to get . . . even started discussing [civil rights legislation] until September anyway. You've got to pass your tax bill and, uh, uh,

you've got to pass some of your other bills. And, uh, uh, September's just about the time. You'll have so many night sessions before you get cloture. So the only big problem is saying to the Baldwins and to the Kings and to the rest of them, "We give you a moral commitment."

Johnson: Then I'd turn all the, every moral force in this country, loose on it.

Sorensen: I think that's a good suggestion.

Johnson: I want to talk to the president about this and about the supersonic bomber. Do you want to take one minute on that?

A transitionless rhetoric of this sort signals one of two things—a speaker who makes no distinctions or a speaker who only makes distinctions. As a philosopher Lyndon Johnson was probably the former; as a practical politician he was clearly the latter. Because his world was so thoroughly rhetorical, he thought all things possible. He tended not to make philosophical distinctions—separating the true from the untrue—because he judged truth to be a product of dialectic, not of ontological certainty. He did not distinguish between the political and the nonpolitical because he could not conceive of such a distinction. Because he was such a good politician, he separated the prudent from the imprudent, the possible-now from the possible-later, the short-term gain from the long-term gain. Because he had seen so much change in his life, he tended to welcome it, the grander its scale the better. Because he came to know people in their infinite variety, he tried not to judge their personal predilections, just cope with them. In these ways and more, Lyndon Johnson was a politician. His conversation with Ted Sorensen demonstrates it. But for many, Lyndon Johnson was also a troubling politician. His conversation with Sorensen demonstrates that as well.

CONCLUSION

If we can believe popular reports in the press, the voices on the call-in radio talk shows, and legion social commentators, nobody likes politics. People do not like politics because its practitioners dissemble, because they make such an unholy row when disagreeing with one another, and because they spend so much public money. Nowhere has this been more true than in the United States, where government has been especially distrusted. Although Americans, like all people, are more than willing to accept the fruits of representative government, they do not like to pay for them. And though they find politics distasteful, they find politicians themselves downright repugnant. They feel that politicians are effete, since they use their brains and not their muscles to make a living and because politicians are willing to discuss core emotions out in public. Above all, Americans detest the lying in politics. They do not understand how enlightened public policy can be built atop legerdemain or how civic virtue can be insured by leaders so lacking in personal virtue. Americans have waxed and waned on this score, as different politicians have caught their fancy, but normally they feel most secure when their legislatures are not in session. Political double-dealing may fascinate them from time to time, but almost nobody wants a politician in the family.

If politics is a problem, Lyndon Johnson is a double problem. Perhaps more than any other contemporary American, he represented essential politics. In his conversation with Theodore Sorensen, Johnson may well have reshaped important aspects of the Kennedy administration's embryonic civil rights strategy of 1963, and he appeared to have done so rather effortlessly. In overcoming legislative hurdles of this sort, Johnson was rivaled only by his mentor, Sam Rayburn. He was rivaled only by Franklin Roosevelt in the scope of his vision for federal governance. Among recent presidents, he was rivaled only by Ronald Reagan in the clarity of his reelectoral mandate. As a consequence, the stench of politicalness clung to Lyndon Johnson as it has clung to few. As Jim Heath once remarked, Mr. Johnson "was accused of being 'too much' or 'only' a politician, the implication being that the person in the White House should be somewhat above politics."[28] Surely this is curious—to accuse a politician of being a politician. But people seem to have a special problem with Lyndon Johnson because they have trouble with politics itself.

As we have seen here, politics for Lyndon Johnson was the modernist/capitalist mandate, pure and simple. We have seen, too, that his modernism was a curious mixture of the masculine and the feminine. It was masculine in that it measured governmental success by empirical, not philosophical, standards and because it saw competition as the root of all good. It commodified people and ideas easily and happily, just as earlier forms of modernism had commodified automobiles and baby buggies. When he complained to Ted Sorensen that their boss, John Kennedy, had "passed nothing" thus far, Johnson betrayed his own image of manhood, an image curiously responsive to the criticisms of politicians-as-sissies he had heard as a young man in rural Texas. But Lyndon Johnson was also responsive to his mother's teachings and so his highly sociological brand of politics came naturally too.

These forces—the masculine and the feminine—collided powerfully in his conversation with Ted Sorensen, lending an irrepressible energy to his talk. And energy is just what modernism promised long ago, energy capable of reworking old forms of commerce and, hence, old social, moral, religious, aesthetic and, inevitably, political routines as well. This is what Lyndon Johnson shows us better than most: that modernism has consequences. "If you want better schools," says Mr. Johnson, "you will have to learn to speak financially." "If you want better families," says Mr. Johnson, "attend to the material." "If you want less racial discrimination," says Mr. Johnson, "you must trade dams for civility." And to his postmodern challengers Mr. Johnson would say: "Talk of *différance* if you like, but I shall end redlining; concern yourself with the surplus of meanings if you will, but I will create jobs; decry the hegemonic order if you must, but I shall put it to use."

If the Johnson-Sorensen conversation is a problem, it is a problem only because modernism is itself a problem, even for its most direct beneficiaries. Although some of modernism's unsavory side effects can be cloaked, expediency is not one of them. That is why Lyndon Johnson's rhetorical instincts were so important; he understood that when people turn away from functionalism they often turn toward romanticism, modernism's precursor. And so he showed a good deal of creativity when suggesting how Mr. Kennedy could stage-manage his civil rights legislation and how the nation's political geography could become that legislation's scenery. Because romanticism so often stresses emotional and not ideational linkages, Mr. Johnson often switched topics and moods when speaking, confident that the flow of his argument would overwhelm the defenses of even the most fastidious listener. The blunt summary, then, is that Lyndon Johnson put romanticism to work.

As Ralph Lane demonstrated thirty years ago, the American people are ambivalent about wordiness, especially in politicians.[29] They sense that words are too often a chimera shielding the known, the true, from being seen. And yet these same people can still be captured by the spellbinder whose oratory gives them a richer sense of purpose and who makes their everyday lives seem grander. Lyndon Johnson was hardly a spellbinder, but he was an imposing rhetorical creature one-on-one. Relentlessly, feverishly, he worked in behalf of modernism, trying to make it seem less grasping than it sometimes seems. As a result, he created a daunting political legacy. But his greatest legacies are those of modernist archetype and rhetorical tactician. Although Lyndon Johnson's personality makes it easy to treat both of these legacies as unworthy, it is hard to imagine how his brand of politics could have been done better. The perversity of that irony would not have been lost on Lyndon Johnson.

CHAPTER 6

The Invention of Nixon
Edwin Black

We all invent ourselves. We cover our bodies with cloth and regulate our language. We "prepare a face to meet the faces" that we meet. There is nothing revelatory in the acknowledgment of self-invention. Indeed, it risks banality.

We accept as a given, as a necessary foundation for civilized life, the existence of a whole and complex moral economy founded on the acknowledgment of self-invention. If we were not somehow at least participants in the formation of our identities, it is hard to see how we could be accountable for our actions. The issue is central to a current controversy over social policy in the United States: whether an exogenous condition—environmental adversity, or developmental deprivation, or cultural deficiency—can absolve misconduct. In order to hold people responsible for what they do, we must also regard them as, to some significant extent, responsible for what they are. Doing and being are inextricably linked in our conceptions of one another.

Moreover, we have the examples of admirable people whom we cannot begin to understand except as self-invented. Abraham Lincoln, who will serve in this chapter as the great model of the presidency, is the supreme example. The reduction of Lincoln to his origins and influences is inconceivable. A condition of our admiring his character, as anyone's, is our believing that character to be, somehow, if not exactly a choice, then a product of choices: at once the manifestation of a human being and the creation of one.

So to observe that Richard Nixon invented himself is to observe merely that he shared with the rest of us a psychological process as common as breathing or digesting. A shrewd commentator once observed of the president: "He acted a part, playing a role he himself created in a way that fit only one actor. Even more, he fashioned *himself* so that he could play it. He created . . . the public person. . . . " [italics in the original] The president of whom that commentator was writing was the president of France, Charles DeGualle. The commentator was Richard Nixon. As the biographer Stephen Ambrose remarked of that comment, "Nixon was surely giving us an excellent self-portrait."[1]

Because of the complex moral economy that undergirds self-invention, the subject of Nixon's self-invention brings us to issues that are more general and enduring than the career of one man. The career of that man, however, is an instantiation of those issues, an avenue into their exploration. Nixon's life was illustrative, even potentially monitory. And if we are to extract from that life whatever lessons it may teach us about the rhetorical presidency, if we are to use, if we are even, for our own moral purposes, to exploit a public career, our orientation to Richard Nixon becomes an attitude of clinical impersonality.

Criticism that begins in detachment can easily end in cruelty. That is why we must remind ourselves that there was a relationship between the real human being called Richard Nixon—the organism of flesh, blood, and sinew; the breathing creature who processed nutriments and perceptions—and the idea of him that lived in the minds of a public. He was a man, not a fiction. But to a greater extent than most of us, he fashioned himself to be a concept. His having become a dehumanized object of diagnostic inquiry was not, initially at least, the work of psychoanalytic commentators, or historians, or biographers, or rhetorical critics, or any other of the hundreds of people who have written about him. The objectification of Nixon—the treatment of him as an artifact rather than as a human being—began with Nixon. He did it to himself. He chose to make himself an instrument of his own ambition, to discipline his impulses to order for mass consumption, to offer himself for public approval. It was he who decided to pursue a career that was not comfortably consonant with his temperament. It was he who decided to forego privacy for himself and his family and to seek the majesty of an institutional personification. He not only willed his own artificiality—we all do that—but he willed that it dominate the whole of his life, so that his public image became one to which his sense of himself had to adapt instead of, as in most of us, the reverse. The fabricating of Richard Nixon was an eighty-one year project, and it was unceasing for its duration.

The willfulness of Nixon's inventional enterprise was most visibly manifested in his tense rhetorical comportment. More than two decades ago, in an essay on the 1972 presidential campaign, I tried to observe some features of that comportment. Self-quotation is a tacky practice, but perhaps it will be forgiven in a critique so concerned as this one is with narcissism:

> Nixon's smile is a tiny bit late . . . one can see his eyes tell his mouth to smile, and since the smile has come from his eyes instead of his spine, we know that he has willed it.
>
> One can see the willfulness in his walk. The legs are stiff; the arms are rigid; the stride is not a single motion but a sequence of discrete motions; the body is slightly crouched, like a wary boxer's. We can find the same characteristics in people who wear leg or back braces, and whose conscious minds must instruct each step.
>
> Most distinctly, it is in his discourse. "Let me make one thing perfectly clear. . . ." "Let me say this. . . ." The discourses are full of statements about the discourses themselves. The compositional machinery—things like transitions and internal summaries—are just a bit clumsy, just a bit conspicuous.
>
> The man is not inventing a speech. He is inventing a man inventing a speech.

Nixon's tics and quirks were not the only symptoms of his self-consciousness. The diagnosis is supported by another empirical datum:

Richard Nixon's public discourses—and especially his presidential discourses—were inordinately self-referential. Never mind those discourses that occurred in circumstances in which we would expect an abundance of self-referencing: justifying one's candidacy during an electoral campaign, for example, or defending oneself against accusations of wrongdoing. Nixon did talk about himself voluminously in those sorts of discourses, but the circumstances prompting the discourses demanded his reflexivity, and in talking about himself, he was doing no more than being relevant. On other occasions, however, when self-referencing would seem not only gratuitous, but even rhetorically inadvisable, Nixon still talked about himself.

Take, for example, one of his most intensely studied speeches, the address to the nation of November 3, 1969, on the war in Vietnam, sometimes called the "Silent Majority Speech." It was a speech that Nixon himself wrote and of which he was proud. In one of his books, he called it "both a milestone and a turning point for my administration." Discussing it in another of his books, he was effusive with superlatives: "We had the biggest television audience ever for a Presidential speech. The reaction by telegram, letters, and telephone was the biggest ever. My approval rating went up eleven points, the biggest increase as a result of a Presidential speech in the history of the Gallup poll."[2] Yet, the speech is strikingly reflexive. It begins and concludes with the focus as much on Richard Nixon as on the crisis that wracked the country.

Among the several lively commentaries by rhetorical critics on the speech, Hermann G. Stelzner was especially perceptive in noting how much of the discourse is a story that has Richard Nixon as its hero.[3] In addition to the overarching narrative that Stelzner recorded, there is an abundance of other self-referential material in the speech. In its introductory section, Nixon invited the audience to consider the political benefits that he—Nixon—nobly denied himself by refusing to withdraw from Vietnam, and in the concluding part of the speech, Nixon invited the audience to consider his own emotional commitment to ending the war. In both sections of the speech, Nixon seems to forfeit some of the advantage he had in being president of the United States by reminding the audience of the partisan campaign that had brought him to the presidency. Strategically, these are curious choices, and their very curiosity highlights the reflexivity of the discourse.

Six months later, on April 30, 1970, Nixon again addressed the nation about the war in Southeast Asia, this time to defend an American incursion into Cambodia. And again, if one reads the speech with special attention to the use of the first-person singular, one must be struck by its reflexivity. The final third of the speech—a section that one would expect to be especially important because of its proportion and its placement—is concerned with Richard Nixon: his motives, his probity, his prospects for reelection.

When we add to the discourses on so ostensibly impersonal a subject as the Vietnam War the discourses that we would expect to be more reflexive, and that are perhaps even better remembered—the Checkers speech, the press conferences on the California governor's election and on Watergate, the Watergate speeches, the farewell to the White House staff, the resignation speech, the books, which include no fewer than three memoirs— what we have, in the end, to contemplate is a substantial inventory of prose works not just largely *by*, but also largely *about* Richard Nixon.

It is inconceivable that Lincoln, for example, or Wilson or Eisenhower would have talked as much as Nixon did about himself. Lincoln, in fact, seemed intent on extinguishing his own presence in the speeches that he gave after the Civil War started. The Gettysburg Address and the Second Inaugural are barren of self references—the latter, awkwardly so.

Nixon invented a public man: nothing unusual in that. But then he admired his handiwork. The invention of the public persona was an act of craftsmanship common to celebrities, but the favorable judgment of that invention was, finally, an aesthetic judgment. It was an expression of bad taste. It was vanity.

The issue of vanity occurs in the context of a public-private distinction. The public and private realms are separately governed by overlapping but distinguishable codes of decorum and morality. Vanity in a public figure is an intrusion of personal values into civic life. The political expression of vanity consists of a particular marking of public deeds by private motives. Such markings violate the overriding scruple that governs the entire public-private disposition, which is that wherever public and private codes are different, they shall remain different; that an unsanctioned intermixture of public and private motives is itself a transgression of political decorum.

The sources of or reasons for Nixon's vanity are matters for speculation. One can never finally understand the formation of a human personality. One can, however, sometimes identify likely influences that are, at the least, compatible with the personality that is formed. In Nixon's case, our suspicion is drawn to his religious grounding and to his parents.

Quakerism is an unpretentious religion, simple and rigorous. It is an unlikely seedbed for vanity, but it is a human institution, and so it is not without its baleful potentialities. One of its central tenets is that each individual human being is personally connected to God and has the capacity for becoming a medium of divine disclosure. Quakerism is predicated on the centrality of self, and it insists on the personal interpretation of religious events—even of what, to the believer, would be supernal interventions. That intensely personal attitude has often fortified an extraordinary moral courage, exemplified in American history by the heroic adherence to principle of Quakers during the slavery controversy and during our wars. But that same attitude can also countenance a septic egoism. To regard one's own voice as potentially a vehicle for divine pronouncements is an invitation to an extreme of self-regard, and that self-regard may be as well expressed in an exorbitance of modesty as an exorbitance of pride.

Nixon was also influenced by parental models of steady certitude. Frank Nixon was a father noted for his contentiousness and bluster, but he lavished attention on his son. And Hannah Nixon was a mother who practiced the quiescent virtues of Quakerism with a reticence of unnerving ferocity. Frank Nixon especially armed his son early with confidence in his own judgments.[4]

Richard repaid his parents with affectionate accounts of them in his memoirs and with his virtual canonization of them in his farewell to the White House staff. But even in his obituary descriptions of his parents' final moments with him, his ego required that he cast himself in the central role.

Nixon wrote of the final hours of his father's life: "'Dad, you've got to keep fighting,' I said. His last words to me were, 'Dick, *you* keep fighting.' The next day, he died at the age of seventy-five." Three pages later in the same book he wrote of his last talk with his mother. It occurred just prior to a surgical procedure that destroyed her mental faculties for the remaining two years of her life. He had lost the election for the governorship of California, and his career was at a low point: "I said, 'Mother, don't give up.' She pulled herself up and said almost sternly, 'Richard, don't *you* give up. Don't let anybody tell you you are through.'"[5]

"*[Y]ou* keep fighting," said the dying father in 1956; "don't *you* give up," said the gravely ill mother in 1965. It is, of course, possible that his final conversations with his parents were as similar to one another as these accounts propose. People who are long married are reputed to come to resemble one another, and so perhaps they can even coincide in their last words. It is possible.

Moreover, there was scarcely a moment in his life when Nixon did not consider himself embattled, fighting for survival. Indeed, his writings, over a fairly long period of time, are pervaded by the motif of battle, almost to an obsessive degree. The image was an epistemic metaphor for him: it represented his way of comprehending politics.[6] Many of his intimates came to share that strenuous view of him. It is not surprising. He was, after all, a persuasive man.

The very first biography of him, the only known copy of which is in the Whittier College library, is an unpublished specimen of puffery written around 1953 by a resident of Whittier, Richard Gardner. It has the oxymoronic title, "Fighting Quaker." The oxymoron's application to Nixon—perhaps even the oxymoron itself—was borrowed by Gardner from O. C. Anderson, who was the principal of Whittier High School when Nixon was a student.[7] Nixon was known as a fighter—early to his high school principal, later to his college football coach, later still to his admiring constituents in the California Twelfth Congressional District. It was the role in which he often presented himself, even to himself. So, maybe his father and his mother, independent of one another, each irrecoverably sick, were truly preoccupied not with the fate of themselves but with the ordeals of their son, the gladiatorial issue of their loins. It is possible.

Yes, it is possible that each of those final conversations really did occur, and that each of those conversations really did focus on the resoluteness of Richard rather than on the sick old person in the hospital bed whose tenuous hold on life was the central motive of the scene. But it is also possible that those two conversations with the dying parents, if they were not deliberate fabrications, were recounted from the memory of a man whose omnivorous ego could nourish itself even by the deaths of his father and his mother. That too is possible.

And while we have mortuary subjects before us, let me breach an even more delicate matter. Consider the death of Pat Nixon. The funeral is on television. The mourners are assembled. The room is quiet. And then you see Richard Nixon escorted in, and this once-powerful figure, this arbiter of the destinies of nations, has come to be simply an old man, convulsed in uncontrollable weeping. No matter what the duration or intensity of your distaste for Nixon, you have to be moved by his anguish, by his common, human grief. And yet, and yet—in later reflection on the desolating scene, it occurs to you that you have seen something wrenchingly personal, that you have *seen* it, and that it is odd that you have seen it.

Who made it a public ceremony? Who allowed television cameras into that tightly monitored space?

It is unthinkable that Richard Nixon's display of sorrow was not genuine. A woman who had stood by him for fifty-three years was dead. Her daughter's biography of her had portrayed her, with utter plausibility, as tested beyond endurance.[8] But never once, amidst the stringencies of a lifetime, had she wavered in her public fidelity to his ambition. And now she was with him no more. Of course he would weep.

Moreover, at eighty years of age, having survived so many losses, so many dangers, so many extinctions, why should he care any longer about appearances? For whom would he display a brave face? Was there anyone anymore who merited his acting or who could recompense him for it? And yet, and yet—who arranged that his agony should be public?

Pat Nixon was buried on the grounds of the Nixon presidential library in a tomb for which he had made assiduous provision. The distinguished company in attendance at the funeral was ornamented by two other former presidents of the United States. And the television cameras were there to broadcast it all.

Was he, whose first book was titled *Six Crises,* he who mastered crisis and prided himself, deservedly, on the mastery, was he, even in that crisis of bereavement, calculating a masterly effect? Or did he, in the agony of his deprivation and in the composure of his old age, at last not give a damn about appearances?

These are impolitic matters to address. No critic has the right to be clinical about lamentation, to probe rude fingers into the psychic wounds of loss. But our consideration here is entirely public evidence, and it was Richard Nixon who made it public. Nixon's griefs were not private griefs that were privately grieved. The dying words of Frank and Hannah were published in a book that professed the authorship of Richard Nixon and that was diligently promoted by Richard Nixon; the funeral of Pat was televised from a sanctuary controlled by Richard Nixon. His parents' dying words, his sorrow over the death of his wife: these are matters that we could not know if he had not informed us. And what does his complicity in our knowing say about his motives, and his values, and the voracity of his ego? What does it say about the relation between this champion of convention and our conventional inhibitions about the public display of private emotions?

Nixon's project of rehabilitating his reputation occupied the final twenty years of his life. It was a project that had some success. The harsh memories of Watergate had faded, and at his funeral, the eulogists found much to praise. But if, in that project of rehabilitation, Richard Nixon was able to turn to rhetorical advantage the deaths of his father, his mother, and his wife, then one may ask if there was anything at all that he was not willing to invest in his dream of himself.

Christopher Lasch, in a book with the suggestive title, *The Culture of Narcissism*, remarked Nixon's "theatrical conception of politics," and "his ability to distinguish a convincing performance from a poor one" in his political encounters.[9] Nixon was an expert at seeing through bluffs. He repeatedly proved himself a connoisseur of skepticism, especially in the Hiss affair and in his dealings with foreign governments. He had, after all, been discharged from the navy in 1945 with a small fortune that he had gained by playing poker, a game that is not won by the gullible. But Nixon's shrewd skepticism was one of the few talents that he did not turn upon himself. Reflexive doubt was not in his repertoire of incredulities. He believed in himself, which meant that he believed in his capacity to engage events, to become whatever the hour required him to become. And he believed in his own motives.

Certainly he never seemed to distrust the festering resentment that occasionally erupted during his public career and that pervaded the White House tapes and the late memoirs. He never questioned the rectitude of his animosities. Nixon did not seek to subdue his malevolent impulses but only his enfeebling ones. The only thing he had to fear was fear itself.

He was, as he repeatedly assured us, not a quitter. For decades, that was one of the recurrent motifs of his public discourse.[10] The message of his life was that he cared about his reputation. It was to him an object to be cultivated. It was not just an implication of his actions but the point and purpose of them.

Lincoln, by contrast, practiced an authority of self-effacement. He subordinated himself to the office; he disappeared into his principles. And even FDR and Reagan—two irresistible charmers—seemed comfortable in the presidency—too secure to display worry about reputation. Reagan was even able to play at self-depreciation. But Nixon adverted continuously to the first-person singular; he persisted in elaborating narratives in which he was the central character. He was too manifestly earning or retaining the office quite to occupy it.

When Robert Bork was a nominee for the United States Supreme Court, he appeared before the Senate Judiciary Committee. Senator Alan Simpson, whose unctuous interrogation of Bork had been larded with flattery, asked him: "Why do you want to be an Associate Justice of the United States Supreme Court?" Bork proceeded to describe the cerebral and honorific satisfactions that the job would enable him to savor. "It would," he said, "be an intellectual feast."[11]

The response was less than transcendent. The question, from a senator friendly to Bork's nomination, was an open invitation, and a higher-minded witness could have reacted with the proclamation of a credo, as David Lilienthal famously did in comparable but more hostile circumstances in 1947.[12] Especially given the political opportunity—the invitation to eloquence—that the question presented to Bork, it would not be surprising if his porcine reply caused even toughened senators to flinch.

Nevertheless, Bork's answer merits attention. He did not announce himself as driven by some ideal. He represented his own ambition as, simply, self-indulgence; but that response, impolitic as it was, had an almost refreshing candor, especially in a proceeding in which candor is so rare. More important, the answer may have crudely comported with Bork's version of conservatism. He could have argued—and not without justification—that to occupy an office of government in order to serve a set of abstract principles would have been to conduct power with indifference to palpable realities, to ignore the texture of the world. There is a powerful argument to be made that the dedication to an ideal, no matter how exalted, has often led to stupidity and sometimes to brutality, that the pursuit of utopia has been, at bottom, the curse of this bloody century.

It can be further argued that to suppose oneself immune to personal appetites and capable of selfless service to an ideal is a dangerous delusion. And so, in a perverse way, Bork's answer may have been a principled answer.

There is an element—actually a defining element—of what we now call conservatism that sanctions the pursuit of selfish interests, that predicates itself not only on the inevitability of egocentricity but, finally, on the civic virtue of surrendering to it. The issue is one of social policy: Which should have priority, the individual or the social unit? There is no more important issue that a politician can address. And insofar as Nixon was actuated by such concerns, his egoism, like Bork's, was perversely principled.

But even so, the pursuit of private interest is supposed to occur only in the venue of private life. If Bork's response to the senator's question was discomfiting, it was not because he proposed to indulge an appetite, but because he proposed using a public institution—the Supreme Court—to do so. And that same fusion of private and public ambitions, that same failure to discriminate between the person and the office and to assign priority to the office was present in Nixon's obsession with himself.

It is understandable that someone who is in a continuous process of self-invention might display egocentricity, if not, indeed, vanity. However, the matter is complicated by the fact that self-invention, like rhetorical invention, can occur in more than one way.

Invention can be formulary; it can conform to preexisting rules. Most of us create ourselves in a largely formulary fashion, adhering to the conventions of family, class, and culture, observing rules and customs, respecting pieties, willingly accepting the mediocrity of social compliance for the consolation of social acceptance and the security of social order.

There is another, subtler, perhaps more complex, kind of invention that is more nearly characteristic of Nixon, an invention that has less to do with conforming to rules than with adapting to challenges. He created himself situationally, seeking and engaging one crisis after another so that in the tension of adversity he could experience the pulse of identity.

Of course, Nixon was not autonomous. He chose a career in politics; he elected to be elected. His self-invention, therefore, was every bit as implicated in social expectation as is the most rule-addicted conformist's. But it is significant that among the collectivities to which he oriented himself, his most vivid references were his adversaries. The hundreds of campaign speeches, the White House tapes, the memoirs: all teem with enemies—some effete, others arrogant—who scheme and conspire and traduce. Entire professions and classes of his compatriots were subject to his anathema in excoriations that were as colorful as that rigidly contained man could make them.[13] His affiliations, on the other hand, were passive and nameless and voiceless—"the people," a "silent majority," an aggregate without a face.

Nixon never stopped inventing himself. His ceaseless quest for betterment—the improvement not of his character but of his condition—resonated with an abiding chord in American culture. It may be to his credit that he was never self-satisfied, never complacent, but that he cared to the end about the opinions of others. And yet there is something sad about it too. It is sad that an old man who had known glory was never to know sufficiency.

Nixon's last speech in public office—his resignation—was unrepentant and characteristically self-absorbed. The speech represented his presidency as a pilgrimage toward peace. Peace was a destination that Nixon never reached within himself. It is doubtful that he ever even undertook the journey. Chronically dissatisfied, incurably unreconciled with his own imperfections, he continuously struggled for a transformation, but of his image rather than of himself. That image—an artifact of guile and television—finally became himself. His appearance was his reality.

One of the most revealing examples of Nixon's late, post-Watergate self-invention is a passage in his last memoir, published in 1990. He is pondering the prospects for the renascence of his reputation—a theme that entwines the entire book. As so much of his work is, the passage is a meditation on method:

> The quicker road to "rehabilitation" would be to exploit the inevitable public sympathy that comes to even the most controversial public figure with the onset of old age. It would be easy to play the kindly, omnipresent elder statesman, attending Rotary conventions and Boy Scout jamborees by the score, offering the same warmed-over platitudes to audience after audience, and appearing before the TV cameras whenever I was asked to offer free, unsolicited advice to the President on the latest international or domestic crisis. . . . to stop being a villain in some people's eyes, I would have to become a deadly bore in everybody's eyes. I could be less controversial but also less relevant, or I could remain controversial but retain a certain amount of influence. I chose the latter, more difficult path. I am not saying that as a result I am always right and others always wrong. But

the person who thinks before he speaks and speaks only when he has something meaningful to say, instead of answering spasmodically every time someone asks him for his opinion, is far more likely to make a real contribution to solving the many problems we face as a nation.[14]

Seventy-seven years old, and he was still rejecting what would be "easy," still choosing "the more difficult path." And in a book that is rife with warmed-over platitudes, he announces that he will not lavish "warmed-over platitudes" on Rotarians and Boy Scouts.[15] But during his years in what he enjoyed calling "the arena," were not the values of Rotarians and Boy Scouts the values with which he associated himself? Now, at last, he bares his contempt for them. And in that bilious candor, he discloses that his link to some of his most devoted followers was just another abandoned piety, just another one of the tactical adaptations from which his persona was constructed.

If Citizen Nixon's life had a "rosebud" in it, it may have been a letter that he wrote at the age of ten to his mother, who was absent from him. Hannah Nixon kept and cherished the letter, and after her son became famous, she showed it to a Nixon biographer as an example of how bright a lad he had been. In the letter, the boy imagines himself to be a dog:

Nov. 12 1923

My Dear Master:

The two boys that you left me with are very bad to me. Their dog, Jim, is very old and he will never talk or play with me.

One Saturday the boys went hunting. Jim and myself went with them. While going through the woods one of the boys triped *[sic]* and fell on me. I lost my temper and bit him. He kiked *[sic]* me in the side and we started on. While we were talking I saw a black round thing in a tree. I hit it with my paw. A swarm of black thing came out of it. I felt pain all over. I started to run and as both of my eyes were swelled shut I fell into a pond. When I got home I was very sore, I wish you would come home right now.

Your good dog

Richard

Roger Morris, a gifted student of Nixon's early years, writes of the letter,

"Obviously modeled on a children's dog story, it was the pitiable cry and fantasy of a lonely boy."[16]

Fawn M. Brodie, a psychohistorian, reviews the comments of other biographers concerning the letter and advances her own:

> There are other such letters in the presidential archives. But the "good dog" letter written by Richard Nixon at age ten is likely to be the most celebrated. [James David] Barber sees it as a fantasy full of symbols, "a tale of hurt, panic, and depression." [David] Abrahamsen sees in the imagery "a high level of confusion and despair." Both Barber and Abrahamsen suggest that the "very old" dog, Jim, may be Richard Nixon's father.
>
> The letter raises many questions, not the least of them being what kind of mother would permit its publication. . . . If nothing else the letter demonstrates how early he had begun to exaggerate the wrongs inflicted on him by others—a compulsion that affected his whole life.[17]

These are grim interpretations: "the pitiable cry and fantasy of a lonely boy," "a tale of hurt, panic, and depression," "confusion and despair," an exaggeration of the "wrongs inflicted on him by others—a compulsion that affected his whole life." But is it not possible that Hannah's naive pride in the letter is, after all, the most sensible reaction?

Let us begin by rejecting, even in a child, a simple equation between symbol and referent. The suggestion that the old dog, Jim, who will neither talk nor play with young Richard, may be Richard's father is gratuitous. We lack independent evidence of Richard's relations with his father at the time of this letter, but we have ample evidence that Frank Nixon was an extraordinarily attentive—even doting—father during Richard's adolescence and beyond, and we have no reason for supposing that this close relationship had not always been there. Frank attended Richard's debate practices and football practices, he cared for the boy during Hannah's absences, he worked closely with the boy in the family store, he continually engaged the boy and his brothers in political discussions at the dinner table, he encouraged the boy's interests and ambitions. Frank Nixon emerges from the testimony of those who knew him as a loud, dogmatic, abrasive man but an utterly devoted father, and while the ten-year-old boy may still have written his "good dog" letter in a pout over some slight, what evidence we have is against his feeling resentful at paternal indifference.

Moreover, the claim that "the letter demonstrates how early he had begun to exaggerate the wrongs inflicted on him by others" is unsupported by the evidence. Even if we assume that the letter expresses wrongs that the boy believes were inflicted on him, we cannot know that those wrongs were exaggerated without knowing, first, what exactly were the events that provoked the letter, and, second, what constitutes exaggeration in the report of a ten-year-old boy. We have neither the information nor the perspective that can warrant Brodie's interpretation of the letter.

The letter represents itself as the composition of a dog, not a boy. By inventing a fictitious canine author, the boy has disassociated himself from the report contained in the letter. Is it likely that a child, especially one who already "exaggerated the wrongs inflicted on him by others," could so objectify his grievances that he would be able to fabricate a nonhuman spokesman for them? Is incipient paranoia compatible with detachment and exogenous attribution? Does not paranoia, in fact, go in exactly the opposite direction: as a tendency to interpret events in terms of oneself rather than in terms of other beings, real or imagined? The issue here is not whether the mature Richard Nixon "exaggerated the wrongs inflicted on him by others." The issue, rather, is whether this letter is probative for such a claim.

Consider the text. Consider that it is the text of a child. It displays a remarkably precocious capacity to imagine the world from the perspective of another. Note how consistently the point of view is sustained: He has fixed the size of the dog in relation to the boys, the angry response of the dog, the retaliation of the boy to the dog, the hitting with the paw. What is seen in the tree is not called a beehive, but "a black round thing," a description that is more faithful to the representation of a dog's perception. And the dog's falling into a pond because its "eyes were swelled shut" is a splendidly imagined touch. The letter sustains a fine mastery of point of view.

The letter really is evidence of young Richard's intelligence, and the "kind of mother" who would "permit its publication" would be one who would accurately see what the bleak diagnoses of the biographers overlook: that only a child of extraordinary capacities of imagination could have executed so skillful a tale. If the letter is psychologically precursive at all, then it would have to be seen as early evidence of a talent, crucial to negotiating skill and important in politics, to see the world as another being sees it, a talent, in sum, for epistemic empathy.

Is it a sad letter? Of course it is. The kid misses his mother. Is it full of violence and pain? Again, of course it is. Violence and pain are not uncommon in children's stories. It should provoke admiration for the boy's talent that he is able to recapitulate in his own little story some of the salient characteristics of children's stories in general. And does the letter prefigure the psychological defects that would later undermine the public man? Only in the indirect sense that the talent for epistemic empathy, which that letter and much of the subsequent career displayed, failed him during Watergate, and so gives us a way of characterizing a strategic deficiency in his response to the impending destruction of his presidency. But that the letter is probative of some moral failure is wholly implausible.

Nixon's epistemic empathy enabled him to sense the vulnerabilities of others. He was shrewd in detecting the points of weakness in his rivals and adversaries. In the course of his career in politics, he developed a shark's nose for blood.

It is easy to understand why Nixon's biographers put such an interpretive weight on the letter. Looking back at what centuries of cultural tradition require us to see as a formative period, we come upon this moving, unguardedly expressive writing by a child who was to become one of the most deviously private men in American political history. It may be the single recorded instance of unforced candor in the lifetime of the man, and so one is tempted to extract from it every photon of illumination possible of this enigmatic figure. But however much we may savor this rare relic of an uncalculated moment in Richard Nixon's life, the letter does not warrant a belief in his innate corruption, nor does it license the inference that his public persona was the abscessed tumefaction of his childhood's psychic wounds. Nixon is not to be so easily absolved.

The mother-deprived child's ability to imagine himself a dog finds later expression in the maladroit young man's ability to imagine himself an athlete, and the power-driven mature man's ability to imagine himself into a series of Nixons, old and new. The "good dog" letter manifests an extraordinary capacity that served him for the rest of his career. It was a capacity to conceive of alternative conditions of being, and then to create himself in conformity with those conditions. But it was an imaginative capacity that came to be constrained by Nixon's vanity, subservient always to his ego, to the fugitive demands of the moment, and to his crippling obsession with crisis and contention.

Nixon's bit of juvenilia brings to mind another work that has play with the minds of animals: Isaiah Berlin's brilliant study of Tolstoy, *The Hedgehog and the Fox.*[18] It is a work that in its maturity and sophistication could not be farther removed from the "good dog" letter, but it is a work that has a suggestive application in the present context. The title of Berlin's study is based on a fragment from the ancient Greek poet, Archilocus: "The fox knows many things, but the hedgehog knows one big thing." Berlin's essay pivots on the distinction between two kinds of intellect: the foxlike kind, which teems with ideas, and the hedgehoglike kind, which is focused and concentrated.

The ten-year-old Richard Nixon imagined himself a dog. He was close. He had the family right (Canidae), but he was mistaken about the genus (*Vulpes,* not *Canis*). Nixon was a fox.

He was not drawn to the realization in himself of one great idea. Rather, his measure was always relative to the trials of the moment, and, having resolved the crisis at hand, he turned with relish to the next crisis, prepared to engage it on its own terms, and to yield himself to its tactical requirements. He was an ad hoc man.

Lincoln too was a self-creation, but Lincoln was a hedgehog. He single-mindedly shaped one towering character and indelibly associated it with one towering issue. The crucibles through which he passed strengthened, purified, and condensed his definition, and made it more vivid. Instead of interpreting each crisis as a test of himself, Lincoln rather interposed moral values between himself and the condition that he confronted. One consequence was that his persona fused with those values in the public mind, and he became less the image of a man enduring a test than the embodiment of civic virtue seeking its fulfillment. Even his moments of self-regard seemed humble because they were subordinated to the moral vision with which he came to be identified.[19]

Lower on the scale, John Kennedy and his handlers had an understanding, however cynical, of the arrangement whereby the whisper of indirection can be made to outsound a bellow of self-promotion. *Profiles in Courage* was not, like *Six Crises,* autobiographical. Instead, it concerned heroic statesmen and induced the reader to contemplate the values that Kennedy implicitly admired. We were invited to think Kennedy a good man not because he assured us that he was but rather because he exalted good things. He let his reputation be an implication of his choices.

Nixon's preoccupation with self-creation made him impatient with modesty. It brought him to talk of himself too much, to solicit attention to his struggles, to his defeats and triumphs. He sought repeatedly to address us directly on the subject of what we should think of him, and the effort had two consequences, both inimical to his reputation. One effect was that the only values with which he was able to associate himself were either commonplace or transitory, and they left him unusually vulnerable to any tests of his rectitude. The other effect was that he developed for his reflexive claims no grounding that was independent of those superficial values. He habitually reenacted, even as a mature man in the presidency, the callow role of the Sunday-school boy who courts our favor by telling us of the temptations he has abjured. There was no projection of virtue or heroism to which he invited comparison. He sought to influence the substance of our judgment of him without thinking to affect its form.

Because he did not lavish expensive acquisitions on his wife and daughters, and because a certain austerity attended his personal style, and because his awkwardness did not lend grace to his appearance, and because he conspicuously lacked the lusty appetites of his two immediate predecessors in the presidency, and because he identified himself with the pious restraint of the Protestant middle class, we did not associate Nixon with self-indulgence. But his self-indulgence was boundless. He made the justification of his own personality one of the principal themes of American politics for a quarter of this century. Once the Hiss case had played itself out, Nixon himself became an issue transcending any impersonal issue that he addressed. He saw to that. It was the paramount achievement of his public life.

CHAPTER 7

Reagan, Vietnam, and Central America:

PUBLIC MEMORY AND THE
POLITICS OF FRAGMENTATION

G. Thomas Goodnight

The collapse of Saigon in the spring of 1975 marked the close of America's longest, most bitterly contested, and notoriously unsuccessful foreign military intervention. Traditionally, the end of a war is marked by memorialization—parades, flag waving, and patriotic oratory. But Vietnam was fixed in memory less by public celebration than by Richard Nixon's hollow pronouncement of "peace with honor." That unrestricted presidential intervention was no longer tenable the war had made clear. What foreign policy could take its place was not. Less than a decade later, civil strife in Central America—a revolutionary struggle in El Salvador, the fall of the Somoza regime, and the transformation of Nicaragua into a leftist state—renewed public debate on the question of presidential power and American foreign policy.

United States intervention into Central America never stirred public sentiment to the extent of Vietnam. This covert war sparked no counter-cultural movement, no mass demonstrations, and far fewer nightly news broadcasts from the scene of war. The sporadic public attention accorded to events in El Salvador and Nicaragua belied the intensity and bitterness of the debate within federal institutional fora, however. For the better part of the 1980s, the prospects of armed intervention and the contingencies of foreign aid to Central America inflamed passions, fragmented party align-ments, proliferated moments of distrust, cynicism, and betrayal, exploded in constitutional crisis, and left American institutions of governance weak-ened substantially—less able to shape consensus on foreign or domestic issues. In short, Central America became "the most controversial foreign policy issue of the 1980s."[1]

A protracted and destructive institutional battle, the Central American controversy was so ferociously contested precisely because it constituted "a struggle between the executive and legislative branches over what America's role in the world should be and who should determine it."[2] As each com-peting branch of the federal government worked to unify and impose its own stamp on policy, institutional spokespersons crafted rival narratives that strived to contextualize policy choices and international events in light of past examples of success and failure. The vortex of this controversy over policy, influence, and history swirled around a defining historical anal-ogy—"the lessons of Vietnam." Who, what party, and which branch of government were responsible? What should have been learned from the intervention? And, most important, how could it be assured that such a tragedy would never happen again? This chapter explores a decade of pub-lic argument over these questions as they formed a central dynamic of the Central American controversy.

SHARED POWERS
AS RHETORICAL CONSTRAINT

Foreign policy in the United States is a responsibility of the executive and congressional branches of government which share constitu-tional power. This shared power "has been a frequent issue of contention" throughout American history, and scholars expect that "the struggle be-tween Congress and the president over foreign policy will continue so long as the Constitution lasts." The "invitation to struggle" for authority is a result of the founding fathers' "ambivalence about the appropriate balance between swift action and clear command on the one hand and popular support and checked and balanced power on the other." The president and Congress must address foreign affairs conjointly because neither can conduct policy alone. As Clifford Krauss concludes, "while the Constitution granted Congress the power to declare war, it appointed the President Commander in Chief. It was left up to the two branches to work out the details."[3]

Rhetorically, a shared power is the product of ongoing private and public deliberations about the responsibilities and constraints among branches of government. To share power is to acknowledge and contest the public actions and opinions of other political actors whose formal consent is requisite to the conduct of policy. The language of such political discussions is developed in ongoing legal, ideological, and institutional disagreements. When such arguments graduate to open debate, they shape and revise public memories of the episodes of United States foreign policy.

Common recollections of foreign policy events are anchors for public support within and across generations. Members of the executive and Congress alike call forward historical analogies both to decide prudentially and to negotiate strategically the legitimate uses of power. The choice of historical precedent—together with how its interpretation, bearing, force, and popularity are legitimized—provides common ground for institutional action under the rubric of a shared power. At times versions of history converge and help constitute consensus. At other times history is unsettled and marched into a contest over policy and power.

A public controversy is a trial in which institutional actors engage discussion and debate in an arena of shared power. Arguments from history provide contested narratives of the appropriate uses and distribution of decision-making authority. The historical analogy that framed the Central American debate—the comparison of Nicaragua and El Salvador to North and South Vietnam—constituted more than a colorful figure of speech or even a prudential guide to decision making. Rather, the Vietnam analogy raised the stakes of the policy debate to the level of a struggle to define the legitimating narratives of institutional power. Who would shoulder the blame for Vietnam—Congress or the executive branch of government? Which side should be trusted in making foreign policy? What political party would establish the prevailing narrative of American history? This chapter examines executive and congressional strategies in framing policy choice in the context of public memory.

The strategic resources of contesting public memory go as far back in western history as the writings of Herodotus and Thucydides, who formed historical understanding, respectively, into a dialectic of archetype and paradigm. Kuzminski observes that history regarded as archetype finds significance in present events as they unfold a pattern of expectations stemming from an originating moment of action. Traditionally, this view is at the core of conservative political conviction. Kuzminski concludes, "History for the Right is a repository of value, a panorama through which certain values are displayed; and since the value of history as a whole cannot be displayed (for who could get outside of history to contemplate it?), it is only the recurring values displayed within history that matter."[4]

For the Left, history is a series of incidents that are propelled by the correlation of influences in evolving contexts. "In this view, nothing is significant in itself; nothing has any intrinsic content. Instead, anything that appears does so solely as an intersection of relations, as an abstract function."[5] What strikes the liberal as important is not locating policy within a singular, immutable order of historical events. Rather, the liberal wishes to discover the similarities and differences between a representative example (or paradigm) and a particular policy up for decision at the moment. Differences in magnitude, intensity, and place, for example, may be correlated among examples to confirm a direction for policy.

Perelman and Olbrechts-Tyteca confirm Kuzminski's observation. They find that the Left tends to prefer abstract values which policy choices can approximate but never exhaust. The Right understands events more in terms of concrete values—that is as unfolding activity that incarnates basic values.[6] But Perelman and Olbrechts-Tyteca remind us that predispositions toward values stand as presumptions or starting places of argument. Thus, it would not be out of line to find conservative and liberal preferences for historical interpretation exchanging places when the circumstances' warrant it.

Presidents do in fact sometimes craft foreign policy against what appears to be a natural ideological alignment. Additionally, advocates often strive to co-opt opposing grounds by seeking to combine (with various levels of success) the rhetorical resources of archetype and paradigm. The

Central American debate engaged in reversals, ambiguous interplay, and re-reversals of established ideological presumptions. As such, it provides a study in the politics of fragmentation.

The subsequent critique reenters the struggle over Central America and public memory of the Vietnam War in order to observe the battle for dominance within United States public institutions. Discussion will focus on how ideological alignments, government policies, and world events became inscribed within evolving and competing historical narratives. Thus, the chapter endeavors a rhetorical history—a study of contested memory and of the uses of time in the service of power.

1981—BEGINNINGS OF CONTROVERSY

The debate over Central American policy is a legacy of the dramatic clashes at the turn of the century, when Europe and the United States were fast moving to divide up the world into dominions of rule and economic dominance. Long before the advent of the Cold War, Congress and the president were at odds over policy in Latin America. Then liberal republicanism sought to constrain the policy of the Big Stick and the White Man's Burden. For anti-imperialists of the 1890s, democracy could be fostered only by example, diplomacy, and encouragement. Intervention, in the name of imperial rule, was not to be countenanced, especially in our own backyard. For pro-imperialists, Latin America was a chip in the game of politics among nations. Repelling foreign interests, as well as sustaining domestic peace and order, were reasons enough to justify repeated American intervention—including the twenty years of occupation of Nicaragua by United States troops. While many of the turn-of-the-century arguments resurfaced in the 1980s, there were surprisingly few that spoke to the specific history of the relationship between the United States and Central America. The past was left mostly to itself, as debate concentrated on the significance of murky present events.[7]

In 1978 President Carter authorized distribution of funds by CIA operatives to forces opposing Nicaraguan leader Somoza. With the ouster of that regime in July, 1979, Carter offered aid to the Sandinistas. Congressional conservatives, fearful that Nicaragua would become a base through which Cuban supplies would flow to leftist rebels in El Salvador, required as a condition of aid that Carter certify to Congress that Nicaragua was not supporting rebels before he distributed aid. Nicaraguan support of insurgency did cease for a time, but apparently the regime bowed to Cuban and FMLN pressure and began to funnel support to El Salvadoran rebels. Just before leaving office in January, 1981, Carter suspended U.S. aid to Managua. Ronald Reagan "came to the White House determined that Nicaragua had to be saved from Soviet-Cuban expansionism, otherwise the dominoes would fall in Central America." Nicaragua was a test case of the new American doctrine of Soviet rollback. This doctrine was espoused in global fora by administration spokespersons such as Jeane Kirkpatrick and Alexander Haig. Because it was an exemplar of a key foreign policy principle, the administration sought to make Central America "the most important place in the world."[8]

In February, 1981, a State Department White Paper declared that the El Salvador insurgency had been "transformed into a textbook case of indirect armed aggression by communist powers through Cuba." Soon, thereafter, the Reagan administration cut off a loan program offered by Carter and went to Congress for counterinsurgency aid, including a request to approve fifty-five American advisers in El Salvador. At an initial administration press conference the president had to rebut the first of a long line of public questions stemming from troubled public memories of Vietnam. When asked if we were getting into a situation that could not be easily resolved, Reagan responded: "No, I don't think so. I know that this is a great concern. I think it's part of the Vietnam syndrome, but we have no intention of that kind of involvement."[9]

Within Congress, discussion was beginning on aid, too. Former U.S. Ambassador White warned that "if we put any advisers into El Salvador we would become embroiled in a Vietnam-type experience." To Representative Clarence D. Long of the House Appropriations Committee, the request for "help" suggested a pattern of mistakes that should not be repeated. "You see," he admonished, "you are setting up a scenario" where an official might claim that "even if the arms flow is halted, the United States will continue to provide economic and military aid to Salvador's ruling junta. Now, I think this indicates an Administration which is doing very much—making the same mistake as my own Democratic administration did 18 years ago."[10] Reluctantly, Congress began to fund El Salvadoran military aid; but, just as Congress had imposed conditions upon Carter's request for Nicaragua, so it required the Reagan administration to certify that human rights abuses in El Salvador were declining.

The administration's successful request invited questions born from recent, bitter memories of another intervention. On March 3 Walter Cronkite asked the president, "Do you see any parallel in our committing advisers and military assistance to El Salvador and the early stages of our involvement in Vietnam?" "No, Walter, I don't," Reagan replied and went on to say: "I know that that parallel is being drawn by many people. . . . What we're actually doing is, at the request of a government in one of our neighboring countries, offering some help against the import or the export into the Western Hemisphere of terrorism, of disruption." Still, the analogy was so suggestive that Al Haig, the president's chief spokesperson, reported that "we have to cope with it [the Vietnam analogy] by reiterating on every occasion what our objectives are." Even the United States military found the analogy informative and objected to prospects of escalation, for it "feared, as well, that any effort aimed at direct confrontation would, as in Vietnam, wither the promised fruits of a massive rearmament program."[11]

Throughout the fall of 1981 Reagan conducted secret negotiations with the Sandinistas which, unfortunately, resulted in little but hardened feelings between Washington and Managua. In December of 1981, the president expanded Carter's secret finding to authorize covert action by the CIA "to disrupt arms shipments into Nicaragua and to harass what the order called the 'Cuban-Sandinista support structure' in Nicaragua and elsewhere in Central America." In March of 1982, the American-supported Contras sabotaged two bridges in Nicaragua. The Sandinista government declared a state of emergency, commencing a struggle that would fragment politics in Nicaragua and the United States for over a decade.[12]

1982—THE BOLAND AMENDMENT

President Reagan addressed the conflict formally at the Organization of American States on February 24, 1982. While public attention gathered around the issue of whether and when United States troops would be sent into the region, the speech left American options open while setting out the ideological tone and tactical dilemmas of administration policy. Of the conflict, Reagan said in his Caribbean Basin speech:

> Very simply, guerrillas, armed and supported by and through Cuba,
> are attempting to impose a Marxist-Leninist dictatorship on the people of

El Salvador as part of a larger imperialistic plan. If we do not act promptly and decisively in defense of freedom, new Cubas will arise from the ruins of today's conflict. We will face more totalitarian regimes tied militarily to the Soviet Union—more regimes exporting subversion, more regimes so incompetent yet so totalitarian that their citizens' only hope becomes that of one day migrating to other American nations, as in recent years they have come to the United States.[13]

The Cold War hues of this rhetoric are familiar. A crisis brought about by Soviet surrogates is declared at hand and the necessity of response looms. Note, however, unlike many previous presidential addresses that followed such rhetoric with an announcement of military intervention, Reagan's speech ended only with a call for "increased security assistance" to "help friendly countries." Thus, the tension arises—and would remain throughout the debate—between featuring an immediate, great, and extremely dangerous threat to national security and eschewing overt military means of resolution. What was the reason for this paradox of exigency and restraint? A Gallup poll completed in mid-March found that two out of every three " 'informed Americans' feared the situation in El Salvador would develop into 'another Vietnam.' And only 2 percent of the public thought that the United States should send troops to help the government in El Salvador."[14] The gap between administration ambition and public support created an opening for opposition.

The covert war in Nicaragua came to public attention in a series of news reports in late 1982. Acknowledging that "the exact extent of U.S. involvement with the Contras is unclear," the press nevertheless spoke of the "fearful talk of war" in Central America.[15] These reports galvanized Congress into publicly affirming limitations to presidential power that had already been set in place by secret annexes on an appropriations bill.

Thomas Harkin (D-IA) began the debate by proposing to cut off all military aid to forces "carrying out military activities in or against Nicaragua." Identifying American-supported Contras as the "remnants of the evil, murderous National Guard," he implored: "In the name of all that is right and just and decent, we should end our involvement with this group." Rising in support, James Leach (R-IA) sounded the guiding lesson from history that would sustain the opposition throughout the debate. "Great power interventionism as the last two decades have taught us, is simply counterproductive." It was for House liberal Barbara Mikulski (D-MD) to bring the Vietnam parallel into public articulation. Boldly she put the argument: "Now we are about to precipitate a regional war in Central America. I do not want to see that, and I do not want to see us cause another Vietnam." According to the representative, Vietnam is the exemplar of a pattern that pushes the United States on the wrong side of national liberation movements when it sides with antidemocratic regimes that flourish anticommunist credentials. The result of supporting corrupt regimes is always failure. "We made this mistake in China 40 years ago," she said. "We made this mistake in Vietnam and we made it throughout Asia. For God's sake, let us not make this same mistake in Central and Latin America."[16]

Subsequent speeches in support of the Harkin amendment suggest how the Vietnam analogy achieved archetypal force. John L. Burton (D-CA) found a convergence of past and present in a moment of urgent choice: "JOHN STENNIS stood on the floor of the U.S. Senate and said when you send these mechanics you will send the American flag. When you send the American flag you send an American commitment and you send our honor and certain things will happen. If my colleagues read the speech by the distinguished Senator from Mississippi, it looks like a history of Vietnam except it was written in advance."[17] To Burton, history was running in reverse again because the words, spoken in favor of Central American intervention, were replaying a pattern that his old friend Stennis had warned would be played out once before. The rhetorical force of archetype here resides in the recollection of forgotten knowledge and in the inventive capacity to transform public memories into timely warnings. Hence, for congressional liberals, Vietnam provided the synthetic form imparting names and identity to present policy choice.

Representative George Miller (D-CA) provided the first of a great number of speeches that would find precise historical parallels in the unfolding patterns of present events. "You are now on notice," he said of Contra support. "This is not speculation about another Vietnam. This is a first step of our Vietnam." Such recognition morally compels action. "Some of us came here to stop Vietnam," he recalled. "And here is a chance to stop the new one. The action is taking place, the money is being spent, the advisers are being sent, payments to third parties are taking place . . . military sales to one government are taking place so those arms can be sent to the Sandinistas, and our hands are supposedly clean." Miller ended his speech with a sense of urgency that brooked no compromise: "This is the last opportunity you will have of this Congress to cut off an unacceptable and illegal and an immoral action."[18] Otherwise, the United States again would sink into the quagmire.

Even as speeches from the floor talked in terms of first steps and moral ultimates, a compromise was worked out in the cloakroom. An amendment by Edward P. Boland, head of the House Intelligence Committee, seemed to do nearly the same thing as Harkin's proposal. The Boland resolution asserted that it was the will of Congress that no aid could be given "for the purpose" of overthrowing the Nicaraguan government. Since intentions could be debated, while weapons and money went forward, proponents of Contra aid raised no objections. Despite this loophole, the amendment was to play a significant role in shaping parameters of debate. As a public constraint, the amendment affirmed a consensus concerning no more Vietnams and provided a context for legitimate congressional oversight.

At the very moment Congress was constraining Central America within a public historical narrative, the administration exercised its power to take covert action—thus fragmenting, for a time, the historical narrative of foreign policy and shared power between Congress and the president. Reagan signed a secret national security finding on November 16, 1982, stating that "covert activity was in the national interest" in "interdicting" Nicaraguan support for the El Salvadoran revolutionaries.

1983—THE LESSONS OF VIETNAM

Early in April, 1983, press reports made clear that the Contras' war-making ability had been enhanced by U.S. military aid, the Boland amendment notwithstanding. Reports estimated that these forces entering Nicaragua had grown from 1,500 to 10,000 in a single year. Seeking to clarify United States policy, *USA Today* asked the president: "I think a lot of Americans wonder if you are getting us into another Vietnam. I think that's the general worry there—something that's secret, and we quietly slip in before we realize we're there. Are we?" The president answered petulantly, "No. And there is no comparison whatsoever in this situation and Vietnam." Further, the president had to reassure the press that he was following this principle in line with congressionally affirmed policy. "We are not doing anything to try and overthrow the Nicaraguan government," he claimed.[19] If not Vietnam, what historical comparisons could frame the legitimate aims of administration policy?

To answer this question, Reagan and his supporters reached into the grab bag of American history to bring forward an array of contexts that might help define policy. In a rare presidential speech to a joint session of Congress on April 27, 1983, the administration sought to justify its Nicaraguan policies by linking Contra aid with global security through the use of historical example. "In a European crisis at least half of our supplies for NATO would go through these areas by sea," he said. "It's well to remember that in early 1942, a handful of Hitler's submarines sank more tonnage there than in all of the Atlantic Ocean." The president then went on to describe the situation as different today, but only insofar as Cuba enables the Soviets to base submarines in the hemisphere. "If the Nazis during World War II and the Soviets today could recognize the Caribbean and Central Americas as vital to our interests, shouldn't we, also?" The two examples are forwarded to serve the purpose of confirming a general principle, namely that the defense of sea-lanes is a strategic necessity. Both historical examples, each in its own way, affirms the need to pursue prudent self-interest in a world defined by threats. But the examples are drawn from a region of public memory that fails to offer the most compelling definition of the situation. The line that drew the loudest applause that evening—"Let me say to those who invoke the memory of Vietnam, there is no thought of sending American combat troops to Central America."[20]

Presidential supporters could not wait to pile on the historical examples. Phil Gramm of Texas thought that the most salient experience was the American Revolution. Just as the French objective then was "to encourage us to tie down British troops here in the Americas, even though our own chief interest was in fighting for our freedom," so forces should be trained in El Salvador to fight Nicaraguans who wanted to train rebels to fight elsewhere in Central America. Admitting that the metaphor was a bit confused, he found the whole debate to be merely a "problem in semantics."[21]

Henry Hyde (R-IL), continuing the thinking, found World War II to provide a comparison to his liking. Queried the exasperated Hyde: "If it was Hitler, my God, we glorified the French underground, did we not? We did not think they were immoral or indecent, did we? We thought they were great people. We thought they were doing a great job because Hitler was the enemy. Now that it is the Commandantes of the Sandinistas, somehow it is not just gentlemanly to engage in covert activity."[22] Although conservatives insisted upon calling their allies "the resistance," the conflict seemed to be on such a small scale as to give World War II analogies only limited currency. Rather, the roster of Cold War shibboleths was trotted out: Poland, Afghanistan, Angola, Guatemala, Chile.

At this point, it seemed that the conservatives' argument tried to shape itself into archetypal form but failed. Don Ritter (R-PA) took seriously the invocation of the president's analogy from the Second World War:

> What we are saying is that somehow if we pull the rug out from under those who are fighting tyranny, we will somehow come up with a safer situation in Central America, safer for us, safer for the people.

> This is precisely the argument that Neville Chamberlain and company made when Hitler was rampaging prior to the outbreak of hot war in Europe, that let us not offend the gentleman. Churchill was consistently castigated in the Parliament for offending Hitler.

> Mr. Chairman, the end result of this policy is to secure in perpetuity the Sandinista type of tyranny, the Soviet-Cuban bridgehead on the mainland of this hemisphere.[23]

The Munich analogy, well-honed in countless foreign policy debates throughout the Cold War, exhibits the conservative archetype of failure. Its dynamic of tragedy is much different than the liberal view.

Analysis of speeches by Mikulski, Miller, and Burton reveals that the liberal archetype of failed foreign policy speaks to a situation where intentions, events, and reasons are at odds—entering into history monstrous wrongs to self and others for the best of purposes. The chief failure in such historical narratives is a lack of foresight and intelligence. For Reagan, Hyde, and Ritter the narrative of foreign policy failure is lodged in a weakness of will that engenders self-betrayal in a moment of moral confrontation. Although enticing, conservative spokespersons could not follow the form to its completion, however. Analysis of Ritter's speech suggests why.

Archetypal narratives spin historical episodes into definitive stories, moving past events into the present by evocation of a timeless horizon. Often, the use of such stories in deliberative address constitutes a warning. The analogy works to identify a moment in time where choice failed and to remind the audience that such a decision is looming again. The motivational thrust of such address urges the public to remember and to avoid making the same mistake. No one can quibble with Ritter's assertion that bad choices were made at Munich, but even if one were disposed to agree that Ortega is the spiritual heir of Adolf Hitler, the analogy requires a proportionately dramatic response.[24] In this case, the form is restrained from such completion by a prior consensus—the Boland amendment. So, while conservatives wished to unleash their favorite archetypal warnings, they were crippled by a common rhetorical constraint. How effective is Ritter's conclusion? "Each of these individuals [Contras] would lay down his arms and the arms of their group tomorrow if free elections would occur in Nicaragua. Each of these individuals is not interested in the overthrow of the government." This statement forces one to consider the possibility of the French resistance tossing away life for freedom in order to sit down for an earnest conversation with Adolf Hitler. The analogy is absurd on its face. Rhetoric that moves in ultimate terms through archetypal form can be completed only by proportionate action. Anything less runs the risk of exposing argument as bombast. Yet, in 1983 the shared power of foreign policy barred either the administration or Congress from pursuing its policies to the fullest. The administration did manage to increase secretly the size of the Contra forces to about eighteen thousand soldiers, but it also failed to increase public support for its intervention.[25]

1984—MINING THE HARBORS

By 1984, American aid to armed forces fighting in Nicaragua had been dispatched for some two years. However, the goals of administration policy were "never clearly stated in public, and the congressional debate during 1983 did not clarify the issue."[26] Facing constraints set by Boland, administration officials had to deny repeatedly that the purpose of Contra support was to overthrow the government. Instead, the word *pressure* was used as a covering term for covert activities that had drifted from interdicting arms shipped for El Salvador to spreading civil violence in Nicaragua.[27] Congressional liberals had built a case against administration policy by weaving a pattern of public expectations that United States intervention in Central America would proceed as a series of negative Vietnam-like experiences. The events of 1984 would both confirm and deny these expectations.

The administration moved to co-opt opposition by couching its objective in the language of the Kissinger Commission. This prestigious group had recommended publicly that aid to Central America be tied to human rights progress—a goal championed by Congress. Moreover, requests for substantial monetary increases and a quintupling of military advisers to El Salvador were wrapped in the legitimizing rhetoric of assuring democratic elections. Yet, no compromise gesture could escape the inevitable comparison with Vietnam. Christopher Dodd (D-CT) talked about administration requests in terms of "a progression that seems to follow historically."

> My concern is that when we are talking about this sort of slow, ever-escalating involvement in El Salvador, innocently enough, beginning, as we do in many places, with military attachés, and then it goes to advisers, none of that is really objectionable. What is wrong with advising people who are allies in a conflict . . . ? Then it comes to reconnaissance flights and support. That is hard to argue against, too, I suppose, to help them out. Obviously, you lose some of the fellows on the reconnaissance flights, and you have to give them protection.
>
> That is where we are in El Salvador. We have moved from the innocence of just an attaché to the adviser, to the trainer, to reconnaissance, and now to having a significant military force on the bordering country, to financially supporting a group of counterrevolutionaries, as they are called, in Nicaragua.[28]

The argument is a classical "slippery slope" objection, but what gives it force is the public memory of Vietnam, an intervention where the conflict escalated in just that way.

Napoleon Duarte's successful spring election dimmed fears of another Vietnam-like Diem catastrophe in El Salvador. For the moment, it appeared that Central America would not fall into regional warfare. Yet, even with these successes the covert war expanded. A series of explosions off the Nicaraguan ports of Cortino, El Bluff, and Sandino suggested that the Vietnam analogy was not merely an imagined concern. Just as the Congress was uninformed of events in the Gulf of Tonkin twenty years earlier—events which enabled the Johnson administration to gain political support requisite for escalating troop involvement—so Congress was uninformed of CIA activities in the harbor mining. Both houses of Congress passed a resolution that the mining should be stopped. The World Court found the activities a violation of international law. Political support for aid in Congress began to evaporate, and condemnations of administration policies were strong.

Reagan supporters became strident in their own rhetorical response. Oklahoma Senator David Boren went on the offensive: "Some have used the Vietnam experience to argue for complete isolationism. They seem prepared to criticize any possible use of American power, under any circumstances or in any circumstances or in any part of the world. Such a policy would render the United States impotent in the eyes of the world. It would encourage our adversaries to test us and would increase the risk of conflicts."[29] The rhetorical problem with Vietnam as archetype, correctly pointed out by Boren, is that it admits of no exception in a world where exceptions are generally the rule. The liberals had a powerful analogy to ground deliberative warnings and to provide a pattern of recognition for each seemingly inconsequential foreign policy step, but the archetype could not inform decisions that required the positive projection of power. In United States history there is a word for such a foreign policy stance: isolationism.

Reagan quickly exploited this theme, labeling the liberal opposition as the "new isolationists." Still, rather than take the master analogy head-on in public (as many right-wing academics had been doing for some time), Reagan drew forward rhetorical resources from the experiences of an older generation.

> There are those in this country who would yield to the temptation to do nothing. They are the new isolationists, very much like the isolationists of the late 1930's who knew what was happening in Europe but chose not to face the terrible challenge history had given them. They preferred a policy of wishful thinking, that if they only gave up one more country, allowed just one more international transgression, and surely sooner or later the aggressor's appetite would be satisfied. Well, they didn't stop the aggressors; they emboldened them. They didn't prevent war; they assured it.[30]

The historical moment that for Reagan casts its shadow on the present is surely one of the most haunting in recent memory; and in its narrative form, the late 1930s becomes a story of monstrous evil and a failure of international will. No doubt the comparison found resonance with an older generation. This counteranalogy defines liberal opposition as callow—even cowardly—of course, while reserving to the Right the ground of steely-eyed realism. So, that spring, a plethora of examples from the book of power politics filled the halls of Congress.

Arguing against an amendment that would have banned the use of U.S. military forces in Central America, John P. East (R-NC) pleaded with the Senate not to "micromanage" foreign policy. "Invariably," he claimed, in this type of debate "opponents say there must be a political solution, in citing Vietnam. Of course, as Duarte has pointed out, if you do not have the military shield, you will not have a political solution; you will have a military solution" imposed by Cuba or the Soviet Union. Citing the military solutions ultimately imposed on Cambodia and South Vietnam, East drew his own analogies: "If you allow Nicaragua to become the model in Central America, El Salvador will fall, Costa Rica will fall, Honduras will fall, Guatemala will fall, and Belize will fall."[31] But for $21 million in foreign aid the fabled dominoes of the Cold War would begin to crash.

Although few public officials resurrected the domino theory that year, the first public cracks began to appear in the "lesson of Vietnam." Henry Hyde's speech in the summer debate suggests how Vietnam as a guiding policy analogy began to be undermined and reversed.

> Back in 1956 in Hungary when the freedom fighters rose to resist the Soviet Union, the Soviet tanks rolled in and we were spectators except for the Voice of America urging them to fight on.
>
> In 1961, the Bay of Pigs—train 'em, arm 'em, encourage 'em, and then walk away, pull the rug, pull the plug, abandon them.
>
> Saigon, 1975—I can still see our helicopters lifting off the embassy roof with the tears and the arms outstretched of the people who believed in us, who trusted in us, recessed into the distance as we abandoned them.
>
> And now—train the Contras, urge them to get in those mountains and fight for freedom, and then abandon them as we are doing today and as we have done before.
>
> Arm them and abandon them on a party line vote. No food, no medicine, no ammunition, not even moral support. We barely leave them a prayer.[32]

There is much that deserves comment here.

In war, abandonment of an ally is worse than an act of ingratitude. It is a confession of cowardice. Hyde's theme of abandonment is a slur cast on the character of the opposition. His statement, viewed with Boren, Reagan, and East's charges of isolationism, shows a developing partisanship anchored by alternative archetypal explanations. Yet, Hyde pulled back his commitments to ultimates at the end of the speech. Following the rhetorical logic of the Boland amendment, Hyde argued that the thrust of his analogy was to show that force is necessary to create the will for negotiation.

Congressional liberals were not in the mood to listen to alternative historical comparisons. In the previous years the comparison between Central America and Vietnam had been a matter of public conjecture, an argument based upon interpretation, probabilities, and future contingencies. The harbor explosions constituted direct evidence of secret, illegal United States involvement. A moment of duplicity had now revealed itself. They recalled a similar moment when a manufactured international incident led Congress to legitimate administration ambitions at the Gulf of Tonkin. They would not be hoodwinked twice, and so a resolution was offered to prevent sending troops to the region.

Joe Biden (D-DE) found in the contrast between a covert war and the absence of public support for intervention a case of "generational amnesia." To him Vietnam was to be remembered for demonstrating an essential truth: that at the very least people should know what is being undertaken in foreign policy and have the chance to sign on. The secretive, elite decision making—the "arrogance of power," as it was once called—was again making a shambles of democracy. "I have had it up to here, and my own generation has had it up to here," Biden said. "I do not want to hear about the Vietnamization of El Salvador or any other place in Latin America. I ran for this job because of a war in Vietnam, and I swore I would never vote to send any American into combat, unless two conditions prevailed before they were sent: One, there was an absolute clear definition of what their mission was and some reasonable prospect of accomplishment; and second, they had the full faith and support of the United States of America behind them. . . ." Christopher Dodd agreed. Remembering that after years of rancorous debate "Congress never once authorized" the Vietnam intervention, Dodd argued that it was now the duty of his peers not to "duck the issue."[33]

Texas Senator John Tower was not of the Vietnam generation, and he could not have agreed less with Biden's view of history. Agitated by the repeated references to Vietnam as a policy failure, he said in a public forum what revisionists had been writing for some years.

> Much has been made of Vietnam, but let me say Vietnam was not lost by our gallant soldiers, sailors, airmen, and marines who perished in that conflict. Vietnam was lost under the Capitol dome in an amendment very, very similar to the one offered by the Senator from Massachusetts that proscribed the use of American Armed Force in or over Vietnam. This was an open invitation to North Vietnam to mount a conventional attack with armor and everything against South Vietnam.

> For God's sake, let us here tonight not convince the elements hostile to the United States and hostile to friendly governments and hostile to people in Central America who aspire to self-determination that they have an open invitation to proceed at will while the Congress debates whether or not to permit the President to defend our interests in the hemisphere. . . .[34]

This was the answer to the Vietnam analogy. The lesson was not that the United States had lost the war but that America was betrayed. Of course, this argument begs a number of questions, not the least of which is whether a full-blown United States invasion of the North could have been successful or the carnage worth its policy goals. But the force of the argument is gathered from an alleged impropriety that questions the meaningfulness of the sacrifice of American servicemen and women killed and wounded in the war.

While the summer debate continued, a captured Contra manual surfaced. It directed Contra activity toward political assassinations and the overthrow of the Nicaraguan government. The manual put into doubt administration assertions that the spirit of the Boland amendment was guiding United States paramilitary forces. Not even administration claims, made later that fall, to have uncovered crates of Soviet Migs in Nicaraguan ports could snap Congress into line. As economic aid for the Contras dwindled, the administration "turned to the NSC [National Security Council] to coordinate continuing covert assistance." Congress for its part narrowly failed to pass a resolution banning use of troops, but it authorized only a meager $14 million in aid, and that aid was predicated upon unified congressional authorization—a condition that everyone knew would not come to pass. With elections on the horizon, Congress did not fund the so-called freedom fighters, but neither did it wish to make itself vulnerable to the claim that it had "lost Central America."[35]

1985—THE REAGAN DOCTRINE

In 1985, the debate grew in complexity and acrimony. Reagan returned to Congress with a request for more aid, but this time the request was placed in the context of a proposal to support a sixty-day cease-fire and church-mediated negotiations between political factions within Nicaragua. While the proposal was being considered without great enthusiasm by most in Congress, Daniel Ortega chose to visit, among other foreign capitals, Moscow. Caught in a vice between a peaceful gesture from the president and evidence of the long-asserted Moscow link, Congress voted $27 million in what the Senate called "humanitarian aid." In fact, "there was little doubt among most senators that the actual effect of the funding was to resume United States support for a paramilitary operation." Said Senator Edward Kennedy simply, "This is more money for more war."[36]

As the policy grew in complexity, arguments over its historical grounding and present scope became increasingly controversial. The president entered his own version of history into the mix. Sandwiched between answers about Nicaraguan policy, the newly reelected Reagan offered his views on "the great tragedy" of Vietnam. American soldiers "were fed into this meat grinder, and yet, no one had any intention of allowing victory," he said, and continued in a somewhat contradictory fashion: "Well, the truth of the matter is, we did have victory. . . . We didn't lose that war. We won virtually every engagement." The only problem was that "when the administration in Washington asked the Congress for the appropriations to keep our word, the Congress refused." The president concluded: "And so, we didn't lose the war. When the war was all over and we'd come home— that's when the war was lost."[37] Reagan had hazarded public airing of this view only once before, in his 1980 presidential bid, and dropped it when the public registered a hostile response. This time the gambit met with more success.

Emboldened by the presidential landslide, legislative supporters of the administration followed the lead. The man from Missouri, John Danforth, put it this way:

Nicaragua is not another Vietnam. Nicaragua is in our own backyard. It is in a region of the world which has historically been within the sphere of U.S. concern. The Monroe Doctrine was developed to relate to just this part of the world. One of the lessons of Vietnam is that there is a domino theory, that when one country falls, other countries tend to fall as well.

It is my view . . . [that we must] face up to a very real problem—to recognize the threat of Nicaragua to the rest of Central America, and eventually to Mexico itself—and to provide the kind of assistance which would give us some hope of nipping this problem in the bud at an early stage before it gets out of hand.[38]

In this rather inelegant bit of oratory, the senator seems to argue that the Vietnam analogy is imperfect, but that the difference proves that United States international interests are more legitimate and chances of military success greater in this hemisphere. That few public spokespersons had engaged in such public discussion prior to Reagan's reelection suggests, in part, the degree to which the archetype held sway; that comparisons were beginning to be made implies that as the debate extended, the historical analogy lost something of its privileged status.

Even so, there is a peculiar irony at work in Danforth's rhetoric. Although the senator tries to redraw the lesson logically, the language of Vietnam continues to resurface as the domino metaphor is played in a Central American scenario. The conservative arguments appeared to be driven by the need to magnify the importance of present policy. Conservatives had to show prospects of disaster equal to, if not more important than, the liberal position—a position that counseled restraint based on the inevitability of failure, if intervention were pursued. The result of the revamped domino theory was a rhetorical posture called the Reagan doctrine.

The Reagan doctrine was drawn from themes of the first administration and articulated in the 1985 State of the Union speech in which the president "advocated U.S. aid to anti-Communist guerilla proxies as a cheaper, more politically tenable option for achieving national security aims than the direct commitment of American armed forces."[39] In short, the doctrine argued, as New Jersey Congressman Jim Courter claimed, that "history shows there is no evidence of a Communist revolution ever being reversed because of the good intentions of democracies or because democracies are willing to abandon those who are fighting for freedom." The consequences of Communism are irreparable. "Sandinista dictators mean to lock Nicaragua permanently under the Brezhnev doctrine," Louisiana Representative W. J. (Billy) Tauzin warned, "just like Poland, Hungary, and Czechoslovakia."[40] Thus reappeared the conservative archetype. The present, within this form, is always on the verge of loss, and only prompt, forceful action and enduring resolve will prove sufficient to the contest.

Armed with this doctrinal version of history and contemporary events, Reagan launched out on a Southern speaking swing to woo congressional democratic support. Gushing over the president's oratory, Newt Gingrich called restriction of Contra aid a vote for unilateral disarmament. Robert Michel (R-IL) warned more disturbingly of a "flood of refugees," observing that "down South, the streets are filling up." In the spring of 1985, Nicaraguan aid was transformed into a litmus test of the Reagan doctrine and so it became a highly partisan issue. As Elliott Abrams put it, "If people see that Americans are not going to move against the Sandinistas in our own backyard, what will they do ten thousand miles away?"[41]

The Reagan doctrine, as a historical narrative, blots up potential policy objections by strategically framing the meaning of present events. The doctrine calls for the application of *pressure* on Leftist regimes.[42] However, waging "low-intensity conflict" (as guerrilla warfare and domestic terrorism were called by the administration) applies decidedly nondemocratic means for democratic ends. This contradiction was a core objection for the Left and went to the heart of the Vietnam analogy. To offset it, administration allies continued to insist that the only goal of the Contras was participation in government and that it was the Ortega regime which refused to share power. Thus, an elastic justification for aid is created. When the Ortega regime made inclusive gestures toward the opposition, it was heralded as the result of *pressure* and judicious use of United States aid as a *carrot-and-the-stick* in stimulating negotiations. When the Ortega regime made hostile gestures toward the opposition, Congress was blamed for restricting Contra support and sending the wrong signals. When Contra leaders failed to provide military victories in the field, the administration said that the issue was primarily political anyway. When the Contra-instigated civil violence failed to rally popular support, the administration pointed to the historical grip of Communism in other nations and called for more *pressure*. Thus, the Reagan doctrine created an evolving historical narrative within which present events could be rationalized endlessly.

Whatever the merits of this rhetorical strategy, moderation is not among them. The president took things a little too far and reopened an avenue for dissent when he named the freedom fighters as "the moral equivalent of the founding fathers."[43] Further, on April 17, a Contra document was leaked suggesting "direct application of U.S. military force" as an "eventual option." Both episodes opened opportunities for rebuttal.

At this point in the debate, the liberal argument appears to shift somewhat—away from the exclusive use of Vietnam as an archetypal warning and toward the accumulation of recent historical examples to assess events defining the conflict. Edward Kennedy found in the *carrot-and-the-stick* rationale a change in administration goals—forbidden by the first and second Boland amendments. He said:

> No longer are we operating under the illusion that, by assisting the Contras, the United States is simply trying to halt the flow of arms from Nicaragua to the guerilla forces inside El Salvador. No longer are we told that we must support the Contras to pressure the Sandinistas into restoring basic freedoms inside Nicaragua. No longer is the purpose of the President's policy in any doubt: President Reagan wants Congress to support the Contras because he supports the aim of the Contras—to overthrow the Government of Nicaragua by force.[44]

In this example, the lessons of Vietnam begin to recede. Examples are drawn from more immediate history. Kennedy concentrates on delegitimating the elaborate public rationalization for administration activities by negating the administration's own interpretations of a series of actions taken within the conflict.

Kennedy, too, swiftly reverses the lionization of the Contras. "No longer is it possible to believe that the Contra commanders are the moral equivalent to our Founding Fathers," he said. "In fact, it is a travesty to compare Enrique Bermudez to Thomas Jefferson or John Adams or James Madison. On the contrary, there have been repeated and reliable reports of gross atrocities by the Contra combatants, of prisoners being executed, of innocent women and children being raped and mutilated, of civilians being murdered."[45] The equation of Contras and American patriots was soon muted in administration rhetoric.

Throughout the debate the Left had reported incidents of human rights abuses. The Reagan doctrine gave these violations new saliency. In promising to promote peaceful negotiations, the administration had created an excellent ploy for military aid, but it had also created a context by which the outcome of its efforts and the qualities of its actions could be measured—no matter who was to blame. Still, at the end of 1985 more funding was accorded the Contras, for the newly elected president would not be denied. And still, the funding was not enough, as the NSC continued and expanded its range of covert activities inside and outside the United States.

1986—INVASION AND
THE NEW MCCARTHYISM

In 1986, United States policy reached a crisis. Partisanship exploded in Congress. Seeking $100 million of additional funds, the president took to the nation's airwaves and on March 16 delivered a message of danger in Central America. Bringing the Reagan doctrine to bear, he claimed that the United States had sought a mediated settlement only to be met with a Nicaraguan-Soviet buildup of arms. Jim Sasser of Tennessee provided a response: "This is the heart of our difference with the President," he claimed. "He proposes a wider war in Nicaragua, now. As the father of a 17-year-old son, I say, Mr. President, let's not rush blindly into that quagmire. We've done that before." Sasser underscored this warning with a contemporary example: "When we are divided, as we were in Beirut, we fail. With tragic results."[46]

The House, unpersuaded by Reagan's pleas, turned down the request for aid, but two days later the administration claimed that Honduras had been invaded by Nicaragua. Citing emergency powers, the president released $24 million and claimed the intentions of the Sandinistas to be manifest. Although the opposition noted that there had been literally hundreds of border skirmishes before, that "hot pursuit" was a frequent operation with few permanent consequences, that the numbers involved had been overestimated, and that the Honduran government itself had to be induced to accept the aid, still the context of crisis had been set for the appropriations debates.

That spring, Vietnam took on qualities of a partisan shibboleth. Like

Munich, Yalta, and China—all favorite names of failed foreign policy episodes for the Right—Vietnam was condensed, elided, and hurled again and again by congressional opponents to exact political costs. Liberal hardballer Patrick Leahy (D-VT) put it flatly: "The American people remember Vietnam. They remember seeing on the evening news how that country was destroyed—the picture of weeping mothers and fathers holding the bleeding, lifeless bodies of their children. They do not want that tragedy replayed in our own hemisphere." Austin J. Murphy of Pennsylvania reduced the lesson to this: "We spent 50,000 lives and a trillion dollars in defense of a democracy in Vietnam. Yet, when we left there was still no democracy and still no threat to our national interest." Mark Hatfield (R-OR) joined in the vituperation. "Here we are, once again, old men creating a monster for young men, young Americans, to destroy. What a waste of life, what utter disregard for the lessons of history."[47] But there was more to it than mere name calling. The charged language of the debate sank into a drama over how public memory itself would be shaped.

An exchange in the House illustrates how memory overshadowed policy in driving the debate. New York Representative Robert J. Mrazek acknowledged reasonable differences between Vietnam and the present intervention, but then he went on to add: "I know the president calls it a noble war, but it was an experience in which my generation of Americans were asked to fight a fledgling democracy, and we had 55,000 Americans dead, 500,000 wounded, we spent several hundred billion dollars there, we sowed the country with agent orange, we admitted to killing 3 million Vietnamese, and when we pulled out, that country collapsed like the rotten house of cards that it always was." Mrazek's speech raised conservative hackles, leading to a different claim to history. Said Representative Don Ritter: "Vietnam today is a slave state. The gentleman seems to be thinking somehow that we are responsible for Vietnam being a communized slave society, a society where 500,000 people fled to the South China Sea, where 100,000 people drowned in Southeast Asia, where up to 3 million Cambodians were killed in the greatest genocide the world has known since the Holocaust. And somehow the other side, according to the gentleman, does not come in for any blame. It is the United States, we are responsible. This is the blame-America-first attitude." It is evident from this exchange that the Vietnam analogy had become an avenue of display for stark partisan adherence. In such a context, the web of shared historical narratives requisite to common deliberation unravels. Old political divisions reappear and fresh wounds are made. Taunted Representative Tommy Robinson (D-AR), for example, "These are the same people who said instead of backing our troops in Vietnam we ought to follow those who are spitting on the American flag and burning their draft cards."[48]

The same animosity, distrust, and strident partisanship that character-ized debates over the Vietnam War resurfaced in the 1986 debates, even though this time discussion involved only a handful of American advisers. Indeed, the arguments became so vitriolic that they began to disturb the comity of the House. Speaker Tip O'Neill (D-MA) addressed what he saw as a "new McCarthyism." "The message has been crystal clear," he said. "Oppose the $100 million and you are somehow un-American; you are acting to help our country's enemies. What is really un-American is the charge that we, the elected representatives of the people, do not have the right to do the job we were elected to do. . . . My conscience dictates that I vote 'nay,' not only to the policy but to its tactics as well."[49]

The controversy moved into a strident contest over public memory, in part because the debate had evolved to the point that each side had no-where to go but to challenge the legitimating contexts of opposing narra-tives. Constrained by the Vietnam analogy, advocates tried to produce rationales consistent with avoiding risks of a new Vietnam—however pub-lic memory was to be construed. The liberals had drained the conservative's fear appeals by approving limited aid, thus claiming to be concerned about Communism, too. But they objected that too much or the wrong kind of aid would drive Managua closer to Moscow. The conservatives, for their part, had claimed to be interested in a peaceful settlement and committed to democratic means as well. They blamed liberals for approving too little aid, thereby reducing Ortega's incentives to compromise. Thus, absent consensus, the debate could but turn to denouncing the truthfulness of intentions and competence of judgment for respective parties.

Under this pressure, the historical narratives reversed and veered to-ward what Kuzminski sees as natural ideological grounds. The conserva-tives boldly contextualized the debate within a full-blown Cold War archetype. Thundered California Senator Pete Wilson: "If we turn away now, we may one day have to color red everything between Managua and the Rio Grande. . . . We are asked now to send, not our sons to protect our borders, but money, equipment, and arms. I would hate to look my nephew or his parents in the eye and have to try to explain why when the price was so cheap Congress failed to act." Without a boost in aid, history would follow an inevitable sequence of events. Peter Domenici (R-NM) sorrowfully concluded that in Nicaragua "freedom is dying daily" and when the Sandinistas are strong enough they will look for new victims to "secure their failed political system."[50]

If fear of Communism itself were not enough to motivate support for the president, many conservatives threw in a practical appeal to prompt self-interest. William Broomfield (R-MI) banked that success would rest on probabilities. To him it seemed far more likely that Ortega would accommodate United States interests with pressure than without it. "We must apply the carrot-and-the-stick approach," he urged. To Bob Kerrey this position was all too familiar. It meant that we were willing to promulgate civil violence as long as "body bags . . . did not come back to our homes, as long as it was not our mothers, fathers, brothers, and sisters who were suffering the grief of these losses."[51]

The liberal position supported a small amount of "humanitarian aid" to the Contras, purportedly in order to minimize civil violence and forestall military intervention. The liberals began to contrast this congressionally approved aid with unilateral administration activities. In this context, Central America was discussed—not as fitting under an inevitable archetype of intervention—but as a venture that could be judged by referencing episodes of failed executive discourses.

Executive promises themselves became textualized as markers that signaled a transparent strategy of deception. Congressional liberals again and again referred to the perfidy of Johnson's promise, "We seek no wider war." In fact, many called attention to an echo effect in listening to pro-administration rhetoric.[52] Yet, Democrats did not so much dwell on lessons from the Johnson administration as they spoke of a recent record of lies and deception. Congresswoman Mary Rose Oaker (D-OH) put the issue most forcefully:

> The rationale for this policy has been characterized by half-truths, even outright falsification. They have told us the Pope supports an armed struggle. Mysterious crates contained Soviet Mig fighters. The Contras are the moral equivalent of George Washington and Thomas Jefferson. Now Democrats opposed to the administration's policy, they told us, are

supporters of Havana, Moscow, and worldwide Communist revolution.

None of these and countless other administration assertions are true. Indeed, they are absurd and demean the issue. If history teaches anything, it is that a policy based on misconceptions and fabrications is fundamentally flawed.[53]

Thus, as conservatives revisited archetypal form, liberals turned to contemporary examples to put on display what seemed a twice-failed presidential discourse. Simultaneously, the opposition pointed out a string of policy failure as well. Edward Kennedy (D-MA) drew objections to five years of Contra support without any military or political victories; Spark Matsunaga (D-HI), to the mining of harbors and the condemnation of the World Court; Howard Metzenbaum (D-OH), to attacks on a cattle cooperative and the slaying of women and children by Contras. To liberals these episodes added up to a distorted context of decision making within which, according to Representative Thomas Downey (D-NY), "the diplomatic option has never been fully tried."[54]

Sometimes history itself intervenes into institutional debates by accident and changes the balance of argument. On October 5, 1986, Eugene Hasenfus was captured after his plane crashed on a secret United States resupply mission. In November, 1986, the Justice Department announced that it had uncovered secret activities conducted by the National Security Council and revealed a memo that suggested that arms were being traded to Iran in return for hostages. The president appeared at a press conference to reassure the American people that he would never trade arms for hostages and that the amount of weapons sold to Iran was small, defensively oriented, and could fit inside a single cargo plane. When it became apparent in the ensuing weeks that Iran had received some two thousand TOW missiles and hundreds of parts for HAWKs, the president appointed a special commission to look into the situation and find out what happened.

1987—THE END OF HISTORY

The Tower Commission studied the secret maneuvers of the National Security Council throughout the Reagan presidency. Its conclusion was announced in January, 1987. Said the commission's chair: "I believe that the president was poorly advised and poorly served. . . . I think that he should have followed up and monitored this operation more closely.

I think he was not aware of a lot of things that were going on and the way the operation was structured and who was involved in it. He very clearly didn't understand all that." Congressional allies rushed to support this finding. "What we have here is a mistake, not a scandal," concluded Newt Gingrich charitably. It shows simply that "the president didn't adopt a hands-on approach" toward the NSC, Robert Dole concluded. "There is no Watergate," said Paul S. Trible, Republican from Virginia. "There is absolutely no evidence of criminal misconduct on the part of the president."[55]

However unpalatable, the commission's conclusions were political medicine that had to be swallowed. President Reagan read one of the oddest political speeches in American history to a national audience on March 4:

> A few months ago I told the American people I did not trade arms for hostages. My heart and my best intentions still tell me that's true, but the facts and the evidence tell me it is not. As the Tower Board reported, what began as a strategic opening to Iran deteriorated, in its implementation, into trading arms for hostages. This runs counter to my own beliefs, to administration policy, and to the original strategy we had in mind. There are reasons why it happened, but no excuses. It was a mistake. I undertook the original Iran initiative in order to develop relations with those who might assume leadership in a post-Khomeini government.[56]

To atone for this lack of attention, the president promised to change his management style of the NSC and to get to the bottom of how arms money from Iran became funneled, without congressional oversight, to the Contras in Nicaragua.

Thus to save his presidency, Reagan was cornered into all but abandoning a powerful rhetorical weapon: his claim as president to articulate public memory. For the better part of two administrations, Ronald Reagan had grounded conservative advocacy in the experiences of World War II and Cold War generations. The public memory of the threats of fasc-ism and the challenges at the opening of the Cold War were resources that Reagan drew upon with great authority—even if at times he got the details wrong. After the Tower Commission's report, the historical links were all but broken because the president had to ask the embarrassing questions: What did I know? And, when did I know it? A leader who could not remember how his own policies were made, who had to admit that his heart and his head were not in consultation, could not very well aspire to interpret the sweep of history. And lest the public would forget this fact, Congress undertook a yearlong investigation into the realities of the covert American war and the unshared uses of institutional power.

During 1987, events rapidly outstripped battles in Washington. Although Reagan continued to campaign against Soviet leaders from Stalin to Brezhnev, Gorbachev was in office—winding down Soviet support to Third World surrogates and making gestures of friendship to the West. Within Latin America the Contadora peace process begun in 1983 came to fruition, and five Central American nations reached a regional security agreement. Speaker of the House Jim Wright and Ronald Reagan joined forces briefly to offer an American alternative plan, but the Latin Americans let it be known that they preferred to make their own arrangements. In the winter of 1988 Reagan prepared a nationally televised address on Central America only to be turned down by all the networks on the grounds that the speech contained nothing new. As the world approached the end of the Cold War, the immediacy of the Vietnam analogy began to fade from public memory. The divisiveness of the Central American debate was still fresh enough, however, for the newly elected George Bush to state in his inaugural address: "Our great parties have too often been far apart and untrusting of each other. It's been this way since Vietnam. That war cleaves us still. But, friends, that war began in earnest a quarter of a century ago; and, surely, the statute of limitations has been reached. This is a fact: The final lesson of Vietnam is that no great nation can long afford to be sundered by memory."[57] In 1990 Nicaragua held open elections. The Sandinista party lost. The Central America debate came to an end.

CONCLUSION

When branches of government are constitutionally required to share power, the result is a struggle to shape and control policy.[58] In part, the struggle takes the form of crafting, revising, and extending historical narratives. Thus, historical analogies become deployed to forward a controlling horizon of meaning. Such a context provides a frame for interpreting the causes and consequences of international events. Contests over the meaning and relevance of history ensue when foreign policy lacks consensus. Institutional actors strive to sustain popular interpretations of history in light of policy outcomes and to argue for the relevance of alternative interpretations and frameworks when the unexpected happens.

The Central American debate was a sustained controversy among branches of government and political parties. The argument began during the first Reagan administration amid fresh memories of the political divisiveness and futility of Vietnam. Congressional liberals deployed the Vietnam analogy as a story whose pattern of unintended involvements and misguided decision making provided a fixed comparison with administration efforts. Congressional conservatives and the executive branch tried to unseat this master analogy by drawing upon examples of their own—from the Revolutionary War, World War II, and the Cold War. Few public spokespersons were willing to challenge popular wisdom. Instead, conservatives assembled diverse historical examples to illustrate the principles of power politics.

During the second Reagan administration, congressional conservatives—emboldened by the reelection landslide and an intensified anti-Communist campaign—took the master analogy to task. Conservatives argued that the lessons of Vietnam were not the hopelessness of a "quagmire war," the illegitimate actions of an "imperial presidency," or the domestic divisiveness of intervention. Rather, the primary lessons of Vietnam were said to be the failure of congressional will and the consequences of abandoning United States troops and allies. So conservatives revised Vietnam to fit the master narrative of Cold War betrayal—thereby perfecting the continuity of the Right's own historical narrative.

As the meaning of Vietnam became publicly contested and as Congress itself became implicated in Central American policies, partisanship increased. While the Left continued to contest revisionism by textualizing conservative argument, it also shifted the focus of historical debate to an array of more recent foreign policy episodes. The arc of Reagan policy itself became the locus of indictment. The contested historical narratives undermined grounds for common discussion, fragmented consensus, and expanded the scope and stakes of partisan opposition. It was as if the Cold War had returned.

There is much irony in all this, of course. Even as the ghost of Vietnam haunted the capital, the analogy was becoming distanced rapidly by time and events. On the global stage, the Soviet Union underwent a progressive revision of its foreign and domestic policies. Indeed, at the height of the revival of Cold War rhetoric, the "evil empire" was on the verge of its own collapse. In Central America regional and domestic politics, not United

States intervention, settled questions of stability. Yet, even while American interests met with good fortune, the executive branch became tarnished for its secret activities in Central America. To avoid charges of impeachment, President Reagan had to forget officially—resting responsibility on a managerial lapse. Thus was lost what is arguably the conservative's most powerful rhetorical resource—an unbroken claim to consistent interpretation and use of public memory. In the days of the Johnson administration, this disconnection of executive policy from public legitimation was called "the credibility gap."

The end of the Cold War is yet another turn on the historical wheel. New metaphors replace old as world events lurch and shudder their way toward new Somalias, new Bosnias, and new Kampucheas. It now seems difficult to recall that the language of the Second World War and the Cold War which animated Reagan rhetoric, like the anti-Vietnam arguments that inspired congressional opposition, were all hard currencies of public debate for nearly fifty years. Now, in the post–Gulf War world, rhetorical examples fashioned from these events seem to have an archaic quality. Perhaps World War II, the Cold War, and Vietnam have faded to a region of public memory near the landscapes of monumental history. These once world-making events are no longer fresh enough to fire the public imagination. Yet, the legacy of such moments of controversy live on in the continued restrictions of presidential power, the profound distrust between branches of government, and the incivility and partisanship of contemporary political warfare. The struggle to capture the arc of history, to provide legitimizing narratives of the past, continues. If it is in the nature of a shared constitutional obligation to generate controversies among branches of government over the meaning and relevance of the past, then it must be the duty of critical inquiry to remember such uses of time in the service of power. Only by so engaging the disputed analogies of an era can the contours of rhetorical history be illuminated.

CHAPTER 8

Tragic Fear
and the Rhetorical Presidency:

COMBATING EVIL IN THE PERSIAN GULF

Robert L. Ivie

A year after the fighting in the Persian Gulf ended victoriously for the American-led coalition of forces arrayed against Saddam Hussein, Stephen Graubard, professor of history at Brown University and editor of *Daedalus,* published a scathing critique of failed presidential leadership which, he argued, had culminated deliberately in war. *Mr. Bush's War,* as Graubard entitled his book, portrayed harshly the president's misguided "adventures in the politics of illusion."[1]

Just what, you may be asking, is the good professor's complaint? Is not all politics an exercise in illusion? And is not war itself, as Carl Von Clausewitz observed in his classic treatise, a continuation of politics by other means? The phrase, "politics of illusion," does not even qualify rhetorically as an oxymoron, so why quibble with presidential success?

These are reasonable questions, at least in some degree. They caution us against falling prey either to political or rhetorical naïveté in the naked, idealistic pursuit of truth and justice—especially when the president's critic, as in this case, has revealed his purpose "to grieve over a nation that is today being infantilized, that has lost its way, that must seek again to find it, for others as well as for its own sake."[2]

Yet, the answers to such reasonable, cautionary questions are not so obvious and automatic as they may initially appear. Nor is there virtue in adopting an attitude of blind cynicism toward any and all ethical questions about politics. Prudence dictates a closer look at the issues raised by Graubard's critique of presidential war rhetoric, for his concern over a degenerative nation losing its way at a critical moment in history leads to a theoretical point about the character of the rhetorical presidency which, in turn, carries practical implications for addressing the challenges of the post–Cold War world.

GRAUBARD'S COMPLAINT

Graubard's complaint consists of a few major themes, each developed throughout his book in some detail. In brief, he accuses an unschooled and unprincipled George Bush of taking an important decision without benefit of advice from his secretary of state or any other major adviser—a decision that the president portrayed as heroic and perilous when in fact it was opportunistic and nearly free of any risk to himself or the Republican party. Bush pretended he was Winston Churchill fending off the advances of an Adolf Hitler in the guise of Saddam Hussein, condemning the invasion of Kuwait and mobilizing American forces to stop naked aggression in order to preserve peace and freedom. The president knew, however, that he would defeat the Iraqi dictator either by compelling him to withdraw from Kuwait through threat of military force or by sending American soldiers to dislodge the intruder in what would amount to an easy victory, especially since the Soviet Union was too preoccupied with its own domestic problems to risk intervening on Iraq's behalf.

Bush, according to this critique, falsely portrayed the Persian Gulf operation as perilous in order to exaggerate its importance and aggrandize himself in the image of a risk taker. He hoped by these means to assure his reelection—a strategy of self-glorification he had learned during his vice presidential years of understudy to the master of political illusion himself, Ronald Reagan. "To pretend to be Winston Churchill, making Saddam

Hussein out to be Adolf Hitler," Graubard observes, "was to spin a fable worthy of the master himself [Ronald Reagan]. Someone ought to have ridiculed the effort in its first days. It wildly exaggerated the qualities of Saddam; it wholly robbed Churchill of his true distinction."[3]

This was a phony war, in Graubard's view, that risked nothing (except, ironically, the lives of combatants and inadvertent collateral damage to civilians) and that resolved nothing. It was an exercise in presidential image making, creating the illusion of a courageous leader steadfast in purpose, true to his word, and unwilling to abide dictators. The president managed to rally public support, in part by staging a pseudodebate in Congress, but he succeeded mainly in further degrading an already ailing American political system, and he failed miserably to prepare a floundering nation to play its proper role in the post–Cold War world.

Graubard's critique is harsh and uncompromising, yet worth revisiting in certain of its essential details in order to reveal its dependency on a dubious, although common, assumption about the operation of the rhetorical presidency. This chapter proposes to explore further, then, Graubard's theme of presidential illusion, deceit, and duplicity, which is central to the thesis of failed leadership. Graubard's criticism, I suggest, is at once too severe and too narrow to place the tragic features of Bush's war rhetoric into sufficient relief. Thus, we return now to Graubard for further indications of what, in his view, constitutes the crime of rhetorical manipulation by the nation's chief executive.

Churchill, as Graubard underscores, "was a mythic figure who never compromised with a mighty foe, bringing Hitler and his detestable regime down to ignominious defeat. To be compared with such a man was to realize all one's fantasies, achieving the kind of political status no one would think to question or disparage. The president's words, implicitly if not explicitly, invited such comparison." From the beginning of the Persian Gulf crisis, Bush never expected or desired economic sanctions to dislodge Saddam Hussein from Kuwait. Secretly, without being straightforward either with the Congress or the public, Bush resisted efforts to negotiate an Iraqi withdrawal, "hoping that he would be able to exhibit the resolve his public image so lacked, allowing him to address the matter militarily." Since Congress was in recess during the most critical developments in the Gulf crisis, and since the news media for the most part featured the drama of the unfolding situation, comparing it to the Vietnam War as a potential quagmire and anticipating extensive loss of American lives, myths supplanted parliamentary debate and key questions went unasked. When the president did speak to the country, his rhetoric "substituted cliché for argument, exhortation for analysis" and employed inappropriately the language of World War II.[4]

This "masterful political performance" amounted to "a public relations stunt worthy of the Great Communicator himself," for "Ronald Reagan's White House was George Bush's political nursery" where he learned that "the game of American politics was played by essentially two rules: electoral victory was the only thing that mattered and moral uplift was a potent opiate, more powerful than prosaic truth." Reagan also taught Bush another lesson: "the power of myth, the capacity of an accomplished storyteller to give the illusion of having caused great events to happen." He learned to use the skills of the theater to prevaricate and tell tall tales, to develop a sense of how to manage and manipulate audiences. Such skills replaced any true expertise or knowledge of foreign affairs. Politics, in the age of television, relied instead on deception. The American public had adapted accordingly, desiring "a president who flattered them, knew how to make himself appealing, fabricated tall tales, and cared not at all to instruct, to bore with unnecessary and distressing details of a kind he himself preferred not to know." In short, Bush had learned from Reagan "how to use rhetoric—the rhetoric of religion, ambiguously Christian—to emphasize and celebrate American virtue." Under Reagan, Graubard argues, the presidency had been transformed into a monarchy—"a monarchy of the people, incarnate in [the president]," thus corrupting the policymaking system itself.[5]

Bush, who had been apprenticed to this rhetorical sorcerer, was entranced and thus trapped within "the well-worn Cold War paths trod by Nixon and Reagan," never reflecting on how forty years of Cold War politics had eroded the power of Congress and thus undermined "what had once passed for a polity of discussion." Instead, he was "consumed with winning elections," and he had learned to play to the American myth that war provides solutions, thus making it "an incomparable rhetorical remedy also for internal disasters." What Reagan had achieved with Grenada and Libya, Bush replicated in Panama and Iraq. When the time finally arrived for Congress to engage in its great debate, just five days before the United Nations' ultimatum expired and hostilities were to begin, Bush knew that the outcome of the congressional debate was inevitable, that it "was for the record only; it would change nothing." Then he manipulated the press into "retailing an essentially antiseptic account of the war," disseminating simple arguments and primordial patriotic sentiments." Accordingly, Graubard concludes, Bush's rhetoric of a New World Order "had no content," no perspective on what the collapse of Soviet Communism and the end of the Cold War might enable the United States to accomplish.[6] It was merely a theatrical ploy to goad the nation into war and thereby serve the president's personal political agenda at the expense of larger national interests.

A recurrent pattern of oppositions animates Graubard's angry critique of presidential war rhetoric. It equates rhetoric with myth and both with deception, cliché, exhortation, emotional appeals, manipulation, stunts, storytelling, theater, public relations, lies, flattery, and sorcery. In contrast to these negative pretensions, Graubard laments the lack of debate, discussion, argument, details, analysis, instruction, prosaic truth, knowledge, and true expertise. Moreover, the opposition of these two clusters expresses a constitutional criterion by which Bush's conduct is judged: Congress, the seat of parliamentary debate, was bypassed by the president in favor of directly exhorting the people. The rhetorical presidency, in short, is the real target of Graubard's attack, the source of his lament over the present diminishment of the republic. In this regard, at least, his objection to Mr. Bush's war echoes the concerns of the political scientists who originated the concept of the rhetorical presidency and, I suggest, thereby illustrates a key limitation of that concept, at least for those who wish to understand the full extent of rhetoric's role in the construction of political culture.

THE CONCEPT OF THE RHETORICAL PRESIDENCY REVISITED

The concept in question was invented by James Ceaser, Glen Thurow, Jeffrey Tulis, and Joseph Bessette, who together in 1981 published their landmark essay on "The Rise of the Rhetorical Presidency." Six years later, Tulis developed the key themes of the original essay into a book-length documentation of the roots, emergence, and unfortunate consequences of the rhetorical presidency. Since its inception, the idea of a rhetorical presidency, if not its critique of the deleterious effects of presidential oratory on republican government, has intrigued public address scholars, largely because it seemed to reinforce and extend Richard Neustadt's claim that the power of the presidency was a function of the power to persuade. What better rationale could exist for the systematic study of presidential speaking if speaking was tantamount to governing? As a result, perhaps, public address scholars paid too little attention to the restricted sense of rhetoric employed by those who meant to condemn what they regarded as a breach of the Constitution's original safeguards against demagoguery and "government by mood."[7]

Rhetoric, indeed, is a problematic, degraded form of communication within the theoretical context of the rhetorical presidency. It refers to popular speeches aimed at the masses, the sort of oratory that the constitutional framers regarded with suspicion and wished to restrict to purely ceremonial occasions. "Their fear," according to Ceaser and his coauthors, "was that mass oratory, whether crudely demagogic or highly inspirational, would undermine the rational and enlightened self-interest of the citizenry which their system was designed to foster and on which it was thought to depend for its stability." The founders distrusted pure, direct democracy, even representative government when guided by public opinion, and believed that popular orators pandered to "transient, often inchoate, public opinion." "The founders worried especially," Tulis notes, "about the danger that a powerful executive might pose to the system if power were derived from the role of popular leader."[8]

To the founders the term "demagogue" was synonymous with "popular leader," suggesting an excess of passionate appeals, flattery, and fear mongering. They designed the Constitution to limit the scope of the public sphere in order to assure against majority tyranny and political instability, hoping to avoid social unrest over issues of class, race, and sectional division. Thus, presidents from the early republic through the nineteenth century with rare exception confined their public, deliberative rhetoric to written communications with the Congress where supposedly they could be debated responsibly rather than consumed directly by uninformed popular audiences.

The institution of the presidency underwent substantial change in the twentieth century, beginning with Theodore Roosevelt's administration and crossing the threshold of transformation during Woodrow Wilson's tenure. Fearing class warfare as the potential resultant of the demagoguery of hate (which pandered to the envy of the poor and middle class) and the demagoguery of fear (which raised the specter of socialism to frighten the wealthy and middle class), Roosevelt "adopted a rhetoric of alarm and exaggeration—that is, of untruth," according to Tulis, in order to establish an administrative republic that aimed to preserve the original goals of the founders by providing a "square deal" for society at large, i.e., by "go[ing] after bad individuals and evil corporations" while "chastiz[ing] as demagogues those who opposed wealth as such or the impoverished as such." Thus, Tulis argues, Roosevelt introduced to the institution of the presidency the use of "blatant appeals to passion, demagoguery in its worst guises, if that is necessary to preserve or restore the constitutional order."[9] Drawing on this precedent, Wilson then transformed Roosevelt's bully pulpit into an even more radical instrument of popular leadership.

For Wilson, interpretation of the public will was the responsibility of the president, who was the sole government servant with a national mandate. The president, he believed, should speak directly to the people in order to translate their "felt desires into public policy."[10] Thus, Tulis argues, the ever-present threat of demagoguery intensified with the rise of the rhetorical presidency.

This increased threat of demagoguery resulted from the Wilsonian notion of presidential interpretation, which required the president to intuit the true majority sentiment within the maze of discordant public opinion and to convey that true sentiment in easily understood and convincing language. There lies the rub, in Tulis's view, because "Wilson's desire to raise politics to the level of rational disputation and his professed aim to have leaders educate the mass are contradictory." What makes these two goals contradictory? The first (popular disputation) requires broad, obvious, simplified arguments; the second (mass education) requires the dissemination of actual information. Moreover, Wilson's attempt to distinguish the demagogue from the leader-interpreter as equivalent to the difference between selfish appeals to transitory moods and popular passions versus altruistic interpretations of durable majority sentiments and lasting community interests was theoretically untenable, in Tulis's view, because there was no basis other than appeals to popular opinion itself on which to separate so-called permanent interests from transient whims. Wilson was more interested in constructing an energetic executive than he was concerned about the risks of demagoguery. Thus, he engaged in visionary speech that was inspirational and moralistic in tone and principle as well as policy-stand speech that aimed for specificity without conveying much actual information.[11]

After Wilson, it became commonplace for presidents to appeal to the public over the heads of Congress, hence the danger of an "ever-increasing reliance on inspirational rhetoric to deal with the normal problems of politics." In other words, this corruption of deliberative discourse undermined the deliberative process as a whole and subverted the routines of a mature democracy by substituting passionate appeal for argument, metaphor for debate, and emotional allusion for informed discussion.[12]

Public address scholars, as a rule, have been interested more in the empowerment of presidential oratory represented by the rise of the rhetorical presidency than concerned with its potentially negative implications for the welfare of republican government. As David Henry has noted, they have dedicated themselves primarily to extending the concept of the rhetorical presidency "by delineating its discursive features," i.e., by identifying the persuasive strategies with which the chief executive influences beliefs and shapes the national agenda. Henry himself investigates Ronald Reagan's campaign in support of the Nicaraguan Contras as a "sustained series of persuasive transactions . . . calling forth his mastery of the media, penchant for storytelling, and capacity to define complex policies in simple terms of abstract values." The essential point of Henry's study is to show how the president's strategy featured argument from principle that "define[d] the conflict in terms of abstract ideals rather than concrete circumstances," i.e., to uncover the discursive features that marked Ronald Reagan as the quintessential rhetorical president rather than to assess or lament the impact of his popular discourse on the quality of foreign policy formation and its deliberation.[13]

Similarly, Kurt Ritter applauds Reagan's presidential oratory for its effective use of the available means of persuasion instead of criticizing the Great Communicator for exercising rhetorical leadership contrary to the ideals of the founders. In Ritter's words, "When one analyzes Reagan's presidential oratory within the context of the modern rhetorical presidency and in terms of the classical canons of rhetoric, one discovers that Reagan was a 'Great Communicator' precisely because his speeches did express his own ideology and because he had developed considerable skill in structuring, editing, and delivering those speeches." As a public address scholar, Ritter not only prefers to measure the president by the standard of his oratorical skill but also resents the "elitist perspective on public policy" imposed by Tulis and other critics of the rhetorical presidency who single out Reagan's administration as an instance of oversimplified rhetoric creating a simple-minded chief executive, a realization of the ultimate danger of a president coming "to think in terms initially designed to persuade those not capable of fully understanding the policy itself." Ritter sides with James David Barber, who insists that real knowledge is sometimes simplicity, not always "complexification"—the kind of simplicity that enables a president to communicate with the public.[14]

Two other public address scholars, Karlyn Kohrs Campbell and Kathleen Hall Jamieson, also employ traditional rhetorical forms to examine the operation of the rhetorical presidency. Their generic framework focuses attention on the modes of presidential address peculiar to inaugurals, veto messages, war rhetoric, the State of the Union address, farewell addresses, and other standard message types. This interest in the rhetorical architecture and rituals of the presidency is grounded on the assumption that a president's public communication shapes the national identity. Campbell and Jamieson thus examine the means through which Americans have been invited to assume various roles and identities. They investigate the constitutive force of presidential rhetorical genres, especially as those genres work to create a distinct identity for the presidency and to maintain it as a stable institution. The power of the rhetorical presidency is assumed and its impact on the political culture acknowledged; its rhetorical mechanisms are revealed from the perspective of genre theory. But its consequences for the quality of political deliberation, that is, the problem of presidential demagoguery, remain outside the scope of Campbell and Jamieson's critique.[15]

To their apparent discomfort, then, contemporary public address scholars either ignore the problem of demagoguery featured in the concept of the rhetorical presidency or weakly protest its elitist bias even while citing Ceaser et al. and Tulis to justify the detailed investigation of presidential oratory. The bind in which they find themselves results from an overly restricted sense of rhetoric in Tulis's concept, one in which it is reduced to irrational persuasion and dissociated from reason, knowledge, and true deliberation—the very sense that animates the concept of the rhetorical presidency and the critique it entails, but that is at odds with the assumption generally held by public address scholars and explicitly articulated by

Campbell and Jamieson—that rhetoric is a constitutive force and a source of national identity essential to the operation of the public sphere and the constitution of the polity. Rhetoric, including presidential oratory, in this more expanded sense of the term is equated with the construction of political culture, not an aberration thereof. It is the practice of public deliberation, the only means short of coercion for managing political contingencies. Thus, blaming the problems of republican government on the institutionalization of presidential rhetoric, and more specifically the war against Iraq on George Bush's demagoguery, is misleading. We should instead examine presidential rhetoric for what it reveals about the nation's sense of itself as a people, including its post–Cold War predisposition to engage in combat.

My point is that the theoretical reduction of popular presidential persuasion to demagoguery is misleading, at least in the case of the Persian Gulf War, because such a reduction deflects our attention from a larger problem common to the political culture, a problem not restricted to the rhetorical presidency—one that cannot be addressed structurally by returning, even if a return were possible, to the founder's constitutional prescription of congressional deliberation.

Unlike Tulis, I do not see the rise of the rhetorical presidency as a source of institutional dysfunction. He believes this "fundamental transformation of American politics" has changed the modern presidency into a hybrid of constitutional officer and popular leader, a hybrid that causes a "dilemma of governance." Woodrow Wilson, Tulis argues, experienced the limits of this hybridized office when he appealed to the public over the heads of Congress in order to gain support for the League of Nations, a campaign that failed because Wilson "was compelled to speak in contradictory ways to different sorts of audiences—the Senate and the people at large." Supposedly as a good rhetorician, Wilson engaged in emotional appeals to move the public and then relied on rational, technical arguments to persuade the Congress, resulting in rhetorical situations that contradicted one another—"what was thought necessary to persuade senators would not work to persuade the people and vice versa."[16]

Lyndon Johnson, Tulis continues, encountered the limits of the rhetorical presidency in yet another way. His War on Poverty campaign succeeded with the public in the short run at the expense of failed policy in the long run. As Tulis observes:

In place of an argument indicating why poverty should be considered a national problem, why it required a coordinated program, why present efforts were insufficient or ill-conceived, and why the kinds of legislation suggested by the president fit together as a single program—instead of this, the president offered a metaphor, whose premise provided the answers. If we were at war with poverty, such an effort would require a national mobilization, coordination, extensive executive discretion, and the potential involvement of virtually any social program as vital to the war effort. Wars require these things. . . . The executive branch and Congress then proceeded as if the need and its rationale had been established.[17]

Although Johnson's communication with Congress on this subject took the form of a written message, Tulis observes, it was designed with a popular audience in mind, that is, to arouse a general disposition rather than to delineate a careful rationale for the War on Poverty proposals. Its style consisted of short, easily consumed paragraphs, often no longer than a sentence, and catchy phrases that made for easy sound bites on the evening news. Thus metaphor and passionate appeal substituted for argument and deliberation, resulting in a hastily packaged proposal that ultimately failed as a program.[18]

Ironically, Tulis ends his discussion of Johnson's example with an approving reference to David Zarefsky's "perceptive study" of the rhetoric of the president's War on Poverty campaign. I say ironically because Tulis calls Zarefsky as an expert witness against the rhetorical presidency, quoting him as saying "the very choices of symbolism and argument which had aided the adoption of the [War on Poverty] program were instrumental in undermining its implementation and in weakening public support for its basic philosophy."[19] At best, I would argue, Zarefsky is a hostile witness, and at worst his testimony has been misconstrued, for his critique, as I read it, is not aimed at the institution of the rhetorical presidency but instead at a deeper understanding of policy formation and implementation as a rhetorical phenomenon.

As I have observed elsewhere, Zarefsky's investigation centers on intragovernmental communication and public discourse as an instrument for constructing political reality. His focus is on language and its power to define. He advances a theoretical framework that begins with the assumption that reality is constructed socially through symbolic interaction and that the rhetorical presidency is instrumental in the construction of political reality. If presidential power is the power to persuade, he suggests, "the power to persuade is, in large measure, the power to define" because "the presidency is the primary source of symbols about public issues."[20]

The president as "chief inventor and broker" of political symbols can construct definitions in a number of ways, but three processes are especially important. First, the strategy of dissociation, based on a manipulation of what Perelman and Olbrechts-Tyteca call philosophical pairs, allows a president to redefine strategically a term such as poverty by distinguishing between its apparent form, a lack of money, and its real nature, a culture of deprivation. Second, a strategy of persuasive definition allows the president to shift attitudinal connotations from one term to another through, for instance, a metaphor that labels the antipoverty program a war. Finally, a reliance upon abstract condensation symbols allows a number of divergent meanings to converge, at least momentarily, under one term.

A president, Zarefsky continues, uses definition to shape a context of interpretation that encourages responses "congenial to his purpose." In particular, Zarefsky agrees with his colleague Thomas Goodnight that presidential definition works primarily within the context of a "dialectical tension between the liberal and conservative presumptions" that sustains American politics. Zarefsky suggests as well that defining a situation as a crisis may be the most effective way to weight an issue on the side of the liberal presumption, that is, on the side of the assumption that desirable change can and should be initiated through governmental action. He draws upon Ernest Bormann's notion of fantasy chains to explain how presidential definitions "are picked up and used by wider audiences." The chain is formed when key audiences begin to use the definition and its associated symbols, adopt its vision, and measure progress against its expectations for the future. Such chains are inherently entropic, however, for the strategic ambiguity of the condensation symbols embodying presidential definitions "proves difficult to sustain. . . . A condensation symbol is attractive during the process of enactment [of an antipoverty law, for instance] because people of divergent attitudes may unite by use of a common symbol. But the divergent attitudes do not go away."[21]

To sustain the power of definitions based on condensation symbols, presidential rhetors must actively intervene with redefinitions aimed at adapting visions to changing circumstances. The states of definition and redefinition in presidential rhetoric, as discussed by Zarefsky, are based on Leland Griffin's conception of movements and thus include inception, crisis, and consummation.

Lyndon Johnson, Zarefsky argues, engaged the liberal presumption with mixed results when he defined poverty as a crisis. Characterizing poverty by the condensation metaphor of war, Johnson initially aroused a nation of warriors intent upon vanquishing the real enemy. Soon, however, enthusiasm for the Economic Opportunity Act of 1964 began to diminish because the metaphor "contained the seeds of its own destruction."[22] The metaphor of unconditional war created expectations that could not be met and required efforts at redefinition that threatened the original purpose of the antipoverty program. Thus, the war ended in stalemate.

Zarefsky's critique is of the Johnson administration's antipoverty symbol system, not of the rhetorical presidency—of the metaphor of war specifically, not of rhetorical metaphor generally. His critique focuses in part on the criterion of immediate effects, pointing out where and how presidential symbols fell short of the mark. Ultimately, it brings him to a consideration of the long-range appeal of ideology, i.e., to an assessment of the "impasse of the liberal argument in contemporary American politics."[23] He points to the dilemmas facing modern liberals who attempt to work for significant change within the system. Inevitably, they must justify programs of change with symbols that generate great expectations and thereby denigrate modest achievements, leaving radicals disappointed with the political establishment and conservatives convinced of the need to get government off the backs of the people. By the larger criterion of political pragmatism, he concludes, modern liberalism has so far failed to produce a rhetoric capable of sustaining a persuasive definition of change. In short, the question is not whether to use rhetoric but what rhetoric to use.

Similarly, Leroy Dorsey's study of Theodore Roosevelt's contribution to the birth of the rhetorical presidency concerns itself with how public discourse articulated a policy of conservation of natural resources, not with lamenting the role of rhetoric as an instrument of executive governance. Dorsey, a public address scholar who views the president as the "nation's chief storyteller" and suspends judgment on whether this fact is for the good or ill of the country, shows how Roosevelt was able to reconceptualize the public's sacred histories, specifically the frontier myth, in order to "accommodate and promote new ideological frameworks" that secured "popular support for the conservation of animal life, forests, waterways, and grazing land."[24] Like Zarefsky, Dorsey assumes that presidents govern by speech making, but, unlike Zarefsky, he argues that lasting liberal change can be deliberated and effected through presidential rhetoric.

Tulis's concern over the hybridization of the institution of the presidency stems from a dissociation of rhetoric and deliberation, a dissociation that rhetorical theorists since Aristotle have resisted. It assumes that true deliberation is essentially rational and that congressional decision makers and constitutional presidents deliberate, unlike the public, in a manner that insures against the harmful influence of misguided emotion and fickle feelings. It assumes, for instance, that true deliberation entails no significant ambiguities, sacred myths, or strategic definitions with attitudinal connotations nor any condensation symbols with divergent as well as convergent meanings. Thus, Tulis's concern is elitist, as Ritter complains, but more importantly its rhetorical naïveté undercuts our ability to critique adequately symbolic constructions of reality as they are constituted through the operation of the rhetorical presidency, reified in the deliberations of Congress, and dispersed throughout the political culture. The hybridization thesis, in short, places too much faith on a republican theory of government that reduces rhetoric to demagoguery and, therefore, provides us with too little understanding of the governing representations that constitute the rhetorical republic.

THE PERSIAN GULF WAR
AND THE RHETORICAL REPUBLIC

Frederick Dolan and Thomas Dumm recently launched an attack within the discipline of political science on its antirhetorical bias, arguing that the "struggle over the *representation* of politics in the public spheres of late twentieth-century America has become the single most important force shaping political life in this country, and that the methods and approaches of political science have proved inadequate for the study of the discourses, imagery, interpretations, and desires attached to practices of representation." In their view, a misguided attempt to "get real" by modeling "the gritty business of competing interests, bargaining, and logrolling, as viewed through such methodological lenses as complex correlation study and regression plot analysis," has left political scientists unprepared to cope with "the inherent unpredictability and open-endedness of public life." The United States is a "republic of words," they argue, "which also means, necessarily, a republic of fantasies and images." Thus, the problem of governing such a republic is the problem of governing representations: "of reinterpreting the phantasmagoric mix of images and tonalities, claims and counterclaims, that shape political discourse in the United States today." The essential character of the republic is such that its politics is no longer shaped "by the grammar of a master discourse unquestioningly shared and respected by all."[25] That is, by extension, there are no settled, long-term interests shared by rational decision makers who with careful deliberation can cut through rhetorical flourishes, flattery, and passionate appeals (including the fear mongering of popular public discourse) to keep the nation on a steady course. Instead, we are left to seek answers to rhetorical questions, but in this case questions to which the answers, neither obvious nor certain, are subject to interpretation and fraught with attitude.

In one application of Dolan and Dumm's perspective on the rhetorical republic, Avital Ronell argues that George Bush called upon an army of metaphors and metonymies to justify war in the Persian Gulf. In her view, "the war was less a matter of truth than of rhetorical maneuvers that were dominated by unconscious transmission systems and symbolic displacements," specifically the resurrection of Hitler and displacement of World War II in the Middle East. Thus, she argues, these signifiers on the rebound worked at an unconscious level to reduce everything to an order of sameness.[26]

David Campbell's analysis of the rhetorical republic explores the larger context of interpretation in which specific conflicts, such as the Persian Gulf War, are justified. The issue on his mind concerns the trope of national security—an image of vulnerability involving a question of national identity which, answered in its conventional way, "convinces us that we are always at risk in a dangerous world." Even those who operate under cover of secrecy in the national security bureaucracy, Campbell argues, work within the nation's cultural parameters, in which their constant fear that anarchy and disorder will break out among nations is entertained without a clear fix on either the source of the danger or the nature of the identity that is supposedly at risk. Thus, the texts of the Cold War took on the form of the American jeremiad that institutionalized anxiety as both the end and means of national salvation, resulting in a "struggle that exceeded the military threat of the Soviet Union." Nor did the orientation of the Cold War die with the demise of the Soviet threat. As Campbell observes, the United States deployed the same interpretative practices in the war against Iraq—the first post–Cold War crisis. Such practices "emphasized the zero-sum analyses of international action, the sense of endangerment ascribed to all the activities of the other, the fear of internal challenge and subversion, the tendency to militarize all responses, and the willingness to draw the lines of superiority/inferiority between us and them."[27]

The present "need to articulate a different orientation to the world" leads Campbell to begin work modestly on such a daunting task by examining how the language of the Cold War is "pivotal in inscribing the boundaries of American identity." Noting that danger is an effect of interpretation rather than an objective, knowable condition, and that not all risks are interpreted as dangers, Campbell observes that "the ability to represent things as alien, subversive, dirty, or sick has been pivotal to the articulation of danger in the American experience." Campbell's point parallels Tom Wicker's view of the nation's unabashed "desire to mold other peoples in the American Way," a strong strain of "messianism" combined with "ideological isolationism" by which Americans, unless they retreat from the world, close ranks against eccentricity and dissent as they venture abroad to slay foreign devils and thereby to excise the evils of foreign societies that they most fear in their own. Such is the dark side of the liberal republican tradition. "Witness," Wicker concludes, "the demonization, during the Gulf War, of Saddam Hussein."[28]

But Saddam Hussein *was* evil. I have heard that refrain more than once, even at the annual meeting of the Speech Communication Association in 1994 when a member of the audience reacted to a paper presented by Karen Rasmussen and Sharon Downey, entitled "The Rhetoric of the Gulf War: Restoring American Dominance and Control." The thrust of Rasmussen and Downey's argument was that the Bush administration's justification of the Persian Gulf War served to reduce the ideological tension between altruistic goals and economic self-interest and thus bolstered the national pursuit of global domination. That is, they analyzed the mythic fabric of textual fragments justifying the war in order to show how rhetorically sanitizing the instruments of combat worked to sanctify the hegemonic goals of warfare by eliminating the cultural tension between supposedly altruistic motives and the capitalistic greed of American imperialism. Any exercise of power to achieve dominance must be justified on moral grounds; power cannot be exercised indiscriminately. The end of the Cold War and the lingering effects of the Vietnam syndrome had eroded the credibility of military means for advancing the nation's material interests. Rasmussen and Downey pointed to the construction of a representative anecdote in the administration's Gulf War rhetoric which associated the weapons of war with a degree of precision that transformed them into moral, humane instruments for destroying the enemy's weapons without causing collateral damage to innocent civilians. These smart weapons were characterized as merciful as well as precise and proficient. Thus, the viability of the war myth was at least temporarily restored as the United States entered a post–Cold War era of technological proficiency in which "militarism defines moralism," an alarming turn "because it is dehumanizing, because it dismisses the human struggle intrinsic to war, because it belies questions about the nature and consequences of war . . . [and because] its ideology is governed by a pragmatic ethic validating the precept that 'might makes right.'" In this way, the dialectical tension between morality and dominance, according to Rasmussen and Downey, was rhetorically reduced to the danger point.[29] But Saddam Hussein was *evil*, insisted at least one member of the audience.

This refrain serves both to indicate a key achievement of the administration's war rhetoric and to mark a focal point of rhetorical endeavor on its part. The administration, that is, had to work hard to realize such a seemingly obvious result, to naturalize an essentially weak analogy. As Mark Pollock has argued, Bush engaged in argument from history, systematically structuring a narrative that associated Iraq with World War II and Saddam Hussein with Adolf Hitler in order "to negate the Vietnam War's symbolic power as an obstacle to U.S. military intervention" on such a massive scale. The association with Hitler was necessary in part because the president could no longer demonize Iraq's leader by linking him to the Soviet Union and the international threat of communism. Moreover, the nation was looking for a peace dividend after the defeat of communism rather than a costly new military engagement in the Persian Gulf. Many questioned whether vital U.S. interests were at stake, whether access to affordable oil in sufficient quantity was seriously threatened, and whether oil itself was a just cause for war. The war had to be elevated to a higher plane; Bush therefore transformed it into a test of the national character by, first, separating Saddam Hussein rhetorically from the Iraqi people in order to elevate (or, more accurately, lower) him to the status of Hitler and, second, presenting the Iraqi leader as a threat to world order and civilized behavior. "Now," the message said, "just as the cold war was won and world peace was once more within our grasp, Saddam Hussein threatened to spoil things." As Pollock concludes, "The construction of a narrative in which Munich, not Vietnam, served as the condensation symbol, amplified the stakes of the crisis and legitimized decisive military action."[30]

The point here is not that Saddam Hussein was a saint; he was in many important respects justifiably pronounced evil. The list of atrocities committed by him, or for which he was directly responsible, is long and appalling.[31] The list includes murdering his brother-in-law, serving as an interrogator and torturer for the revolutionary government following the Baathist's brutal killing of General Abdul Karim Qassim in 1963, personally executing senior members of his own Baath party after his rise to the presidency in 1979, the genocidal suppression of Iraqi Kurds, and more. Yes, Saddam Hussein was evil but no less evil before he invaded Kuwait than after; no less evil when he attacked Iran in 1980 and prosecuted one of the most savage wars in modern history; no less evil than when he used chemical weapons against Khomeini's sacrificial wave of child soldiers and immediately thereafter used nerve gas to slaughter civilians in villages throughout Iraqi Kurdistan.

Yet, throughout this reign of terror, both the Reagan and the Bush administrations found ways, mostly secret ways, to provide Saddam Hussein with economic and military aid (including assistance in obtaining chemical and biological weapons), despite the restrictions of federal law and a U.S. arms embargo against Iraq. The Bush administration even went so far as to oppose passage of a U.N. Human Rights Commission resolution criticizing Iraq's use of chemical weapons against the Kurds, and it ignored Amnesty International's April, 1989, report of widespread torture of Iraqi children, children who were routinely subjected to "extractions of fingernails, beatings, whippings, sexual abuse, and electrical shock treatment" as well as "beatings with metal cables while naked and suspended by the wrists from the ceiling" and much worse, including young girls being found "hung upside down from the feet during menstruation" with "objects inserted into their vaginas" and the summary execution of dozens of children from a single village after at least some of the victims' eyes were gouged out. Despite these reported atrocities, the Bush administration reiterated its commitment to deepening and broadening the United States' relationship with Iraq. After Iraq invaded Kuwait, however, the president made much of Iraqi atrocities against Kuwaiti civilians, including the now-discredited charge that newborn babies were thrown out of their incubators. For some reason, George Bush had decided finally to equate Saddam Hussein with Adolf Hitler.[32]

Certainly, the Bush administration could not have changed its mind because Kuwait was America's friend, an ally, a democratic state, or even a neutral party. Kuwait's feudal regime, instead, has been hostile toward Israel, and thus its press has been extremely anti-American. Moreover, the emir of Kuwait cut off oil shipments to the United States following the Six-Day War in 1967 and successfully played the United States off against the Soviet Union throughout the Iran-Iraq war of the 1980s. As Senator Daniel Patrick Moynihan put the matter, "We are not in an international crisis in the sense that events that took place on August 2 necessitate the confrontation of the largest set of armed forces since World War II. Nothing large happened. A nasty little country invaded a littler but just as nasty country."[33]

Surely, President Bush did not change his mind about Saddam Hussein because the invasion of Kuwait constituted a serious risk to America's oil supply. Even if the Iraqi dictator had succeeded eventually in controlling all of Kuwait's and Saudi Arabia's oil, his 21.5 percent of the global output would not serve the purpose of his conquests unless he were able to produce and sell it on the world market. Moreover, new oil reserves are constantly being discovered throughout the world, and new technology is increasing the amount considered economically recoverable.[34] Even the president realized that a war to protect oil reserves was unacceptable to the American public and thus backed away from making that the stated purpose of his crusade.

How, then, was the limited risk of a nasty dictator on the loose in the Persian Gulf transformed into an exaggerated perception of danger to the United States? What danger loomed so large in the president's construction of reality to justify committing the nation to war? The answer, in large measure, involves a problematic representation of American identity. The immediate manifestation of this representation is what Theodore Draper calls "American hubris," an affliction suffered by Democratic and Republican administrations alike. Draper traces the source of this hubris to the Truman Doctrine, which he terms "the original codification of the Pax Americana illusion," that is, the vision of universal ascendancy. By combining "a universal doctrine with limited means of action," he argues, the Truman Doctrine created "a dangerous mixture of illusion and reality" from which the country has yet to recover even after the demise of the international communist threat on which the doctrine depended for its original rationale.[35] Hubris, however, is a sign of fear, tragic fear in the case of the Persian Gulf War, reconstituted in the rhetorical republic for further extension, unfortunately, into the post–Cold War era.

TRAGIC FEAR
IN THE RHETORICAL REPUBLIC

The rhetorical legacy of the Cold War was expressed in the presidential call for a New World Order. This vehicle of exaggerated fear reproduced in the post–Cold War rhetorical republic the tragic identity of a heroic nation which had hardly vanquished the demon of communism only to be confronted by yet another specter of international disorder. The threat was not so much a matter of the actual power of Saddam Hussein as it was a reminder of America's inadequacies as the principal agent of universal harmony in an otherwise unjust and insecure world. The administration's caricature of Saddam Hussein conveyed the image of a Persian Gulf crisis of such magnitude that it constituted a fundamental challenge to the fragile international order. As the president said, "What is at stake is far more than a matter of economics or oil. What is at stake is whether the nations of the world can take a common stand against aggression . . . whether we live in a world governed by the rule of law or by the law of the jungle." And again, in Bush's words, "Iraq's brutality, aggression and violations of international law cannot be allowed to succeed. . . . [W]e've been called upon to help. The consequences of our not doing so would be incalculable, because Iraq's aggression is not just a challenge to the security of Kuwait and other Gulf nations, but to the better world that we all have hoped to build in the wake of the Cold War."[36]

Insofar as Saddam Hussein personified evil, he signified an antagonist capable of exposing America's tragic flaw, its hubris. He represented not only the necessity of slaying the demon figure in order to achieve temporary redemption but also a tacit reminder of the ultimate futility of the nation's heroic mission. Fate, by the logic of this tragic form, dictated the eventual failure of American idealism—the futility of its quest to transform the barbaric world into a civilized haven of lasting peace and universal freedom. Such a failure would be tantamount to the demise of the nation, its very identity the first casualty of cynicism. This was the stuff of tragic fear transmitted in George Bush's call to arms.

The perception of a threat to world order was achieved in Bush's war rhetoric by identifying Iraq's attack on Kuwait as an "unprovoked invasion," an act of "aggression" that required the restoration of the state of Kuwait, "or no nation will be safe, and the promising future we anticipate will indeed be jeopardized." The Iraqi armed forces, he said, had "invaded a peaceful Kuwait," indeed, had "stormed in blitzkrieg fashion" through Kuwait in "the early morning hours . . . without provocation or warning . . . just hours after Saddam Hussein specifically assured numerous countries in the area that there would be no invasion." This was an "outrageous and brutal act of aggression" and, therefore, one of those moments in the life of a nation when "we're called upon to define who we are and what we believe." Moreover, Saddam Hussein, not the people of Iraq, became the sole symbol of aggression. In the president's words, "Saddam Hussein systematically raped, pillaged, and plundered a tiny nation no threat to his own. He subjected the people of Kuwait to unspeakable atrocities, and among those maimed and murdered, innocent children."[37] Kuwait was the innocent victim of a mad man's vicious ambitions. This was a monstrous challenge to world order that only the United States, with the assistance of its allies, could hope to meet.

The focus of the president's narrative on the unprovoked aggression of an evil dictator against a small, defenseless neighbor could invoke the tragic vision of America as a heroic savior only by strategically omitting a number of complicating details. As Edward Said observed: "Saddam Hussein, a dictator of the kind the United States has typically found and supported, was almost invited into Kuwait [by the United States], then almost immediately demonized and transformed into a worldwide metaphysical threat. Iraq's military capabilities were fantastically exaggerated, the country verbally obliterated except for its by-now isolated leader, U.N. sanctions given a ludicrously short run, and then America began the war." The president's rhetoric, Said argued, was "simply undeterred, uncomplicated by any considerations of detail, realism or cause and effect."[38] There was a good deal more to the story than the president bothered to tell.

For instance, the president neglected to take into consideration the history of Iraq's claims against Kuwait prior to Saddam Hussein's rise to power. He ignored the historical claim, first advanced in the late 1930s by Iraq's King Ghazi, that Kuwait was an integral part of Iraq because it had been an administrative subdistrict of the Iraqi province of Basra under the rule of the Ottoman empire until the defeated empire was carved up by Great Britain after World War I, arbitrarily drawing a border that suited Britain's own imperialist interests. This claim had been reiterated by General Qassim during his revolutionary presidency. Iraq under the general's leadership nearly invaded its neighbor soon after Great Britain withdrew its protectorate over Kuwait whose independence was declared in 1961. The dispute extended to a chronic disagreement over the borders between the two countries, leading to an occupation of a Kuwaiti military post in 1973 by Iraqi troops who had crossed the contested frontier, and most recently to Iraq's complaint that Kuwait had pumped billions of dollars of Iraqi oil between 1980 and 1990 from the Rumaila field, which spans the disputed border.

Although such claims against Kuwait do not justify an invasion, it has been noted that "many Arabs believe that Iraq's case against Kuwait is not devoid of all merit." As Glenn Frankel reports, Saddam Hussein's claim "to have redressed a wrong inflicted by British imperialism" is the justification for his invasion of Kuwait that "resonated most deeply in the hearts and minds both of his own people and of the Arab world in general." Denied by British fiat in 1922 access to a viable port on the Persian Gulf, Iraqis harbored a sense of injustice for over three generations that ultimately manifested itself in war with Iran followed by the conquest of Kuwait. Even though Hussein's own Baath Party renounced its legal claim to the whole of Kuwait in 1963 when it was first briefly in power, Frankel notes that many historians and analysts agree that Iraq "never acceded to a specific border-line, and some [experts] believe it has valid historic and strategic reasons for claiming a small portion of northeast Kuwait." Thus, the invasion of Kuwait was not completely unprovoked nor devoid of any historical or contemporary reasons shared by the Iraqi people and other Arabs besides Saddam Hussein. As Sir Anthony Parsons, Britain's former U.N. ambassador and a thirty-year veteran of Middle East diplomacy, has remarked: "In the Iraqi subconscious, Kuwait is part of Basra province, and the bloody British took it away from them. . . . We protected our strategic interests rather successfully, but in doing so we didn't worry too much about the people living there. We created a situation where people felt they had been wronged."[39]

My point is not to side with Saddam Hussein, only to suggest some additional complexities overlooked by President Bush's overly simplified story of aggression and its threat to world order. There are further details that indicate a degree of American culpability, that support the viability of economic sanctions as an alternative to military force, and that question the assumption that only the United States was sufficiently motivated and capable of preserving world order. Further attention to such details, were there space to develop them here without losing sight of my main point, would disperse the focus of evil and undermine the principle of tragedy upon which the presidential call to arms depended for its narrative representation of an extreme threat to international order and mortal challenge to the integrity of the nation. Saddam Hussein would no longer be "troped" merely as the personification of pure evil, and the nation and people of Iraq would no longer be reduced metonymically to a representation of evil in the person of Saddam Hussein. Rounding out the president's caricature of the crisis in Kuwait would diminish his ability to displace attention from the complexities of Persian Gulf history, from the competing and balancing forces at work in that region, from the irony of America's heroic rescue of Kuwait working counterproductively to exacerbate long-term anticolonial antipathies toward Western powers and Israeli allies, and from the embarrassment of the Bush administration's previous policy of aiding and abetting the heinous crimes of Iraq's evil dictator against even his own people.[40]

My point also is not to lay blame on George Bush, per se, at least no more blame than he deserves in his capacity as the nation's chief rhetor. My purpose instead is to call attention to a governing representation of our rhetorical republic that is a dysfunctional vestige of the Cold War era and that transcends the institution of the rhetorical presidency. Neither the Congress nor the mainstream press ridiculed the president's fable, as Professor Graubard wishes they had, because the tragic fear engendered by the caricature of Saddam Hussein cuts to the quick of American political culture and works its will on national motives regardless of the forum in which foreign policy is deliberated. Its influence is evidenced even in the secret deliberations of the national security establishment; experts are no more immune to the perils of such hubris than the general public.[41] The problem is not a function of presidential demagoguery but instead a matter requiring a rhetorical adjustment of political culture that will enable the public and its leaders to interpret and deliberate the exigencies of the post–Cold War era less fearfully.

The rhetorical legacy of the Cold War is a tragic framework of interpretation that constitutes the perils of hubris in the image of a heroic nation struggling globally to redeem itself by contesting the relentless forces of chaos and establishing a New World Order. The very identity of the nation within this tragic perspective requires it to find and fight evil everywhere in the hope of creating and preserving an international utopia of freedom and democratic principles, thereby saving America's own soul and insuring its material security. The nation, that is, experiences a double fear of the consequences of aggression left uncontested and of a failure to prevail over aggression when it is contested. Such tragic fear prods us as a people to continue the fateful struggle against international chaos as if one nation might control the world sufficiently by itself to achieve a lasting and just peace. Thus, the cycle of national redemption through the bloody ritual of tragic victimage perpetuates a futile quest for security through global hegemony. It is the kind of rhetorical representation of the nation that sustains the "delusion," as Theodore Draper aptly labels it, "that the United States has the power to decide matters all over the world," a delusion that most certainly has a "hypnotic effect" but, I would hasten to add, a delusion that addicts us to fear.[42]

The republic's addiction to tragic fear requires both a consciousness-raising critique of its bad rhetorical habits carried over from decades of Cold War discourse and an alternative strategy for representing America's current role in the community of nations. As Draper observes, regarding the first point, the local situation of Greece in 1948 was transformed into a universal Cold War axiom (articulated initially in the Truman Doctrine speech) of protecting freedom globally, a transformation of the local into a universal situation that "was accomplished by the 'domino,' or, as it might have been called, the 'rotten-apple,' principle."[43] The universalization of American policy required a rhetorical strategy of sufficient cultural force to universalize the foreign threat. In this case, the strategy relied on a cluster of conceptual metaphors that associated the foreign threat with fearful images of disease, fire, and a flood of communism spreading to every corner of the earth, images that have since become thoroughly literalized within the republic's rhetorical culture and projected into the post–Cold War era. A deconstruction of such strategies is a necessary step toward reconstituting a less fearful rhetorical republic.

A productive critique of the republic's Cold War rhetorical habits, moreover, entails the cultivation of what Kenneth Burke calls a comic corrective to the tragic framework of the victimage ritual. Indeed, courage is a by-product of adopting a comic attitude toward international affairs, the kind of courage that comes from appreciating the multiple facets of any problematic situation and of realizing the inherent complexities of an adversary's motives. These complexities routinely delimit (rather than exaggerate) the extent of any threat and thereby encourage its constructive resolution through means short of frightened military heroics. They underscore stabilizing factors in the international environment instead of dramatizing the constant threat of chaos, and they warrant governing representations of national security and prosperity devoid of the futile quest to dominate a New World Order or the equally unrealistic wish to withdraw into the fetal position of isolationism. Indeed, the rhetorical cultivation of a comic corrective would transcend the extremes of isolationism and international hegemony, displace the false dichotomy between political idealism and realism, and provide a narrative structure that articulates an ethic of responsible participation in world affairs.[44]

The deconstruction of old rhetorical habits and formulation of a comic corrective for the tragic fear permeating the republic's post–Cold War culture is a considerable project for academic criticism to undertake, one more consequential and potentially productive, I believe, than any we might conceive under the more restrictive notion of the rhetorical presidency which reduces rhetoric to mere demagoguery and prompts public address scholars to investigate presidential persuasion without giving sufficient consideration to the wider implications of its governing representations. The general goal of this chapter, an abbreviated examination of tragic fear in President Bush's Persian Gulf War rhetoric, has been to indicate the potential value of scholarship guided by the notion of the rhetorical republic. Whether it entails research on domestic or foreign affairs, presidential or congressional discourse, public or privileged deliberations, this is a notion that can enhance scholarship on nearly any aspect of the rhetorical presidency. Specifically, though, my goal has been to issue a prolegomenon for an expanded study of the Cold War legacy of tragic fear and the possibility of effecting a comic corrective for our times. Such a project of productive criticism promises to probe the constructive potential of conceptualizing a thoroughly rhetorical republic.

CHAPTER 9

The Rhetorical Presidency:

A TWO-PERSON CAREER
Karlyn Kohrs Campbell

T his chapter represents the convergence of two areas of scholarship—women's studies scholarship energized by the second wave of feminism and rhetorical studies of the presidency. Women's studies scholarship has compelled recognition of the importance of women's roles and activities in human affairs through history; rhetorical studies have focused attention on the significance of the discourse and the symbolism of the presidency as an institution. As a women's studies scholar, I choose to focus on presidential women; as a rhetorical scholar, I hope to demonstrate their importance in understanding the presidency as a rhetorical institution.

As presidential scholars, we are accustomed to thinking of the presidency as a corporate entity larger than the individual incumbent. At a minimum, press secretaries and speech writers have long been recognized as parts of the institution, particularly as viewed rhetorically, and from the very beginning the views of cabinet members have shaped presidential thinking as well as presidential discourse. Until quite recently, however, a key member of that corporation, to whom we now refer as the First Lady, has largely been ignored in presidential scholarship. Interest was heightened by the partnership of Jimmy and Rosalynn Smith Carter; it was piqued by revelations of the influence of Nancy Davis Reagan on both personnel and policy matters. Then in 1992 the presidential election pitted "plump, popular, white-haired, grandmotherly" Barbara Pierce Bush, a woman who seemed to epitomize traditional womanhood, against Hillary Rodham Clinton, a wife, mother, and highly successful attorney. The intensity of the feelings generated by Rodham Clinton's public career and the Clintons' political partnership were reflected in the epithets with which she was attacked.

This chapter offers a framework for understanding why the First Lady-ship is a vital part of the presidency and why it is such a difficult role to play. I recognize that no framework can describe that role as defined by each and every presidential wife or explain reactions to all of them, especially given their variations as individuals and the differing times in which they served; indeed, there are exceptions among them to every generalization.[1] What I offer is an analysis that explains why so many of them have faced severe criticism, and although I often illustrate my claims with materials from the Clinton presidency, I also provide historical parallels.

The role of the First Lady is vital to the presidency because it epitomizes what sociologist Hanna Papanek calls the "two-person career," that is, a profession that by reason of the combination of "formal and informal institutional demands placed on a married couple" precludes a traditional public-private spousal division of labor and requires their cooperative efforts if it is to be pursued successfully. In such a two-person career the wife's functions, depending on her talents, may include "status maintenance, intellectual contributions, and public performance."[2]

As the president's wife, the First Lady has always been expected to manage and maintain the presidential residence. In modern times, she has been expected to espouse a cause or project, an expectation made clear in the questions put by journalists to candidate wives Margot Birmingham Perot and Sybil Bailey Stockdale during the 1992 campaign.[3] Moreover, in terms of public performance, the First Lady functions as a representative of the nation. She is expected to welcome heads of state, preside at state dinners, make public appearances, attend local and national celebrations, and become the patron of selected charities or projects.

These aspects of the role resemble the duties assumed by royal families, which are related to its idealization. In other words, the presidency is a career that entails a certain kind of marital partnership.[4] Presidential spousal relationships are ill-defined because the division of labor will vary with the talents and attitudes of the partners and because the wife's role combines state and domestic duties.

These expectations and requirements hint at the reasons that the First Ladyship is such a difficult role to fulfill successfully. Specifically, the First Ladyship is an ambiguous mixture of public and private functions whose performance almost inevitably offends someone. Moreover, because of the nature of the U.S. presidency, the First Lady and the First Family are viewed as ideals or culture types, a problem exacerbated by the intense press scrutiny they now receive in what Richard Schickel calls our "culture of celebrity."[5] Finally, in political terms, her every word is scrutinized in the belief that she is a reliable sign of the values or underlying beliefs of her husband. Accordingly, she becomes a lightning rod for discontent with his administration or opposition to its stands on particular issues.

THE IMPOSSIBLE ROLE

First, a distinction. Presidential wives challenge the public and press differently than do women candidates for public office. Women candidates ask voters to revise the relationship between women and public power directly. By contrast, presidential wives raise the more problematic issue of the relationship between women, *sexuality*, and power. That is, spouses exert power by virtue of their sexual and marital relationship to the president; their influence is indirect and intimate, a subtle intrusion of the private into the public, political sphere. Accordingly, especially as changes in women's roles have affected that relationship, the press and the public consider and reconsider the relationship between presidential spouses in order to infer the extent and character of a form of influence exerted largely outside public scrutiny.

Anxieties about that relationship are rooted in the history of U.S. women. The U.S. presidency came into being at a time when conceptions of female roles were dominated by the cult of "true womanhood," which defined women as pious, pure, submissive, and domestic and relegated them entirely to the private sphere of the home and to the functions of wife, mother, and housekeeper.[6] The woman who attempted to transcend these limits was censured; domesticity and purity were interdependent. "Public" women, including public speakers and workers, lost their claim to purity and femininity.

Because of its public social dimensions, the demands of the role of presidential wife blurred these distinctions. Martha Dandridge Washington, the first presidential wife, found herself called upon to navigate subtle public-private boundaries. She was to keep the president's house and provide the emotional support of a wife, but she was also to welcome legislators and foreign diplomats and, on occasion, the public. Lady Washington, as she was known, undertook this role with advantages not available to her immediate successors. She had traveled with her husband and the troops during much of the Revolutionary War (one regiment was named Lady Washington's Dragoon). She was almost as widely known as her husband, regularly mentioned in newspapers, a rarity for any female of her time. As historian Carl Anthony notes, however, "it was not public adulation that presented uncertainty for her, but rather a public role." The difficulties she faced prompted a tart comment in a letter to niece Fanny Bassett Washington at Mount Vernon in which she said, "[C]ertain boundaries is [sic] set for me which I must not depart from . . . and as I cannot do as I like, I am obstinate, and stay at home a good deal." Even her style of entertaining drew comment; her rather formal levées were criticized as "awkward imitations of royalty" and, simultaneously, as not royal enough.[7]

Ambivalence about the First Ladyship is a product of the ambiguous combination of its public-private functions, which transcend woman's traditional sphere, and of beliefs about women that reach back to the very beginnings of Western civilization. Nietzsche, philosopher and classical scholar, echoed the views of the ancient Greeks: "Woman is indescribably more evil than man; also cleverer. . . . The fight for equal rights is actually a symptom of a disease. . . . Has my answer been heard to the question of how one cures a woman—'redeems' her? One gives her a child."[8] In effect, both the Greco-Roman and Judeo-Christian traditions, as mythologized in the stories of Pandora and of Eve's role in the Fall, suggest that woman's potential for evil can be contained only if she remains in the home in her traditional roles, but if she moves into the public-political realm, her evil potential can be realized. Apprehensions about the influence of any presidential wife on substantive matters reflect these fears.

As recent presidential wives have demonstrated, spouses inevitably influence substantive decisions. Nancy Davis Reagan affected scheduling, personnel, and policy decisions; Rosalynn Smith Carter was the president's emissary in South America, discussed issues with him at regular weekly lunches, and attended cabinet meetings in order to stay current on policy decisions. Even Bess Wallace Truman, who assiduously avoided the White House limelight, is now known to have had a part in virtually every decision made by her husband. Other wives also influenced policy. For example, Julia Gardiner Tyler lobbied for the annexation of Texas; Sarah Childress Polk was her husband's personal secretary and his primary confidante and adviser during the Mexican-American War; Ellen Axson Wilson supported a D.C. slum clearance bill, which was passed by Congress as a memorial to her. In fact, with the exception of wives who retired from all public activities because of grief or illness (e.g., Jane Appleton Pierce and Ida Saxton McKinley), a significant number of First Ladies perceived their roles as having a political dimension, ranging from Dolley Payne Madison's subtle lobbying of her husband's political opponents to Julia Dent Grant's issuance of press releases.[9]

As everyone agrees, the most significant enlargement of the First Ladyship in modern times was made by Eleanor Roosevelt, who traveled all over the nation as the eyes and ears of the president, lectured, had her own radio show, wrote columns for newspapers, and took stands on controversial issues, notably on civil rights. What is often forgotten is that prior to her husband's election as president, she had an independent career and was active politically.[10]

Reactions to Eleanor Roosevelt's activities highlight the problems such an enlargement creates. Until the Clinton presidency, it was widely agreed that "no other [First Lady] has been so much the center of controversy." Because of criticisms, Eleanor Roosevelt attempted to frame her activities as those of a traditional woman acting as a helpmate to her husband, and she repeatedly issued disclaimers. At one press conference she declared, "I never tried to influence the president on anything he ever did," and she wrote: "There is such a concerted effort being made to make it appear that

I dictate to FDR that I don't want people who should know the truth to have any misunderstanding about it. I wouldn't dream of doing more than passing along requests or suggestions that come to me."[11] In other words, given anxieties about her public role, she felt constrained to minimize her influence and to describe her activities in terms consistent with traditional notions of womanhood.

Wives of presidential candidates whose life histories diverge from traditional roles have experienced similar difficulties. Elizabeth Hanford Dole's experiences in past campaigns are illustrative. She was a federal trade commissioner (FTC) under presidents Nixon and Ford, head of the White House Office of Public Liaison, head of the White House Coordinating Council on Women, and secretary of transportation under President Reagan, and later secretary of labor under President Bush. She took a leave of absence from the FTC to campaign for her husband, the Republican vice presidential nominee in 1976, but still was criticized sharply by John Moss, Democrat from California, chair of the House subcommittee that oversees regulatory agencies, who alleged "a possible conflict of interest because she was in the position of directly or indirectly asking for votes and financial support from persons and corporations over whom she would later sit in judgment." She resigned from the FTC in 1979 when her husband announced his presidential candidacy. In 1987, she resigned as secretary of transportation to campaign for her husband in the Republican primaries. Ann Grimes comments:

> You could hardly find a more telling image of America's befuddlement over sex and work and marriage in the eighties—a candidate's wife spending perhaps a third of a precious personal campaign stop [in Concord, N.H.] arguing that she had a right to be there at all. . . . [S]he had to defend herself for quitting that high-echelon office and taking on the role of full-time spouse of a candidate. Ironically, once she stepped down from Cabinet member to supporting role, some found her less credible than her counterparts on the spouse circuit, whose put-aside careers were less prominent.

Her childlessness also was a "mild, but discernible undercurrent at some events." Finally, Dole supporter Lee Daniels, Illinois House minority leader, introduced her with words that proved especially damaging. He said: "We have an opportunity to elect a *team* president of the United States. We have an opportunity to select a *person* that is going to be as much a part of this government, a *strong* part, a strong *participant,* a strong *person* behind the president, who *believes* in her *husband.*" Grimes writes: "[The] specter of a team presidency clung to Liddy Dole like pesky lint. . . . wouldn't the First Lady role be too confining for a woman with Elizabeth's résumé and ambition? Would she want to give up 'her position, influence, prestige, and salary knowing if her husband wins she will be pushed permanently into second place?' one reporter asked."[12]

Hillary Rodham Clinton's difficulties began during the Democratic presidential primaries. Statements made by both Clintons during these campaigns, emphasizing their partnership, aroused fears. "In January Bill Clinton told a CNN interviewer that he might appoint her to a Cabinet post. . . . At fund-raisers, he used to quip, 'Buy one, get one free!'" When asked to define the role of First Lady, Hillary responded, "[She is a] partner who represents for all of us a view of who her husband is, as well as a symbol of women's concerns and interests at a particular time." These statements, highlighted in an article by Gail Sheehy, heightened fears that the Clintons might establish a kind of co-presidency. Patricia O'Brien, Michael Dukakis's press secretary during the 1988 campaign, comments that "she moved onto the national scene assuming her credentials were an asset. 'If you vote for him,' she proudly said of her husband, 'you get me.' That produced a tremor of national nervousness." Fears about the role she would play as First Lady were exacerbated during the Illinois primary campaign. During a debate Edmund G. (Jerry) Brown, Jr., charged that her law firm benefited unfairly from her marriage to the Arkansas governor. She responded with a widely quoted remark: "I suppose I could have stayed home and baked cookies and had teas." Her next line was not reported by most news outlets: "I chose to fulfill my profession, which I had before my husband was in public life." In an attempt to avoid misunderstanding, she later added: "The work that I have done as a professional, a public advocate, has been aimed . . . to assure that women can make the choices . . . whether it's full-time career, full-time motherhood, or some combination."[13] The line about staying home and baking cookies was widely publicized and aroused hostility among traditional women who saw it as a condemnation of their life choices.

Public anxieties about her role were reflected in polling data. In a *New York Times*-CBS poll in March, 31 percent rated Clinton's wife favorably, 17 percent unfavorably, with 50 percent undecided or not knowing enough to comment. In mid-April in a *U.S. News and World Report* poll, 38 percent said she helped, while 30 percent said she hurt her husband's chances for election. A news story said simply that "too many voters are uncomfortable with her forcefulness, her intelligence, and her quick tongue"; in August her favorable ratings were 33 percent.[14]

The Republican National Convention attempted to capitalize on the fears aroused during the primaries. In a prime-time speech, Marilyn Tucker Quayle, wife of the vice president, reaffirmed her own credentials as a True Woman while implicitly attacking Clinton's wife when she said of her generation that "not everyone believed that the family was so oppressive that women could only thrive apart from it." She added a statement that was frequently quoted: "They're [liberals] disappointed because most women do not wish to be liberated from their essential natures as women. Most of us love being mothers and wives." During the fall campaign she emphasized similar themes: "'Women are different than men: women are women,' she said [in an interview]. 'I find it outrageous that anyone would find that controversial.'"[15]

The attacks had an effect. Reportedly, even Democratic focus groups "tended to perceive Hillary Clinton as a conniving, manipulative spouse," and Mary Matalin, the Bush campaign's deputy director, reported that in their research, focus groups "have a sharper and more clear reaction to the spouses. Barbara is cookies and grandchildren. Hillary is too brassy and coldly ambitious. This leads to too much influence."[16]

A *USA Today*/CNN/Gallup poll immediately following the election on November 10–11 reported that 40 percent said Clinton's wife represents their values and life-styles more than past First Ladies, and 40 percent said she does not; 20 percent had no opinion; however, 25 percent of respondents were concerned that she might have too large a role in the new administration.[17]

Following the election, press aides to former presidential wives expressed their views of the constraints of the First Ladyship. Letitia Baldrige, press aide to Jacqueline Bouvier Kennedy, said: "She can't be perceived by . . . the public or the press as interfering. . . . You don't do it openly. . . . You do it behind the scenes." Merrie Spaeth, a special assistant to Ronald Reagan, said, "It isn't an up-front role." Some aides expressed reservations about a formal government position. "Bobby Kennedy didn't sleep with the president," Mrs. [Sheila] Tate [Nancy Davis Reagan's press secretary] said. "That special relationship resonates differently with the American people." Sheila Rabb Weidenfeld, Betty [Bloomer] Ford's press secretary, said, "[T]he White House is a very chauvinist place. There's no understanding of what to do with the First Lady. The people in the West Wing know there is pillow talk, and they resent it." She added: "When Rosalynn Carter sat in at a Cabinet meeting, there was a lot of criticism, and rightly so. It was the wrong symbolism. It made people wonder, 'Where's the heart? Where's the compassion?'" Sheila Tate commented, "They [the American people] want her to carve out her own niche without becoming power hungry" and described the conflicting expectations as "brutal."[18]

In 1987, David Broder tried to put anxiety about wifely influence in a larger political context when he wrote: "When marriages are partnerships of independent, able and co-equal people and one of them seeks the presidency, new issues are created for voters, for reporters and for both spouses. . . . [T]he Constitution did not envisage the presidency as a dual office, and it is not clear what standards or methods are appropriate for ensuring accountability in the unelected half of these modern marriages."[19] Although his comments seem plausible, we would do well to ask, what are these issues, and in what sense are they new? By law (5 USCS § 3110), since 1967, no member of the president's family may hold a position in or funded by the federal government. The law, sometimes called Lyndon Johnson's revenge on Bobby Kennedy, prevented Gerald Ford's son from working for the Park Service and forced Rosalynn Smith Carter to become the honorary chair of the president's Commission on Mental Health. Even in honorary, unpaid positions, members of the president's family may be called as witnesses in congressional hearings, as Carter's wife was. What issues are raised by these positions that are not raised by other spousal relationships? In particular, recall Nancy Davis Reagan's active role in removing Chief of Staff Donald Regan and in promoting the Reykjavik summit meeting with Gorbachev. Although a wife cannot be fired, only divorced, what prevents her from being removed from or forced out of an honorary, unpaid position?

Criticism of Hillary Rodham Clinton trumpets these fears, dramatically visualized in *Spy* magazine's post-election cover showing a superimposed photo of Hillary Rodham Clinton as an S-M dominatrix. Of special political significance is that husbands of politically active wives are perceived as weak, a point Richard Nixon made about the Clintons. In earlier periods presidential husbands with strong, active wives were seen as henpecked, e.g., James Polk.[20]

THE INSUPERABLE IDEAL

An astute observer commented: "A feminist political wife is a contradiction in terms. . . . It is like a subtle Joan Rivers. It doesn't exist in nature."[21]

The U.S. presidency combines the functions of chief executive and legislative leader with symbolic functions analogous to those of a monarch. As head of state, symbol of the nation, a figurehead who represents the country at home and abroad, the presidency is idealized, and its occupants and their families become models or culture types. They are Mr. and Mrs. America, an ideal First Family expected to represent cherished U.S. values. Writing about the 1988 campaign, Jane Reilly commented: "The politicians have an ideal woman in mind, and the symbol they are using for that idea is 'family.' The earthly manifestation of the idea are the wives." Speaking of First Ladies, Susan Riley asks, "Why does society insist on an archetypal wife, an Everywife, a figurehead with no political power but potent symbolic importance?"[22] Identifying the impact of such idealization, historian Lewis Gould explains:

> Being a First Lady . . . requires a woman to act, if she would succeed, as a mixture of queen, club woman, and starlet. Subject to unrelenting attention, expected to behave impeccably in every situation, and criticized from some quarter for substantive assertion, the wife of a president has all the perquisites of stardom and the rewards of fame. What she is denied is genuine importance as an individual. Celebrity is a trivializing process, and for First Ladies that is the central point of their position. They live on display. While their cage is gilded, their freedom remains severely limited.[23]

Visual images in magazine, newspaper, and campaign photographs illuminate the political significance of First Ladies as culture types. *New York Times* photography critic Charles Hagen quotes *Mythologies*, Roland Barthes's classic study of popular culture, as the basis for his analysis. Barthes wrote that photographs of candidates "offer to the voter his [*sic*] own likeness, but clarified, exalted, superbly elevated into a type." Hagen continues: "As a result, coverage of the candidates' families, whether photographic or on television, more often than not, is conservative and simplistic, both reflecting and reinforcing public attitudes. In the intricate game of images and reality that is at the heart of any campaign, everyone—candidates, editors and the public—tend to reach for the reassuringly familiar." Just how important and conservative campaign photographs are is suggested by Susan Riley, who reports that a "radical faction of the British Labor Party had a novel suggestion a few years ago. It proposed to ban the use of family photographs in campaign literature, on the grounds that such personal information is superfluous, has no political relevance, and creates a disadvantage for gays, divorced and single people, [or] anyone who doesn't fit the nuclear mold yet wants to run for public office. It was an idea of such revolutionary potential that it was immediately squashed by the Labor party hierarchy and denounced from every pulpit in the land."[24] Both the proposal and the reaction to it are revealing. The proposal accurately reflects the ideological role of campaign photographs, and the reaction identifies the profound commitment to patriarchy that such photos represent. The power of the ideal is elaborated by Deborah Tannen, who writes:

> In the typical family photograph, the candidate looks straight out at the camera, while his wife gazes up at him. This leads the viewer's eye to the candidate as the center of interest. In a well-publicized family photograph, [Geraldine] Ferraro was looking up at her husband, and he was looking straight out. It is an appealing photo, which shows her as a good woman, but makes him the inappropriate center of interest. . . . Had the family photograph shown Ferraro looking straight out, with her husband gazing adoringly at her, it would not have been an effective campaign photo, because she would have looked like a domineering wife with a namby-pamby for a husband.[25]

Historian Lewis Gould sums it up this way: "The nation is not altogether comfortable with the idea of autonomous, self-reliant women, and it is comforting to have a cultural symbol of femininity who fulfills the stereotypes of what women should be and do." Referring to reactions to Hillary Rodham Clinton at midterm, Anna Quindlen astutely commented, "Many Americans have underestimated how much of what they see in her is a complex reaction to the changes in the roles of women."[26]

The demand that presidential wives fit a traditional mold and represent an idealized U.S. womanhood has always existed, but merciless scrutiny of them by the press has not. Early presidential wives were rarely mentioned in newspapers, and only an occasional piece appeared in magazines; lack of coverage was a sign of respect. Surprisingly, some very unusual First Ladies were treated positively. Historian Betty Boyd Caroli writes, "The most outspoken and politically involved wife since Abigail [Smith] Adams, Sarah [Childress Polk] received a universally good press from both sides of the fence," although Charles Sellers, a prominent Polk scholar, summed up her role as "secretary, political counselor, nurse, and emotional resource" to her husband. Sarah Polk's tenure as First Lady coincided with the beginnings of the U.S. woman's rights movement at Seneca Falls, New York, in 1848, an event to which she was invited to lend her support but declined. Given the effects of the nascent feminist movement, the unusually powerful role she played, and her explicit rejection of traditional functions, the positive reaction to her is intriguing. (Responding to a comment that the wife of her husband's presidential opponent was a more skilled butter maker than she, she is reported to have said, "If I get to the White House, I expect to live on $25,000 a year, and I will neither keep house nor make butter.")[27] Possibly because it was then unthinkable that such power should have been held by a woman, her influence was disregarded.

Around the middle of the nineteenth century, with the advent of the penny press, the increase in women's literacy, which created a new audience, and the coming of the Civil War, journalism took a more personal turn, and the social activities of presidential wives received considerable attention, much to the detriment of Mary Todd Lincoln. Their intellectual pursuits or their substantive contributions to causes, however, were ignored.[28] The next major change occurred in 1933 when Eleanor Roosevelt became the first presidential wife to hold press conferences.

The contemporary treatment of First Ladies as celebrities began with Jacqueline Bouvier Kennedy, and she was the first presidential wife to have a press secretary. Television, tabloids, and movie magazines, recent additions to the U.S. communications industry, scrambled for details about the lives of the occupants of the White House, a process that continues. Cultural norms define what is newsworthy, that is, what is deviant, dramatic, and controversial. News norms heighten curiosity about any comment or activity by a presidential wife that might be construed as controversial or as a departure from traditional norms and values. Consider the coverage and criticism generated by reports that Rosalynn Smith Carter sat in on Cabinet meetings, a fact that prompted rumors that the "steel magnolia" was telling her husband what to do. Similarly, a journalistic tempest resulted when, following a schoolyard massacre with an AK-47, Barbara Pierce Bush was asked whether assault weapons should be prohibited and emphatically agreed. When her comment suggested the possibility that she and her husband differed on this issue, press secretary Marlin Fitzwater told the press corps that there was "no dispute" between the president and Mrs. Bush on banning AK-47s. Later a spokeswoman for the First Lady delivered the word: "Barbara Bush would henceforth have no comment on controversial political issues." News norms make it far more difficult for a presidential wife to modify or enlarge her role precisely because reporters seek juicy stories that attract viewers and readers by arousing controversy. News norms insured that Hillary Rodham Clinton's activities would be minutely examined for any possible deviation from traditional activities and that such deviations would receive extensive coverage and commentary.[29]

News norms also affect the kind of coverage the First Lady receives. Journalistic treatment of Hillary Rodham Clinton's comment, "I could have stayed home and baked cookies and had teas," is illustrative. It was taken out of context and made to seem an attack on homemakers when, in fact, it was a statement about her carefully avoiding conflicts of interest as an attorney who was the Arkansas governor's wife and about her refusal to shrink her activities to those of the governor's hostess. As Patricia O'Brien comments, "The rest of the quote negated what was provocative, and when the whole quotation makes the sound bite less interesting, it gets dropped."[30] The search for a juicy story leads reporters to create controversy where none exists.

As treatment of Eleanor Roosevelt and others reminds us, Clinton's wife is not the first to be attacked as unrepresentative of some aspect of the traditional ideal of U.S. womanhood. Criticism and praise have been apportioned according to current definitions of femininity. Whatever its meaning, presidential wives face insuperable obstacles arising out of expectations that they are to represent what we pretend is a single, universally accepted ideal for U.S. womanhood.

PRESIDENTIAL LIGHTNING RODS

In her 1936 study of presidential wives Mary Randolph complained that "everything she [the First Lady] says and does is taken as an indication, if not a reflection of the president's attitude toward his political future." In 1992, Charles Black, a senior Bush campaign aide, offered the modern version of that observation when he said that wives "help define the candidacies and the personal styles of their husbands. They are good character witnesses for their husbands." University of Toronto political scientist Heather MacIvor offers another reason for this focus: "Party lines and policies are so trivialized and so unclear that voters are left with a collection of personalities to judge. With all the hype and clutter, spouses can be one solid clue to a candidate's character."[31]

When Gennifer Flowers's charges surfaced during the New Hampshire primary, it was widely believed that only his wife could rescue Clinton's sagging fortunes, and their joint appearance on CBS's highly rated *60 Minutes* on Super Bowl Sunday was a turning point in that campaign. During the interview, however, Clinton's wife made a comment that aroused controversy. She said: "You know, I'm not sitting here—some little woman standing by my man like Tammy Wynette. I'm sitting here because I love him, and I respect him, and I honor what he's been through and what we've been through together. And you know, if that's not enough for people, then heck, don't vote for him."[32] Protests from Tammy Wynette, herself divorced, and country music fans followed, presumably because good (read: idealized) wives "stand by their man."

Accordingly, based on these events, the "suggestion in the Republican [campaign] strategy was that she represents the views Mr. Clinton secretly holds, too, but will not admit." The essentials of the attack were set forth by Daniel Wattenberg in the August *American Spectator* in an essay entitled "The Lady Macbeth of Little Rock." Using unidentified sources ("a Clinton insider," "a Clinton advisor," "a campaign source"), Wattenberg accused her of being a woman of "consuming ambition" and "inflexibility of purpose," guilty of "domination of a pliable husband," who has "an unsettling lack of tender human feeling, along with the affluent feminist's contempt for traditional female roles." He compared her unfavorably to Eva Perón—Evita at least "was worshipped by the 'shirtless ones'"—and to Winnie Mandela as well as to Lady Macbeth. He set about to show that a nice conservative girl (a 1964 Goldwater supporter) from the suburbs of Chicago underwent a "faculty mind-sweep" at Wellesley, quoting close college friend, E. D. Acheson, the granddaughter of (pinko?) Dean Acheson as evidence. Moreover, he used the "anti-corporate, anti-acquisitive rhetoric" of her 1969 commencement speech as a graduating Wellesley senior to condemn her as a hypocrite because she later served on corporate boards and "made out like a bandit" from the fees, according to an unidentified tax expert. That she spoke first in the courtship with Bill Clinton was evidence of her domination of her husband. She represented, not women or children, according to Wattenberg, but a "feminist elite of working mothers." Sexual deviance was implied as her feminist extremism was emphasized by a report that she and her husband took separate vacations, that she often took mother-daughter vacations with Arkansas native Mary Steenburgen, and that San Francisco was a favorite destination. Moreover, her birth name appeared on page one of her 1991 tax return.[33]

Obviously, Wattenberg's article was written to provide conservatives with ammunition for the upcoming presidential campaign. According to Robin Toner, however, at least "twenty articles in major publications this year involved some comparison between Mrs. Clinton and a grim role model for political wives: Lady Macbeth." She was also compared to the Glenn Close role in the movie *Fatal Attraction,* she was said to be "searching for a heart," and she was called a "feminazi," the "wicked witch of the East" (a reference to the *Wizard of Oz*) and a dragon lady (an epithet also applied to Madame Chiang Kai-Shek and Nancy Davis Reagan).[34]

In part, the attacks were an attempt to present Clinton as a wimp dominated by his wife; in part, they treated Hillary and her writings or statements as revelations about Clinton's values. Richard N. Bond, Republican National Committee chair, initiated the attack just before the convention when he "criticized Clinton for taking advice from his wife who would 'liken marriage and the family to slavery,'" a misconstrual of material in a law article she had written. Vice President Dan Quayle alluded to a speech she had given to the American Bar Association convention a few days earlier, to say that "she was evidence that 'the Clinton presidential campaign is clearly in the pocket of the American Bar Association leadership.'"[35]

At the Republican convention Patrick Buchanan denounced her as a champion of "radical feminism," and claimed that "Clinton and Clinton" would "impose a far-left agenda on the nation." Former presidential candidate Pat Robertson asserted that the Clintons "are talking about a radical plan to destroy the traditional family and transfer its functions to the federal government."[36]

The attacks did not stop with the election. The views of extremists give the clearest picture. According to Anna Quindlen, *Flashpoint,* the newsletter of the Living Truth Ministries in Austin, Texas, "identifies Mrs. Clinton as a 'doctrinaire Marxist' who has recruited 'other America-hating subversives for key administrative posts' and who communes with the spirit of Eleanor Roosevelt." Similarly, Lt. Col. James (Bo) Gritz, a Vietnam-era Green Beret and onetime Populist Party candidate for president, is building a community based on fear and hatred of the federal government called Almost Heaven, in Clearwater Valley, Idaho. He "singles out Hillary Rodham Clinton as the font of all Big Government plans to control people's lives. . . . [and] castigates 'homos and feminists.'" Several protest demonstrations have been equally extremist. Tobacco farmers burned the president's wife in effigy. At a health care rally in Seattle demonstrators carried banners that read "Heil Hillary" and howled "Stop the Bitch." At a clinic in Arkansas protestors carried posters depicting Hillary Rodham Clinton with the label "Abortion Queen," although she holds quite conservative views on that issue. A letter to the editor reported attendance at a lecture during the health care debates at which the lecturer projected a slide depicting the First Lady superimposed on a Playboy bunny, and asked, "Do you trust this woman with health care reform?"[37]

If a 1995 *Frontline* report on the Clinton presidency was accurate, from the beginning of his political career, Bill Clinton has aroused intense reactions, provoking significant parts of his constituencies to dislike him.[38] Admittedly, the attacks on the president also have been intense, but my judgment is that the attacks on his wife have been and continue to be even more extreme. In fact, at first glance they seem irrational and wholly inappropriate.

By now, however, some of the reasons for the displacement of opposition to the president, to his policies, and to government generally onto the First Lady should be clear. Violating the norms limiting the activities of "true women," Hillary Rodham Clinton has continued to function as her husband's partner, including having an office in the West Wing of the White House. Indeed, she has muddled the public-private dimensions of her position by extending her public social role into policy-related political activities, flaunting her competence and her right to take stands on controversial issues related to health care reform. In spite of this, she is loved and respected by her husband, whose affection and respect clearly demonstrate that he is a wimp who is dominated by her. Obviously, then, she is the true author of all of the controversial policies of the Clinton administration and, because she espouses liberal positions, she (and other women like her?) can be held responsible for many of the federal policies that her critics despise (affirmative action, environmental regulations, and the like).

That she merits harsh criticism is evidenced by her involvement in political matters, which proves that she is impure and evil. Not only does she violate the traditional ideal of U.S. womanhood, but she also symbolizes an entirely different ideal—a feminist ideal—that celebrates the diversity of women's talents and life choices. Because she symbolizes the synthetic rather than the simplistic character of women's roles, no public representation of her will be perceived as satisfactory. If she appears in *Vogue* magazine (December, 1993) posed elegantly in a simple black dress, she will be attacked: "Her photo spread in *Vogue* bludgeoned the fledgling identities of girls who were beginning to believe that maybe it wasn't all-important that they be sex objects." Alternatively, when she poses for the cover of the *New York Times Magazine* in a white suit, the accompanying story entitled "Saint Hillary" impugned her religious concerns as overly zealous and suggested that what she talked about as the "politics of meaning" was vague and impractical. With over ten different hairdos at last count,[39] the First Lady can hardly be said to project a unified image, much less an ideal, of U.S. womanhood.

Hillary Rodham Clinton is only the most recent U.S. example of the problem she epitomizes. (Maureen McTeer, the frankly feminist wife of former Canadian Prime Minister Joe Clark, is another nearby example.) The studies of presidential wives by Carl Anthony and Betty Boyd Caroli demonstrate that many of her predecessors were politically active and that most were attacked for some violation of an invisible boundary circumscribing woman's sphere. Ironically, although she, like her immediate predecessors, has dedicated her life to the service of her husband and his career,[40] neither the press nor the public seem to find that an acceptable motive for her actions. But make no mistake about it, the treatment of this First Lady is not an aberration; her problems are merely those of all First Ladies writ large.

PART 3
Critique and Commentary

CHAPTER 10

Presidential Rhetoric:

WHAT DIFFERENCE DOES IT MAKE?
George C. Edwards III

The literature on political rhetoric is burgeoning. Interest in the field can be seen in the new book series begun by several publishers, the interdisciplinary outpouring of research, and the establishment of a program in presidential rhetoric at Texas A&M University.

Students of political rhetoric have many objectives. Some examine rhetoric for what it reveals about speakers' goals, while others focus on speakers' strategies in manipulating symbols to achieve those goals. Yet others view rhetoric as a window to the ideas, thought processes, and psychological make-up of speakers. Some scholars are interested in investigating the ethical choices involved in speech.

All of these topics are worthy of investigation. Underlying most of the work on political rhetoric, however, is the premise that rhetoric matters—not just to the speaker, but, most importantly, to the audience.

Although students of political rhetoric might contend that they are not concerned primarily with the impact of rhetoric on listeners, the assumption of the influence of rhetoric is pervasive in the literature and central to the justification of rhetoric as a field of study. Would anyone in the field of political rhetoric be content arguing that rhetoric is worth analyzing even though it has little or no impact on the audiences at which it is ostensibly aimed? Why would we care about questions such as strategies or ethical choices if the strategies and choices had no impact on the audience? In addition, can we justify a field of study on the basis of employing rhetorical analysis to understand the inner workings of a personality when the scholars who do so are lacking in credentials for engaging in psychological analysis?

Since the premise of the influence of rhetoric on the audience is so central to the field, it is important that it be properly justified through rigorous analysis. Unsupported assumptions can be dangerous. They may be in need of refinement to properly explain the influence of rhetoric. If they are seriously in error, they may direct scholars into unproductive lines of inquiry. If assumptions are discovered to be completely without justification, the legitimacy of a research enterprise may be undermined.

Thus, it is important that we understand the logical structure of inferences regarding the impact of rhetoric and whether these inferences are justified.

THE ASSUMPTION OF THE IMPACT
OF RHETORIC IN THE LITERATURE

How do scholars of presidential rhetoric arrive at their inferences regarding its impact? What evidence do they offer on their behalf? To obtain answers to these questions, we need to examine literature on presidential rhetoric. This is not the place for a full literature review, so I have selected seven books by leading members of the presidential rhetoric research community.

The authors represent both the communication and political science disciplines and have focused on a range of presidents and historical eras. These works do not necessarily compose a representative sample of the literature on presidential rhetoric, but they are representative of the best work being done in the field and provide a valuable sense of the treatment of the question of the impact of rhetoric.

Zarefsky

David Zarefsky's primary emphasis in his exemplary study of the Lincoln-Douglas debates is on the reconstruction and assessment of appeals—"the rhetorical dynamics within the text"—and he includes in this emphasis studying "the ability of particular argument patterns to reflect or modify the pre–Civil War political culture."[1]

In general, the author is careful not to make assertions about the impact of the debaters' rhetoric, but there are exceptions. In the chapter on conspiracy arguments, he concludes that conspiracy arguments were taken seriously by audiences, that Lincoln's charges against Douglas that he was plotting to spread slavery everywhere were "effective," and that Douglas's charge that Lincoln was part of an abolitionist plot to abolitionize both parties was his "strongest and most successful in the campaign."[2] No evidence is offered for the first and last of these conclusions, and a letter from a Lincoln supporter comprises the evidence for Lincoln's success.

Zarefsky also argues that Lincoln was effective in undercutting Douglas's national appeal by demonstrating that it rested on ambiguous statements that North and South could interpret differently, that the speakers' use of historical analysis "exerted force and influence" on the public platform, that the moral arguments of Lincoln may not have been effective, that conspiracy arguments sensitized listeners to the fact that differences between the candidates mattered and made their later arguments more credible, and that Douglas won because he convinced Illinois voters that Lincoln was a radical.[3] Evidence on behalf of each of these assertions is lacking, however.

At the same time, the author argues that "there is little reason to believe the debates changed many votes," and that they did not have much effect on the political landscape. The *American Almanac,* a reference work of the time, did not include the debates among the two hundred most important events of 1858. He also points out that there is serious question that the audience followed the arguments closely—or that it could even hear them—and that fatigue was likely to have taken a toll on listeners' attention.[4]

So which is true? Did some of the arguments of Lincoln and Douglas influence voters, or did they simply serve to reinforce the public's predispositions before the debate? We do not know.

In the end, it is important to show that the debates had important consequences. Thus, the author argues that they demonstrated the possibilities for discussion of fundamental issues. They transformed the audience into a *public* [italics in original], a community in which common interests can be discovered and given form through discourse. "Public argument revitalizes a political community by coaching public judgment."[5] Once again, no evidence is offered that any of this actually happened.

Tulis

In *The Rhetorical Presidency* Jeffrey Tulis places presidential rhetoric within the larger context of changing conceptions of the political order in an admirable and successful effort to integrate the history of ideas with the study of political institutions. He views presidential rhetoric as both a reflection and an elaboration of underlying theories of governance.

Most of the work is a careful description of the changing nature of presidential public rhetoric as it moved from a focus on popular instruction of constitutional principle and the articulation of the general tenor and direction of presidential policy to the advocacy of particular policy proposals.

Tulis is a close student of the rhetorical presidency, but he is not enamored with it. In chapter 6 he employs short, provocative case studies of Woodrow Wilson's campaign for the League of Nations and Lyndon Johnson's efforts to obtain the passage of his War on Poverty. His goals are to examine the limits to both what presidents can accomplish through popular leadership and the system's ability to function under the auspices of a theory of popular leadership.

He recognizes that there may be limits to what even the most skillful presidents can accomplish through rhetoric. He argues that "Woodrow Wilson's campaign to found a League of Nations failed because he was compelled to speak in contradictory ways to different sorts of audiences." Yet the author clearly believes that presidential rhetoric can exert a powerful political influence. "The rhetorical presidency makes change . . . more possible." It was Ronald Reagan's rhetorical skill that got SDI established, tax reform passed, and the budget cut. He concludes that "rhetorical power is a very special case of executive power because simultaneously it is the means by which an executive can defend the use of force and other executive powers and it is a power itself."[6]

Why should we have confidence in such conclusions? Not because the author offers systematic evidence for them. There is none. In chapter 4 he indicates that many forces affected the passage of the Hepburn Act, but he concludes that Theodore Roosevelt successfully appealed over the heads of Congress to the people.[7] How do we know that Roosevelt's appeals obtained public support for his legislation? We do not. Roosevelt's rhetoric may have been quite effective, but in the absence of evidence or any potential to falsify the proposition, we have no reason to accept such a conclusion.

The author is also fearful that the power of the rhetorical presidency has deleterious effects on the U.S. polity. Lyndon Johnson's campaign on behalf of his War on Poverty is his archetypical example of the use of rhetoric not only to obtain passage of legislation but to subvert the deliberative process as well.[8] Once again, the point is well worth considering, but before we condemn rhetoric (and its power for mischief), would it not be reasonable to establish its impact more clearly? It is not enough to simply assert an influence for LBJ's public relations efforts, especially in the face of his long record of failure to arouse the public in support of his policies.

Hart

Roderick Hart picks up where Tulis leaves off. His concern is the nearly ten thousand instances of presidential speech between the day Harry Truman took office and the end of 1985. Hart's data base is impressive and represents an immense research effort, and the author exploits his data in a wide variety of ways.

Hart clearly believes that speech is a powerful tool of presidential leadership. One of his key conclusions is that "public speech no longer attends the processes of governance—it *is* [italics in original] governance." In chapter 3, entitled "Speech and Power," the author argues that the "remarks of presidents exert influence not found in the speeches of others," and that "[t]he speech of presidents is more powerful than most." Presidential speeches give them personal influence, help them maintain political relationships, and help focus the public's attention.[9]

In the concluding chapter, the author joins Tulis in a negative appraisal of the rhetorical presidency. He finds that, among other consequences, the emphasis on public speech makes presidents too powerful. Congress is increasingly docile to the president, perhaps because members know how powerful a rhetorically skilled president can be. Presidents, he says, have used rhetoric to move legislation forward, prolong war, build personal reputations, alter party fortunes, and influence the public.[10]

Yet he is able to offer no systematic evidence that rhetoric is related to public support. And it is difficult to imagine how anyone can conclude, for example, that Congress is docile or that presidents have been able to prolong war through their rhetoric. It certainly did not help Lyndon Johnson in Vietnam, and George Bush felt a hostage to public opinion as he hurried the end of the Gulf War despite reaching astronomical heights in the polls.

At one point Hart argues that a speech President Nixon gave in China in which he spoke of his daughter in hopes of encouraging China to dismantle nuclear weaponry "became unusually powerful social action" in terms of the president's prestige and our relationship with China.[11] The fact that China did not dismantle any nuclear weapons seems not to matter, nor does the complete absence of evidence that Nixon's rhetoric affected either his prestige or U.S.–Sino relations.

Often the author makes a strong assertion, unencumbered with qualifications, about how presidents think, but he fails to support it with evidence. For example, he writes that "presidents use speech to convince themselves and others that they are not impotent." The next sentence reads: "One anecdote should suffice to make this latter point." When he examines the rhetorical efforts of Presidents Johnson and Nixon, he concludes that although it is unclear that speech gave them power, at least they acted as if it did. How do we know this? The author turns psychologist and explains, without the benefit of proof, that they relied on speeches "to establish their authority over their opponents and . . . it made them feel safe from their opponents and better about themselves."[12]

Clearly, Hart wants his readers to believe that rhetoric is an important element of presidential power and plays a significant role in their personal psychologies. He may be correct. Yet he provides us with little reason to have confidence in his inferences.

Medhurst

Martin Medhurst has carefully studied the rhetoric of Dwight D. Eisenhower. He concludes that "many of Eisenhower's accomplishments can be traced to his ability to inspire, in the American people, faith and confidence in their president." Eisenhower, Medhurst shows us, employed rhetoric "as a strategic weapon of policy making" to influence the actions of others. Moreover, we learn that Eisenhower drew repeatedly on the persuasiveness of his image and the reservoir of respect and goodwill for him during his presidential years. Indeed, the author tells us that Ike had a "charismatic hold on the public."[13]

Given the importance of rhetoric to Eisenhower and the assertions about its value as a persuasive tool, we might expect to gain an understanding of the extent and circumstances of its influence. Instead, we find a masterful analysis of Eisenhower's rhetoric and rhetorical techniques. We do not, however, learn how they advanced the president's goals.

Aside from arguing that Ike "scored a stunning rhetorical victory" over Stevenson in 1956 as a result of his rhetoric and citing a decline in support for cessation of nuclear testing, little connection is made between rhetoric and successful persuasion. Indeed, we learn that public challenges (a rhetorical technique) were ineffective. In the 1958 midterm elections, "Try as he might, Eisenhower could not dispel the sense of vulnerability, fear, and dissatisfaction that characterized the national mood." His efforts to deal with Sputnik and the alleged missile gap were ineffective. Although the president repeated many of the themes from 1954 and 1956, the circumstances were different. Nor was he successful in moving the public to support Richard Nixon for president in 1960.[14]

Thus, we are left in a quandary. We have learned a great deal about Eisenhower's rhetoric, and we have some impressive assertions about its importance in public policy making. Yet we do not have evidence to support those assertions, and we have some evidence that Eisenhower frequently failed to persuade his audiences to support his views.

Windt

Theodore Windt is a firm believer that "discourse is a source of power for presidents." He points out that presidents can make some issues more salient than others and have the option of "going public" to marshal support for their policies. "In national affairs presidents establish the terms of discourse." He even goes so far as to say that presidents can define something as a crisis and "presidents can depend on tremendous public support for whatever policy they pursue in situations they deem 'critical'."[15] In other words, they define incidents or issues as a crisis and obtain support for their response.

Later in his book Windt gives us some examples of the power of presidential rhetoric. He tells us that President Kennedy's speech on the Berlin crisis "was so frightening that it produced a climate of fear and foreboding among Americans. One cannot stress too greatly that it was the rhetoric—not specific acts—that created the effect." Thus the speech created "political reality." In addition, he argues that Kennedy's rhetorical efforts to change the assumptions about policy differences on issues between the U.S. and the Soviet Union ushered in the era of détente, and that his June 11, 1963, speech on civil rights "aroused a nation."[16]

In none of these cases, however, does the author provide any evidence whatsoever of a changed public opinion, nor does he trace any such change to the president's rhetoric. His inferences may be correct, but in the absence of credible evidence or consideration of alternative explanations, they are difficult to accept. Moreover, we know, for example, that in many crises, public support for the president does not go up at all,[17] and, as we will see, the public frequently fails to follow the president's lead.

Smith and Smith

Craig and Kathy Smith are quite explicit regarding their orientation toward presidential rhetoric: "We regard public persuasion as a crucial dimension of presidential leadership . . . we want to explore the significance of what presidents say and how they say it."[18] There is no question that readers of Smith and Smith's *The White House Speaks* will learn much about what presidents say and what strategic challenges they face as they choose their rhetorical approaches to issues and events.

Showing the significance of what presidents say and how they say it is something else, however. Typically, the authors describe what was said and then attribute significance to it—without benefit of systematic evidence or consideration of alternative explanations for a presidential success or failure. In chapter 3 they contrast President Ford's speeches on his pardon of Richard Nixon and his plan for amnesty for draft evaders. The premise of the entire discussion is that the president's rhetoric affected the public's response and could have altered the acceptance of the controversial pardon. Yet no evidence at all is provided to support the underlying argument.

In their analysis of the battle over the ratification of the Panama Canal Treaty, the authors tell us what opponents and President Carter said about the treaty. But what are we to make of the rhetoric? They repeatedly imply that the rhetoric they have been describing is important (why else describe it?), but they never explicitly deal with the issue. In the conclusion, they assert that it was the treaty fight that enabled the New Right to win control of the Republican rhetorical agenda,[19] a sweeping generalization that requires, one would think, at least some supporting argument. But there is none.

The authors make all sorts of claims on behalf of presidents and their "political jeremiads." They assert that "jeremiadic logic enabled Ronald Reagan simultaneously to establish the centrality of his personal presidency and to cut back the federal government." Yet they provide no evidence that the president's logic had this consequence, and we know that he was not able to cut back the federal government. Regarding Jimmy Carter's famous "crisis of confidence" speech, they argue that his lack of support "can be traced to mishandled elements" of his speech. Perhaps, but they do no tracing to support their case. In their discussion of John F. Kennedy's 1963 speech on civil rights, the authors tell us what he said, implying that it was important, but then drop the subject entirely.[20]

Sometimes the authors' assertions, implicit or explicit, are clearly wrong. For example, they argue that the "rhetorical form of a presidential address has political consequences." As an example, they assert that Ronald Reagan's "addresses unified most Americans" with his storytelling. They offer no evidence for such an assertion, and it certainly flies in the face of what we know of Ronald Reagan's public support. On the average, he was approved by just 52 percent of the public and was the most polarizing of presidents in the past four decades.[21] His public support will be discussed in more detail later in this chapter. The point here is that *assuming* consequences of rhetoric risks making substantial errors.

Campbell and Jamieson
Karlyn Kohrs Campbell and Kathleen Hall Jamieson reveal their view of the power of rhetoric in the title of their book, *Deeds Done in Words*. They argue that "presidential rhetoric is one source of institutional power, enhanced in the modern presidency by the ability of presidents to speak when, where, and on whatever topic they choose, and to a national audience through coverage by the electronic media."[22]

To their credit, the authors address the issue of providing evidence on behalf of their assertions about the importance of rhetoric in general and its impact in specific instances. They argue that "in most instances" they have documented their judgments of presidential speeches with outside evidence, but they also point out that "it is extremely difficult to link rhetorical acts and effects causally."[23]

Having made this point, they state that "external measures of effects are an inadequate basis for evaluation." Instead, they propose to evaluate a speech on how well it is adapted to achieve its ends and identify outstanding examples of a type of message. Just how they will know when a speech has actually achieved its ends in the absence of these external measures, much less what constitutes an outstanding example of such a speech, remains a mystery. Equally perplexing is how the authors determine how rhetoric serves the institutional ends of the presidency.[24]

What is especially striking in what follows is the *lack* of documentation of any kind on behalf of their assertions regarding the effects of presidential rhetoric. It is difficult to imagine the standards of evidence they are employing, since they never discuss standards and their footnotes are essentially barren of evidence. (I encourage readers to examine them.) The only place in which they actually refer to evidence in the text is Gerald Ford's speech on his pardon of Richard Nixon. There they cite a statement from Ford's memoirs that he did not succeed in healing wounds, and they make a reference to reporters questions to the president asserting that voters displayed their displeasure with the timing of the pardon in the November, 1974, elections.[25] Given all the public opinion data easily available on the issue of the pardon and all the rigorous studies of the 1974 elections, one might think the authors would choose to look at systematic evidence. But they do not.

There are myriad other assertions about the power of rhetoric. Inaugural addresses unify the audience by reconstituting its members, and Lincoln's first inaugural address created "a respect for thoughtful deliberation by the citizenry." State of the Union messages create a national unity, sustain the presidency, tie together the past, present, and future for the public, reassure the public, adjust Congress and the public to new circumstances, and in general are "an important weapon" in the struggle for power, a "great persuasive force," and "the greatest opportunity to exercise legislative leadership." The authors continue, "When presidents fulfill ceremonial functions, they define and refine the national ethos and the nation's values, and they instruct the citizenry and Congress in their roles as members of the polity and, in so doing, weave the fabric of a shared national heritage and identity."[26]

Presidential war rhetoric "constitutes the audience as a united community of patriots" and enlarges the president's freedom of action. (It is so powerful that it poses a continuing threat to the nation's democratic principles.) Ronald Reagan's speech in response to the Tower report was "effective." And rhetoric to forestall impeachment can define the terms of the debate.[27]

How do we know these things? Unfortunately, the authors do not present findings or carefully structured, compelling arguments based on systematic evidence. Instead, they make assertions. There is no consideration of alternative explanations for the 1974 election results (such as disgust over Watergate) or for any other consequence they discuss. Apparently, we are to accept their conclusions as articles of faith.

In each of these books, then, the authors explicitly or implicitly operate on the premise that the president *can* employ rhetoric to lead the public. He may not do a good job of it and fail to move opinion, but the potential is there. At the same time, the authors often fail to provide evidence to support either their broad premise or its application in specific instances. Given the centrality of the premise of the power of rhetoric to the field of rhetorical studies, it is appropriate to inquire whether such an assumption is justified.

THE LIMITS OF RHETORIC

The topic of the rhetorical persuasiveness of presidents is an enormous one, and space is limited in one chapter. Thus, it is necessary to narrow the scope of our inquiry, and I have chosen to focus on Ronald Reagan to investigate whether a broad assumption of rhetorical influence is warranted.

Reagan is a best-test case for the premise of rhetorical influence. In contrast to Reagan's two immediate predecessors, the public viewed him as a strong leader. He overwhelmingly won a second term in office and became the only president in the past third of a century to win and complete two terms. This seeming love affair with the public generated commentary in both academia and the media about the persuasiveness of the Great Communicator. If we cannot find evidence of the impact of the rhetoric of Ronald Reagan, then we have reason to reconsider the broad assumptions regarding the consequences of rhetoric. More importantly, we may need to reevaluate the methodology of research on presidential rhetoric and the questions we ask regarding it.

Perhaps the most important potential consequence of political rhetoric is moving the public—changing opinions, mobilizing citizens into action, and placing new issues on the public's agenda. In his farewell address on January 11, 1989, Ronald Reagan reflected on his tenure in office: "They called it the Reagan Revolution, and I'll accept that, but for me it always seemed more like the Great Rediscovery: a rediscovery of our values and our common sense." As Haynes Johnson put it, "In believing in him they were reaffirming a belief in their nation and in themselves."[28] The question for us is whether Ronald Reagan moved the public to support his clearly identifiable political views. Or was he the agent around which already existing conservative thought coalesced?

In an earlier work, I have outlined two contrasting views of presidential leadership. In the first the president is the director of change, establishing goals and leading others where they otherwise would not go. A second perspective is less heroic. Here the president is primarily a facilitator of change, reflecting and perhaps intensifying widely held views and exploiting opportunities to help others go where they want to go anyway.[29]

The director creates a constituency to follow his lead, whereas the facilitator endows his constituency's views with shape and purpose by interpreting them and translating them into legislation. The director restructures the contours of the political landscape to pave the way for change, whereas the facilitator exploits opportunities presented by a favorable configuration of political forces.

Reagan's Coming to Power

The evidence suggests that Ronald Reagan, like presidents before him, was a facilitator rather than a director. The basic themes Reagan espoused in 1980 were ones he had been articulating for many years: government was too big; the nation's defenses were too weak, leaving it vulnerable to intimidation by the Soviet Union; pride in country was an end in itself; and public morals had slipped too far. In 1976 conditions were not yet ripe for his message. It took the Carter years, with their gas lines, raging inflation, high interest rates, Soviet aggression in Afghanistan, and hostages in Iran, to create the opportunity for victory. By 1980 the country was ready to listen.

Martin Anderson, Reagan's first chief domestic policy advisor, agrees: "What has been called the Reagan revolution is not completely, or even mostly, due to Ronald Reagan. He was an extremely important contributor to the intellectual and political movement that swept him to the presidency in 1980. He gave that movement focus and leadership. But Reagan did not give it life." Anderson goes on to argue: "Neither Goldwater nor Nixon nor Reagan caused or created the revolutionary movement that often carries their name, especially Reagan's. It was the other way around. They were part of the movement, they contributed mightily to the movement, but the movement gave them political life, not the reverse." As journalist Haynes Johnson put it, Reagan "was the vehicle around which conservative forces could and did rally, the magnet that attracted a coterie of conservative journalists and writers and ambitious young economic theorists who proclaimed sacred dogma and argued theoretically pure positions."[30]

William Niskanen, one of the members of Reagan's Council of Economic Advisers, concurs, writing that several developments in the generation prior to Reagan's election set the stage for substantial change in economic policy. As he saw it:

> lower economic growth, rising inflation, and increasing tax rates led to a popular demand for some change in economic policy. . . . reduced popular confidence in the government increased the appeal of policy changes that would reduce the role of government in the American economy. Several complementary changes in the perspectives of economists and an increasing number of empirical studies shaped the choice of policies to meet these concerns. [Thus,] there was broad bipartisan agreement in Congress by the late 1970s for the direction of change in each of the major dimensions of federal economic policy.[31]

Therefore, "the institutions, procedures, and people were in place to support the monetary objectives of the new administration" (increased attention to the money supply rather than money growth).

> All that was missing was a president who could shape a coherent economic program and articulate the rationale for this program to Congress, the press, and the American public. For most voters Ronald Reagan was the logical candidate and the logical president for the time. For over fifteen years he had articulated a quite consistent set of views that appealed to an increasing share of the electorate. . . . There are few periods in American history for which a president so closely matched the current demands on this role. Few presidents have had a greater opportunity to guide and shape federal economic policy.[32]

More systematic data support the view that Reagan had a receptive audience. Stimson concluded that "movements uniformly precede the popular eras." The conservative winds of the 1980s were "fully in place *before* the election of Ronald Reagan." He was the beneficiary of a conservative mood, but he did not create it. Similarly, Page and Shapiro found that the Right turn on social welfare policy took place *before* Reagan took office and ended shortly thereafter. Davis also found that pro-defense and antiwelfare conservative trends had occurred by the late 1970s, before Reagan's nomination. Mayer produced similar findings, while Smith found that liberalism had reached a plateau by the mid-1970s.[33]

There is another aspect of Reagan's coming to power that is of direct interest to us. Although he was the preferred candidate of the American people in 1980 and 1984, Reagan was also the least popular candidate to win the presidency in the 1952–88 period. His supporters displayed an unusual degree of doubt about him, and he was disliked with unprecedented intensity by those who opposed him.[34]

Reagan Governing

Thus, Reagan arrived at the White House on the crest of a preexisting tide of conservatism that he helped to articulate but not to create. What happened after he took office? Was he able to use the bully pulpit to move the public to support his policies if it was not already inclined to do so?

Reagan knew better. In his memoirs he reflects on his efforts to ignite concern among the American people regarding the threat of communism in Central America and mobilize them behind his program of support for the Contras.

> For eight years the press called me the Great Communicator. Well, one of my greatest frustrations during those eight years was my inability to communicate to the American people and to Congress the seriousness of the threat we faced in Central America. . . .
>
> . . . Time and again, I would speak on television, to a joint session of Congress, or to other audiences about the problems in Central America, and I would hope that the outcome would be an outpouring of support from Americans who would apply the same kind of heat on Congress that helped pass the economic recovery package.
>
> But the polls usually found that large numbers of Americans cared little or not at all about what happened in Central America—in fact, a surprisingly large proportion didn't even know where Nicaragua and El Salvador were located—and, among those who did care, too few cared enough about a communist penetration of the Americas to apply the kind of pressure I needed on Congress.[35]

Numerous national surveys of public opinion have found that support for regulatory programs and spending on health care, welfare, urban problems, education, environmental protection, and aid to minorities increased rather than decreased during Reagan's tenure. But support for increased defense expenditures was decidedly lower at the end of his administration than when he took office.[36] (This change may have been the result of the military buildup that did occur; the point remains, however, that Reagan wanted to continue to increase defense spending, but the public was unresponsive to his wishes.)

In the realm of foreign policy, the president, as we have seen, was frustrated in his goal of obtaining public support for aid to the Contras in Nicaragua. But the problem for Reagan was broader than this. Whether the issue was military spending, arms control, military aid, and arms sales, or cooperation with the Soviet Union, public opinion by the early 1980s had turned to the Left—*ahead* of Reagan.[37]

Finally, Americans did not move their general ideological preferences to the Right. Indeed, rather than conservative support swelling once Reagan was in the White House, there was a movement *away* from conservative views almost as soon as he took office. According to Mayer, "Whatever Ronald Reagan's skills as a communicator, one ability he clearly did not possess was the capacity to induce lasting changes in American policy preferences."[38]

Thus, Ronald Reagan was less a public relations phenomenon than the conventional wisdom indicates. He had the good fortune to take office on the crest of a compatible wave of public opinion, and he effectively exploited the opportunity the voters had handed him. Yet when it came time to change public opinion or mobilize it on his behalf, he typically met with failure. As press secretary Marlin Fitzwater put it, "Reagan would go out on the stump, draw huge throngs, and convert no one at all."[39]

Comparing Reagan with Margaret Thatcher

We can increase our confidence in the validity of these findings if we can find evidence regarding a similar leader in a similar era. Fortunately, we can examine the impact of Margaret Thatcher on public opinion in Britain. We have another strong conservative leader holding office at about the same time as Reagan.

The results are much the same. In a series of studies, Ivor Crewe has analyzed the support for Thatcherite values, policy beliefs, and leadership style, using opinion polls by MORI, Gallup, and the British Election Surveys (1970–83). He concluded that with the exception of privatization, there was no evidence that Prime Minister Thatcher converted the electorate on the central values of strong government, discipline, and free enterprise during her first term. In addition, there was no increase in the Conservative vote, partisanship, or party members in the 1980s. Similar findings are reported in studies by John Rentoul and John Curtice.[40]

RESEARCHING THE IMPACT OF RHETORIC

It seems clear that we cannot assume rhetoric, even in the hands of the most skilled rhetorician, directly influences public opinion. However, *I am not arguing that presidential rhetoric has no influence on public opinion or public policy.* I am arguing that we do not know nearly enough about the impact of rhetoric, and we should not assume its importance. We need better questions and better evidence.

Questions

As Tulis and Zarefsky, among others, have pointed out, the impact of rhetoric may be in realms other than that of the general public.[41] The real influence of rhetoric may be on elite debate, journalistic coverage, and congressional deliberation. It might be that to the extent presidents lead public opinion, it is more often by articulation of widely held views and pointing out their application to some policy area, than by educating the public about causal connections related to policy. All of these questions are important and well worth investigating.

For example, presidents are continually engaged in an effort to structure the choices regarding issues before Congress. If they succeed in framing issues in ways that favor their programs, presidents set the terms of the debate on their proposals and, thus, the premises on which members of Congress cast their votes. Often, however, they fail.[42]

Once again, we cannot *assume* that rhetoric has an impact. We cannot simply assert that even though we cannot find an impact of rhetoric on aggregate public opinion, it has one in other arenas. This is a hypothesis, not a finding in which we can have confidence.

Before we can discuss the impact of rhetoric in a meaningful way, we require answers to questions such as the following:

Under what social, economic, and international conditions is presidential rhetoric most likely to affect opinion?

What is the relative impact of rhetoric on elites and the general public?

Which types of persons are most likely to be affected by presidential rhetoric?

On what issues are presidents most likely to be influential?

For how long will any presidential influence on public opinion hold?

How does the nature of the opposition affect the influence of presidential rhetoric?

To what extent and under what conditions does public rhetoric structure elite decisions?

If presidents can influence public opinion, are they only able to reinforce opinion or can they change it?

Are presidents able to mobilize citizens to political action?

Evidence

It is difficult to determine the impact of any social action, especially if it occurred as long ago as, say, the Lincoln-Douglas debates. Nevertheless, without an effort to present evidence to support inferences of the influence of rhetoric and an estimate of the certainty of our inferences (based on the evidence), we can have little confidence that the claims made for the impact or importance of rhetoric have validity.

What would evidence look like? One might start with public opinion data. Researchers certainly do not have to stick to the aggregate level of the nation, however. Poll data can be disaggregated easily to investigate the nature of the effects of rhetoric on different types of persons listening under different circumstances. Polls can also inform us about the political activity of citizens.

Like any data, poll data must be handled skillfully. It makes little sense, however, to make inferences about mass public opinion or some segment within it and then ignore the best evidence we have about that opinion.

There are also ways of measuring elite opinion *systematically*, and the expressions of those opinions in and outside of the halls of government. For example, we have well-established techniques for systematically coding the content of the media. Thus, we can examine the media to determine whether it responds to the president's efforts to emphasize some policy areas over others and to characterize problems or the president's solutions to problems in particular ways.

These suggestions are only the tip of the proverbial iceberg. Creative researchers have always developed measures to meet their needs. *The issue for students of rhetoric is not lack of information, it is the unstated premise that these scholars have no need for it.* Moreover, an abstract desire for information makes little difference if it is not brought to bear on the inferences scholars make.

CONCLUSION

A possible objection to my call for greater rigor in studies of presidential rhetoric is that this is not what scholars of rhetoric do. After all, they tend to be humanists, not social scientists, and they have their own way of treating their subject.

Such an objection is without merit. What researcher would argue that he or she is happy to make inferences but is uninterested in whether they are valid? There is no inherent nonstylistic difference between quantitative work characteristic of the social sciences and the qualitative research typical in the humanities. All good research derives from the same underlying logic of inference, and the rules of inference are as applicable to qualitative as to quantitative research.

The standards for judging qualitative work should be clarified and research on rhetoric judged accordingly. It takes much more than a cogently argued point to verify an empirical claim about the world. It is not good enough to maintain that arguments *are* the evidence in humanities, so there is no need to go further. There is no reason that we should accept inferences that cannot be supported with systematic evidence, that cannot be falsified (at least in theory), that fail to consider alternative explanations for an observed effect, and that are not accompanied by discussion of the uncertainty of the conclusion. These standards apply to inferences regarding any effects from any form of communication over any time period.

To some, perhaps to most, this may seem like a tall order. Yet how else will scholars of presidential rhetoric determine which arguments (theories) or assertions about the impact of rhetoric are true? There are many arguments and many assertions. We have already seen that at least some are clearly wrong. Why should *any* inference be exempt from rigorous analysis?

The argument that the world is complex, making it difficult to isolate the effects of rhetoric, is not compelling. Of course the world is complex. Historians, psychologists, economists, sociologists, and political scientists, for example, face equally difficult tasks in their quests to understand their subjects. Every day scholars in these areas have to come to grips with a multitude of causes for the phenomena that interest them. And every day they marshal evidence, consider alternative explanations, and generally make probabilistic statements about the certainty of their conclusions. Why should the field of presidential rhetoric be exempt from the same standards to which other disciplines are held?

Rigor is not an end in itself, however. A rigorous analysis of an unimportant question is largely worthless. At the same time, an unconvincing analysis of an important issue can only be suspect. We require both relevance *and* rigor.

Afterword:

THE WAYS OF RHETORIC
Martin J. Medhurst

When one speaks of the future of the rhetorical presidency, there are at least three possible meanings of the phrase. One might mean the future of the construct as articulated by Ceaser, Thurow, Tulis, and Bessette.[1] Under this interpretation it is the future of the presidential office itself that is being investigated. Such an interpretation might focus on the utility of the construct, its explanatory power, and the centrality or importance attributed to the historical data upon which it is based.

But if one construed "rhetorical" more broadly, as Gronbeck, Benson, and the authors represented in part 2 of this volume do, then the future of the rhetorical presidency takes on a much different meaning. Under this interpretation it is rhetoric as a field of study that is being investigated, with special emphasis on presidential rhetoric.[2] Such an interpretation might focus on the nature and scope of rhetorical discourse, the definition of what it means to be a rhetorical president, the rhetorical constitution of political culture, the ability to use rhetoric to achieve one's goals, and the possibilities that a rhetorical presidency holds for an expanded—and preferably improved—democratic dialogue between government leaders and the citizenry.

Finally, there is a third possible meaning that one could associate with the future of the rhetorical presidency. It is an interpretation that encompasses both of these previous meanings but is broader than either the presidential office or the normal disciplinary boundaries of rhetorical studies. Under this third interpretation "rhetorical" is construed not as a negative descriptor for a problem (e.g., the rhetorical presidency) nor as the parameters of a discipline or subdiscipline (e.g., presidential rhetoric). Instead, "rhetorical" refers to a general way of existing in the world—approaching the world as a rhetorical being who understands that few things in life are given or inalterably determined; one who understands that most things are amenable to choice and to selection from among several competing choices; one who understands that the ability to use symbols carries with it the power both to build and to destroy; one who believes that all of life is the domain of the rhetorical, not merely those formal occasions that call for speech or discourse; and one who comprehends that the truly important questions in life seldom lend themselves to clear-cut answers that can be held with absolute certainty.

To be a rhetorical being is to live in a world of constant change, with misunderstandings, ambiguities, and lack of sufficient evidence one's constant companions. To live a rhetorical life is to be at home with the vicissitudes of human existence. It is to proclaim, along with the sophist Protagoras, that "there are many hindrances to knowledge, the obscurity of the subject and the brevity of human life,"[3] but mankind must nonetheless carry on. For those who hold, as both Isocrates and Cicero did, that rhetoric is an ideal of culture, the rhetorical life becomes just that—a way (*ódós*) of living in the world.[4]

It is perhaps instructive to remember that the earliest Christian sects referred to themselves as "the way." The New Testament is filled with references to the way, the path, the road, and the wayside. Those who pursue the rhetorical life do so from a philosophical, almost a theological, point of view. It is a comprehensive understanding of human existence based on certain presuppositions about human nature, the power of speech, the nature of the good, the ends of human community, and the limits of human knowledge.

These three meanings correspond, in a rough way, to three ways of thinking about rhetoric: as a way of doing, a way of knowing, and a way of being.[5]

When Tulis and Thurow worry about the use or overuse of rhetorical discourse by the president of the United States, they are focusing on rhetoric as a way of doing. They clearly recognize that there is an actional dimension to rhetoric—it seeks to accomplish ends beyond mere self-expression. Tulis's primary concern is that the contemporary ways in which presidents seek to do their job—using popular rhetoric to appeal to mass audiences—is a perversion of the kind of doing envisioned in the U.S. Constitution. The founders, in Tulis's view, did not envision popular rhetoric as a primary, much less the primary, way of doing government business. In Thurow's view one of the functions of rhetoric that was endorsed by the founders was the modeling of character and virtue through public discourse. Although rhetoric addressed to the citizenry was not supposed to deal with detailed matters of policy making, it was supposed to display the character of the speaker, thus presenting a model to the listeners of the virtues necessary to make the republican form of government work. There is, in the doing, a specific kind of end or purpose in mind.

If rhetoric is a way of doing something in the real world, it is also a way of knowing something. Generally speaking, people act on what they think they know. Rhetorical doing is usually predicated on rhetorical knowing. But how do we come to know rhetorically? Several of the chapters in this volume point toward possible answers. Hart and Kendall reveal Lyndon Johnson as a man for whom doing was the heart of politics. But LBJ's advice to Ted Sorensen about how to pass the administration's civil rights bill was predicated on a thorough vision of rhetorical knowing. LBJ knew certain things, not from formal education or reading books but from practical experience: that timing was everything when moving legislation, that certain people had to be on your side, that legislative success breeds more legislative success, and, as Hart and Kendall put it, "political legislation passes when its proponents' and opponents' most human needs are met." Johnson expressed this knowledge in many ways, including his choice of metaphors. Language reveals thought patterns and analysis of those patterns reveals the epistemological presuppositions of the speaker. Because the speaker has come to this knowledge, he invites his interlocutor to share in its secrets and to harness its power—to use this knowledge to do something. This is precisely what Johnson does.

The chapters by Goodnight and Ivie also point to rhetoric as a way of knowing. Goodnight focuses on historical analogy as an expression of popular beliefs *(doxa)* that take on the force of public knowledge. By bringing the Vietnam analogy into the debate over American policy in Nicaragua, both proponents and opponents of that policy contested the meaning of American history. To accept as valid one set of meanings was to chart one direction for Central American policy; to accept the other set was to chart a very different kind of course. Policy was established on the basis of which version of history—which public memory—could be made to prevail rhetorically. It was, after all, through the practice of deliberative rhetoric—argument in the legislative assembly—that policy choices were set forth and, ultimately, votes taken and laws established. The process was thoroughly rhetorical from beginning to end—from construction of the public memory through news stories, photographs, films, memoirs, history books, archival documentation, and the like; through appropriation of that memory in the form of debate, argumentation, examples, personal testimony, and historical comparisons; to the policies enacted as a result of such debates and their instantiation in the specific language of the law. Rhetoric, as Aristotle long ago recognized, is deeply implicated in how human beings come to know and act upon their world.

Ivie's chapter also points to rhetoric as a way of knowing. The symbolic representations used before and during the Persian Gulf War revealed both the thought patterns and cultural presumptions of those in power; those same representations invited the public to understand the situation in ways that were conducive to support of the administration's war effort. By "systematically structuring a narrative" that equated Saddam Hussein with Adolf Hitler and the crisis in the Gulf with a threat to world order, George Bush was able to muster both popular and congressional support for going to war. That he accomplished this by troping Saddam Hussein and metonymically reducing the nation of Iraq to the person of its leader points to the power of rhetoric to structure ways of seeing, understanding, and knowing the world. When such a rhetoric operates within a socio-cultural environment that already sees America as an embattled island of freedom in a sea of slavery, dictatorship, and aggression, it is not particularly difficult to lead audiences to see an impending crisis through the filter of an ongoing struggle for survival. That such a way of "knowing" poses great obstacles for "inventing" a new public memory and new motives for action is the transcendent tragedy of the Persian Gulf War, according to Ivie. Before we can symbolically encompass the world in different terms, we must first rhetorically transform ourselves and our political culture. In short, we must first know ourselves differently before we can expect to learn ways of symbolically constructing other ways that point toward peace rather than war.

To learn new ways of rhetorically constructing the self is to discover new modes of "being" in the world. Rhetoric not only helps us to know and to do, but also to be—to invent and, at times, to reinvent ourselves as the people we most want to be. No president attempted to reinvent himself more often than Richard M. Nixon. But as Edwin Black reminds us, we all invent ourselves; we are creatures who invent our own life stories and then inhabit them. The reflexive nature of this enterprise is central: we first make the rhetoric, then the rhetoric, in turn, makes us.[6] Black illustrates this point nicely in his chapter on President Nixon. Nixon constructed an image of himself and then adjusted his rhetorical behaviors to live up to the image he had constructed. In so doing, he became what he proclaimed. His very being was defined by the image he had rhetorically created. It was a being always embattled, constantly fighting for the right, eschewing the easy pathway, and never quitting. This was the self, the persona, and the political culture inhabited by Richard Nixon. The president's egoism, as Black calls it, left his vision a far cry from the cultural ideal of rhetoric as envisioned by Cicero. Even so, Black's chapter is a good illustration, though a dark one, of living a rhetorical life. Nixon's whole way of being was wrapped up in the choices he made and the way he symbolically encompassed those choices in his various rhetorical endeavors. That he was forever playing the tactician rather than the grand strategist points not only to the tragedy of Nixon but to the dark side of rhetoric when reduced to its most base form—win at any cost, without regard to self, other, or truth itself.

Campbell's chapter on First Ladies is also illustrative of the power of rhetorical discourse to define being. What does it mean to be a lady, or, more to the point, what does it mean to be the First Lady? Campbell examines the criticisms that have been leveled against First Ladies throughout the history of the Republic to reveal deep fissures in what it means to be a lady in general, and the First Lady in particular. That our societal notions of what constitutes a lady are highly political and carry with them certain (sometimes contradictory) expectations makes the role of being First Lady extremely difficult. At no time have these difficulties become more public or been the subject of such sustained political debate as the present. First Lady Hillary Rodham Clinton has been the lightning rod for discussion of what it means to be First Lady—a discussion that closely parallels the ongoing debate over the roles of women in American society.

Historically, the First Lady was circumscribed by two forms of rhetorical invention—invention by type and by sign. She was to participate in the ideal type of True Womanhood and was to serve as a visible sign of her husband's beliefs, values, and attitudes. When First Ladies have played against type or proven to be unreliable or uncooperative signs, they have suffered criticism. A rhetorical chasm has opened between what a First Lady is supposed to be, and what some First Ladies actually are. The ideal, itself a rhetorical creation, has come under increasing assault, as contemporary First Ladies seek to establish a new mode of being in the world, one characterized by what Campbell calls "a feminist ideal." This ideal offers a new rhetorical vision around which to structure a new, more wide-ranging type and an understanding of First Ladies not as signs pointing to their husbands, but as important actors in their own right. Contemporary First Ladies are in the process of establishing a new ideal, and of rhetorically adjusting the ideal to the culture and the culture to the ideal.

Finally, I want to return, briefly, to the chapter by Tom Benson. Benson, too, writes from the perspective of rhetoric as a way of being. He sees technological innovations as opportunities to extend what it means to be president of all the people. He takes as his beginning premise the possibility of politics as "an activity that takes place in a universally available public sphere built upon the context of an actively civic society, implying citizens who recognize and enact their public obligations both locally and nationally, and discursive practices that are by some measure rational, accessible, and reciprocal." In this one sentence, Benson articulates a vision of rhetoric as an ideal of culture. This ideal features a "public sphere," an active citizenry, and rational "discursive practices" that are both accessible to all and reciprocal between the leaders and the citizenry. Such an ideal culture does not, at present, exist. Yet one of the central roles of rhetoric is—and has been for over 2,500 years—to hold forth a vision of a better life, a better way;[7] to make arguments about how to improve civic life; to expose those who would seek to shrink the public sphere or to limit debate therein; and to utilize various discursive practices to maintain contact between and among the many actors in the social drama. And so the future of the rhetorical presidency can also be understood as a kind of political relationship not yet in existence, but one whose outlines and possibilities we can try to imagine. For if we can imagine them, then we can seek to encompass them discursively; and if we can encompass them discursively, then we can argue about our strategies of encompassment. And if we can argue—openly, rationally, passionately, and ethically—then we can recreate the public sphere which is the sine qua non of a truly rhetorical republic.[8]

These three ways of thinking about rhetoric—as doing, knowing, and being—are not, of course, mutually exclusive. They overlap and often reinforce one another. Indeed, the Hart and Kendall chapter is, by itself, a case study of the ways in which these three dimensions intersect and inform one another. By thinking of rhetoric as doing, knowing, and being, we can avoid the pitfall of reducing rhetoric to a cause. Seldom is a single rhetorical endeavor, whether speech, essay, editorial, debate, advertisement, or presidential press conference, ever the cause of anything, especially a thing as complex as political decision making. Oftentimes, of course, we speak as though our language is a causal factor. The very term "persuasion" seems to imply a causal connection between suasory language and behavioral outcomes. We need to be careful, therefore, about how we speak and write about the rhetorical process—one of the messages contained in George Edwards's chapter.

Edwards questions whether scholars working within the constructs of the rhetorical presidency and presidential rhetoric have sufficient evidence to warrant some of the claims they make on behalf of rhetoric's power, influence, and importance. Although some of Edwards's discomfort comes from the narrational form of case building used in both political theory and rhetorical criticism (as opposed, for example to building the case on quantitative measures or statistical inferences), it is still a valid criticism. One ought to have the best available evidence for the claims that one makes, wherever one must go to obtain that evidence. Edwards is on strong ground when he insists on clear arguments supported by compelling evidence and careful inferential reasoning.

Edwards's next moves, however, are more problematic. He seems to want to treat rhetoric as nothing more than a causal factor in a chain of cause-and-effect reasoning. Although he acknowledges that rhetoric might make a difference in any number of ways (some of which he even cites), he nonetheless writes as though the only important way it might make a difference is as a causative factor in persuasion. Starting from this bias, Edwards naturally finds the methodological rigor of political theory and rhetorical criticism lacking. He even goes so far as to assert that "there is no inherent nonstylistic difference between quantitative work characteristic of the social sciences and the qualitative work typical in the humanities." This extraordinary claim, left unchallenged, would equate grammar, rhetoric, and dialectic (the trivium) with music, geometry, arithmetic, and astronomy (the quadrivium). The ancients clearly recognized that the language arts were different from the numerical arts. To the extent that modern social science claims scientific status, the differences between the humanities and the (social) sciences are as stark today as they were centuries ago. Perhaps the greatest point of departure is in the nature of the questions asked.

Rhetoric tends to ask questions about artistry (understood as the rhetor's ability to shape a discourse in conformity with some preestablished theory or model), or intent (understood as the rhetor's motive for speaking or writing in a particular way), or strategy (understood as the match between the rhetor's intent and the artistry displayed in the speech or message), or genre (understood as the rhetor's ability to draw upon preestablished forms that, for a variety of reasons, might have suasory force with the intended audience), or style (understood more as an aspect of argument than as a literary device; metaphors argue, they do not merely adorn), or argument (understood both as inventional resources [argumentative *topoi*] and as the movement from data through warrant to claim), or situations (understood as the relationships among exigences, constraints, and audiences), or audience effectivity (understood as the ways in which rhetoric works to promote and prefer some meanings over others and to serve some social or political interests better than others).[9] Few, if any, of these kinds of questions are amenable to study through the various methodologies of the social scientific enterprise. It is sometimes the case that the findings of humanistic scholarship can be transformed into testable hypotheses, but the only reason one might want to do that is to answer a different kind of question than the one originally pursued.[10]

Since so many of the questions that are of interest to rhetorical scholars revolve around issues of values, morals, personal or public identity, character, public good, political philosophy, and the like, it is not surprising that their research methods tend toward the historical-critical or that the case study (whether conceived microscopically, as in the analysis of a single speech, or macroscopically, as in the analysis of argument across a whole campaign or movement) is the preferred unit of analysis. That historical-critical methods have little in common with modern techniques of social scientific investigation can be easily discerned by reading any issue of the *Quarterly Journal of Speech* or *American Literature* and comparing them with *Political Science Quarterly* or the *Journal of Experimental Social Psychology*. It is not, contrary to Edwards, that one group of scholars is more rigorous than the other. It is, instead, the nature of the questions asked and the recognized means for answering those sorts of questions that determines the approach utilized.

With the "rhetorical turn" now well established in all humanities and most social scientific disciplines, including some quarters of political science, the day is fast approaching when disciplinary boundaries and standard methodologies will be looked upon as relics from a benighted past.[11] Until that time, however, scholars will go on arguing about questions, approaches, methods, and data—and that is how it should be in a rhetorical world, where the future of the rhetorical presidency—and most everything else—is continuously being negotiated.

Notes

Introduction: A Tale of Two Constructs

1. See Edward S. Corwin, *The President: Office and Powers,* 4th ed. (New York: New York University Press, 1957); Clinton Rossiter, *The American Presidency* (New York: Harcourt, Brace, and World, 1960); Richard E. Neustadt, *Presidential Power: The Politics of Leadership* (New York: John Wiley and Sons, 1960); Thomas E. Cronin, ed., *Rethinking the Presidency* (Boston: Little, Brown, 1982); Harvey C. Mansfield, Jr., *Taming the Prince: The Ambivalence of Modern Executive Power* (New York: Free Press, 1989); Stephen Skowronek, *The Politics Presidents Make: Leadership from John Adams to George Bush* (Cambridge: Harvard University Press, 1993).

2. Edwin Black, *Rhetorical Criticism: A Study in Method* (New York: Macmillan, 1965). For a brief history of the development of historical-critical scholarship in rhetorical studies, see Martin J. Medhurst, "American Public Address: A Tradition in Transition," in *Landmark Essays on American Public Address,* ed. Martin J. Medhurst (Davis, Calif.: Hermagoras Press, 1993), pp. xi–xliii. If there was any one event, however, that heralded the advent of presidential rhetoric as a distinct subfield within rhetorical studies, it was the critical analysis of President Richard M. Nixon's Novem-

ber 3, 1969, address to the nation on the war in Vietnam. Four rhetorical critics, writing at four different moments between 1970 and 1972, produced four variant readings of this one presidential speech. See Robert P. Newman, "Under the Veneer: Nixon's Vietnam Speech of November 3, 1969," *Quarterly Journal of Speech* 56 (1970): 113–28; Hermann G. Stelzner, "The Quest Story and Nixon's November 3, 1969 Address," *Quarterly Journal of Speech* 71 (1971): 163–72; Karlyn Kohrs Campbell, "An Exercise in the Rhetoric of Mythical America," in *Critiques of Contemporary Rhetoric* (Belmont, Calif.: Wadsworth, 1972), pp. 39–58; Forbes I. Hill, "Conventional Wisdom—Traditional Form: The President's Message of November 3, 1969," *Quarterly Journal of Speech* 58 (1972): 373–86.

3. The original article by Ceaser et al. appeared in *Presidential Studies Quarterly* 11 (Spring, 1981): 158–71. It was reprinted in Theodore Windt and Beth Ingold, eds., *Essays in Presidential Rhetoric,* 2nd ed. (Dubuque: Kendall/Hunt, 1987), pp. 3–22.

4. Quotations appear in Ceaser et al., "Rise of the Rhetorical Presidency," p. 159. Deleterious effects are discussed on pp. 161–68.

5. See Glen Thurow and Jeffrey D. Wallin, eds., *Rhetoric and American Statesmanship* (Durham, N.C.: Carolina Academic Press, 1984); Jeffrey K. Tulis, *The Rhetorical Presidency* (Princeton, N.J.: Princeton University Press, 1987). For a further elaboration by James W. Ceaser, see "The Rhetorical Presidency Revisited," in *Modern Presidents and the Presidency,* ed. Marc Landy (Lexington, Mass.: Lexington Books, 1985), pp. 15–34. Quotations appear in Tulis, *The Rhetorical Presidency,* p. 4 and Ceaser et al., "Rise of the Rhetorical Presidency, p. 161, respectively.

6. Quotations appear in Tulis, *The Rhetorical Presidency,* p. 18 and Samuel Kernell, *Going Public: New Strategies of Presidential Leadership* (Washington, D.C.: Congressional Quarterly Press, 1986), p. 83–110, respectively.

7. Lloyd F. Bitzer, "The Rhetorical Situation," *Philosophy and Rhetoric* 1 (1968): 6. This essay has been widely reprinted, most recently in Martin J. Medhurst and Thomas W. Benson, eds., *Rhetorical Dimensions in Media: A Critical Casebook,* 2nd ed. (Dubuque: Kendall/Hunt, 1991), pp. 6–16.

8. Bitzer, "The Rhetorical Situation," p. 6.

9. This idea, of course, is not new. See Aristotle, *On Rhetoric,* trans. George A. Kennedy (New York: Oxford University Press, 1991), p. 53.

10. See James David Barber, *The Presidential Character: Predicting Performance in the White House,* 2nd ed. (Englewood Cliffs, N.J.: Prentice-Hall, Inc., 1977); Fred I. Greenstein, *Personality and Politics* (Chicago: Markham Publishing, 1969).

11. See Kenneth Burke, *Attitudes Toward History* (1937; rpt. Berkeley: University of California Press, 1984); Burke, *A Grammar of Motives* (1945; rpt. Berkeley: University of California Press, 1969); Burke, *A Rhetoric of Motives* (1950; rpt. Berkeley: University of California Press, 1969); Richard M. Weaver, *The Ethics of Rhetoric* (1953; rpt. Davis, Calif.: Hermagoras Press, 1985); Weaver, *Visions of Order* (Baton Rouge: Louisiana State University Press, 1964); Chaim Perelman and Lucie Olbrechts-Tyteca, *The New Rhetoric,* trans. John Wilkinson and Purcell Weaver (Notre Dame, Ind.: University of Notre Dame Press, 1969); Chaim Perelman, *The Realm of Rhetoric* (Notre Dame: University of Notre Dame Press, 1982).

12. See Walter J. Ong, S.J., "The Writers Audience is Always a Fiction," *PMLA* 90 (1975): 9–21.

13. For two examples of how fictionalizing an audience can be beneficial to a presidential rhetorician, see Craig R. Smith, "Richard Nixon's 1968 Acceptance Speech

as a Model of Dual Audience Adaptation," *Today's Speech* 19 (Fall, 1971): 15–22; Martin J. Medhurst, "Eisenhower's 'Atoms for Peace' Speech: A Case Study in the Strategic Use of Language," *Communication Monographs* 54 (1987): 204–20.

14. See Karlyn Kohrs Campbell and Kathleen Hall Jamieson, *Deeds Done in Words: Presidential Rhetoric and the Genres of Governance* (Chicago: University of Chicago Press, 1990).

15. For two works that challenge the generic study of presidential discourse, see Halford Ryan, ed., *The Inaugural Addresses of Twentieth-Century American Presidents* (New York: Praeger, 1993); Amos Kiewe, ed. *The Modern Presidency and Crisis Rhetoric* (New York: Praeger, 1994).

16. As I have written elsewhere, "Perhaps it is the case that the explanation that accounts broadly for everything, accounts specifically for nothing." See Martin J. Medhurst, "Public Address and Significant Scholarship: Four Challenges to the Rhetorical Renaissance," in *Texts in Context: Critical Dialogues on Significant Episodes in American Political Rhetoric,* eds. Michael C. Leff and Fred J. Kauffeld (Davis, Calif.: Hermagoras Press, 1989), p. 33.

17. Robert D. King, "Franklin D. Roosevelt's Second Inaugural Address," *Quarterly Journal of Speech* 23 (1937): 439–44.

18. Theodore Windt, "Presidential Rhetoric: Definition of a Discipline of Study," in *Essays in Presidential Rhetoric,* p. xxiii (quotation). For some of the better examples of each type of study, see Kathleen Hall Jamieson, *Packaging the Presidency: A History and Criticism of Presidential Campaign Advertising* (New York: Oxford University Press, 1984); Arthur Miller and Bruce E. Gronbeck, eds., *Presidential Campaigns and American Self Images* (Boulder: Westview Press, 1994); Kurt Ritter and David Henry, *Ronald Reagan: The Great Communicator* (Westport, Conn.: Greenwood Press, 1992); Martin J. Medhurst, *Dwight D. Eisenhower: Strategic Communicator* (Westport, Conn.: Greenwood Press, 1993); Roderick P. Hart, *The Sound of Leadership: Presidential Communication in the Modern Age* (Chicago: University of Chicago Press, 1987); Theodore Otto Windt, Jr., *Presidents and Protesters: Political Rhetoric in the 1960s* (Tuscaloosa: University of Alabama Press, 1990).

19. Ceaser et al., "Rise of the Rhetorical Presidency," p. 161.

20. See Edwin Black, "A Note on Theory and Practice in Rhetorical Criticism," *Western Journal of Speech Communication* 44 (1980): 336.

Chapter 1: *Revising the Rhetorical Presidency*

1. Jeffrey K. Tulis, *The Rhetorical Presidency* (Princeton, N.J.: Princeton University Press, 1987).

2. James W. Ceaser, Glen E. Thurow, Jeffrey Tulis, and Joseph M. Bessette, "The Rise of the Rhetorical Presidency," *Presidential Studies Quarterly* 11 (Spring, 1981): 2. With some revisions, reprinted in Thomas E. Cronin, ed. *Rethinking the Presidency* (Boston: Little Brown and Co., 1982).

3. Tulis, *The Rhetorical Presidency,* chap. 7.

4. Fred Barnes, "Mr. Popularity," *New Republic,* Jan. 8 and 15, 1990, p. 13.

5. "Text of the President's State of the Union Message to the Nation," *New York Times,* Feb. 1, 1990.

6. "Address to a Joint Session of Congress on Health Care Reform, Sept. 22, 1993," *Weekly Compilation of Presidential Documents* (Washington, D.C.: U.S. Government Printing Office), vol. 29, no. 38, p. 1837.

7. Clinton departed from the leadership style in three stages. First, he never fully articulated the principles as such. Even in the first speech the principles resembled labels for clusters of policy rather than reasoned standards for a range of possible policies. Second, Clinton quickly abandoned a routine defense of all but two of his initial principles. Finally, Clinton allowed himself to become wedded in the public mind with his plan. He failed to convince the public to hold his partisan opponents to the standards of his principles because they lost sight of those principles.

8. This is also necessary for the president to establish his authority. For the best discussion of the concept of presidential authority, see Stephen Skowronek, *The Politics Presidents Make: Leadership from John Adams to George Bush* (Cambridge: Harvard University Press, 1993), chap. 2.

9. Institutional partisanship continues to be the principal defect in studies of American politics. I discussed this issue in *The Rhetorical Presidency,* pp. 9–13. Even the best recent book on the presidency, Skowronek's *The Politics Presidents Make,* perpetuates this problem.

10. The best evidence for a realignment is not the partisan affiliation of elected officials but rather the partisan content of the dominant political rhetoric. When Democrats began talking like Republicans, the Republicans had already won. The elections of 1994 made more palpable a realignment that had already occurred well before the election.

11. Compare Kenneth Cmiel, *Democratic Eloquence: The Fight over Popular Speech in Nineteenth-Century America* (New York: William Morrow and Co., 1990) and Roderick P. Hart, *Seducing America: How Television Charms the Modern Voter* (New York: Oxford University Press, 1994).

12. Tulis, *The Rhetorical Presidency,* p. 204.

Chapter 2: Dimensions of Presidential Character

1. Aristotle, *The Art of Rhetoric* (Cambridge: Harvard University Press, 1959), I.11.4.

2. Alexander Hamilton, James Madison, John Jay, *The Federalist,* ed. Jacob E. Cooke (Middleton, Conn.: Wesleyan University Press, 1961), no. 68, p. 461.

3. Ibid., no. 72, p. 488.

4. *The Inaugural Addresses of the Presidents of the United States* (Washington, D.C.: U.S. Government Printing Office, 1952), pp. 1–3.

5. Aristotle, *The Politics* (Cambridge: Harvard University Press, 1944), III, p. xiii.

6. *Inaugural Addresses,* p. 4.

7. Ibid., pp. 5–9.

8. Ibid., pp. 11–14.

9. See Harvey C. Mansfield, Jr., "Thomas Jefferson," in *American Political Thought: The Philosophic Dimension of American Statesmanship,* ed. Morton J. Frisch and Richard G. Stevens (New York: Kendall Hunt, 1971), pp. 23–30.

10. *Inaugural Addresses,* pp. 177–87.

11. Ibid., pp. 189–92.

12. Ibid., pp. 193–96.

13. Woodrow Wilson, "Abraham Lincoln: A Man of the People," in *The Papers of Woodrow Wilson,* ed. Arthur S. Link, vol. 19 (Princeton, N.J.: Princeton University Press, 1942), p. 42.

14. Jimmy Carter, "Inaugural Address," *Vital Speeches* 43 (Feb. 15, 1977): 258. For an excellent analysis of the changes made by Wilson, see Tulis, *The Rhetorical Presidency,* pp. 117–44.

15. Speech of July 15, 1979, *Vital Speeches* 45 (Aug. 15, 1979): 642.

16. Ronald Reagan, "Inaugural Address," *Vital Speeches* 47 (Feb. 15, 1981): 258–60.

17. George Bush, "Inaugural Address," *Vital Speeches* 55 (Feb. 15, 1989): 258–60.

18. *Inaugural Addresses,* pp. 1, 3.

19. Carter, "Inaugural Address," p. 258.

20. Washington is quoted in *Inaugural Addresses,* p. 1. Carter quoted in Carter, "Inaugural Address, p. 258.

21. *Inaugural Addresses,* p. 2.

22. Carter, "Inaugural Address," p. 258.

23. Bush, "Inaugural Address," p. 258.

24. Carter, "Inaugural Address," p. 258.

25. William Clinton, "Inaugural Address," *Vital Speeches* 59 (Feb. 15, 1993): 258–59.

26. James David Barber, *The Presidential Character* (Englewood Cliffs, N.J.: Prentice-Hall, 1985), pp. 32, 445.

27. Ibid., p. 7.

Chapter 3: *The Presidency in the Age of Secondary Orality*

1. Jeffrey K. Tulis, *The Rhetorical Presidency* (Princeton, N.J.: Princeton University Press, 1987).

2. Samuel L. Becker and Elmer W. Lower, "Broadcasting in Presidential Campaigns," in *The Great Debates: Background-Perspectives-Effects,* ed. Sidney Kraus (Bloomington: Indiana University Press, 1962); p. 319 (quotation). On Roosevelt, see Joy Hayes, "Radio Broadcasting and Nation-Building in Mexico and the United States, 1925–1945" (Ph.D. diss., University of California at San Diego, 1994).

3. I review some of these works in the introductions to sections of Arthur N. Miller and Bruce E. Gronbeck, eds., *Presidential Campaigns and American Self Images* (Boulder, Colo.: Westview, 1994). For more of the story, see F. C. Arterton, *Media Politics: The News Strategies of Presidential Campaigns* (Lexington, Mass.: Lexington Books, 1987); W. Lance Bennett, *The Governing Crisis: Media, Money, and Marketing in American Elections* (New York: St. Martin's Press, 1992); A. H. Cantril and S. D. Cantril, *The Opinion Connection: Polling, Politics, and the Press* (Washington, D.C.: Congressional Quarterly Press, 1991); Richard Davis, *The Press and American Politics: The New Mediator* (New York: Longman, 1992); T. R. Dye and Harold Zeigler, *American Politics in the Media Age,* 3rd ed. (Pacific Grove, Calif.: Brooks/Cole Publishing Co., 1989); Murray Edelman, *Constructing the Political Spectacle* (Chicago: University of Chicago Press, 1988); R. E. Gilbert, *Television and Presidential Politics* (North Quincy, Mass.: Christopher Publishing House, 1972); Kathleen Hall Jamieson, *Packaging the Presidency: A History and Criticism of Presidential Campaign Advertising* (New York: Oxford University Press, 1984); Kevin Melder, *Hail to the Candidate: Presidential Campaigning from Banners to Broadcasts* (Washington, D.C.: Smithsonian University Press, 1922); and Tulis, *The Rhetorical Presidency.*

4. For details, see Becker and Lower, "Broadcasting in Presidential Campaigns."

5. This argument about Coolidge as media personality is made by Arthur F. Fleser in "Coolidge's Delivery: Everybody Liked It," *Southern States Communication Journal* 32 (1966): 98–104. See Hayes's argument for FDR's media personality in "Radio Broadcasting." Factual details come from Arthur M. Schlesinger, Jr., ed., *The Almanac of American History* (New York: G. P. Putnam's Sons, 1983).

6. For a collection of short analyses of this event, see Frederick W. Haberman, "General MacArthur's Speech: A Symposium of Critical Comment," *Quarterly Journal of Speech* 37 (1951): 321–31.

7. On Clinton's film, see Bruce E. Gronbeck, "Characterological Arguments in the Bush and Clinton Convention Films of 1992," in *Postmodern Argument: Proceedings of the 8th Biennial SCA/AFA Conference on Argumentation,* ed. Raymie E. McKerrow (Annandale, Va.: Speech Communication Association, 1993).

8. On media events as a special kind of collective experience, see Daniel Dayan and Elihu Katz, *Media Events: The Live Broadcasting of History* (Cambridge: Harvard University Press, 1992).

9. See arguments made in Marshall McLuhan and Quentin Fiore, *War and Peace in the Global Village* (New York: Bantam, 1968), and Walter J. Ong, *Orality and Literacy: The Technologizing of the Word* (New York: Methuen, 1982). See David Horton and Richard R. Wohl, "Mass Communication and Para-Social Interaction: Observations on Intimacy at a Distance," in *Inter/Media: Interpersonal Communication in a Media World,* ed. Gary Gumpert and Robert Cathcart, 2nd ed. (New York: Oxford University Press, 1979), pp. 188–211.

10. For an eighteenth-century example, see Edmund Burke's famous speech to his constituency on the nature of virtual representation in "Speech to the Sheriffs of Bristol," in *British Orations from Ethelbert to Churchill,* ed. Chauncey A. Goodrich (1780; rpt. Indianapolis: Bobbs-Merrill Co., 1963), pp. 292–310. For a discussion of nineteenth-century public opinion, see Frances F. Piven and R. A. Cloward, *Why Americans Don't Vote* (New York: Pantheon Books, 1988).

11. Scott Ratzan, "The Real Agenda Setters: Pollsters in the 1988 Presidential Campaign," *American Behavioral Scientist* 32 (Mar./Apr., 1989): 451–63. On the role of polls generally in American culture, see the special issue on "Polling and the Democratic Consensus" of *Annals of the American Academy of Political and Social Science* 472 (1984).

12. James Carville and Mary Matalin, *All's Fair: Love, War, and Running for President* (New York: Random House, 1994).

13. Clifford Geertz, "Center, Kings, and Charisma," in *Culture and Its Creators,* ed. John Ben-David and T. Clark (Chicago: University of Chicago Press, 1980), chap. 2.

14. Even rhetorics through the ages have recognized that visually oriented verbal language has great power. So, for example, Longinus in *On the Sublime* has this to say: "Weight, grandeur, and energy in writing are very largely produced, dear pupil, by the use of 'images.' (That at least is what some people call the actual mental pictures.) For the term Imagination is applied in general to an idea which enters the mind from any source and engenders speech, but the word has now come to be used predominantly of passages where, inspired by strong emotion, you seem to see what you describe and bring it vividly before the eyes of your audience" (W. H. Fyfe, trans., Longinus's "On the Sublime," in *Aristotle; "Longinus"; Demetrius,* Loeb Classical Library (1960), p. 171. Cf. Bruce E. Gronbeck, "The Spoken and the Seen: Phonocentric and Ocularcentric Dimensions of Rhetorical Discourse," in *Rhetorical Memory and*

Delivery: Classical Concepts for Contemporary Composition and Communication, ed. J. Frederick Reynolds (Hillsdale, N.J.: Lawrence Erlbaum Associates, 1993), pp. 139–55.

15. Edelman, *Constructing the Political Spectacle,* p. 1.

16. Thomas E. Patterson and R. D. McClure, *The Unseeing Eye: The Myth of Television Power in National Politics* (New York: Putnam's, 1976).

17. On subject positioning, see Laura Mulvey, "Visual Pleasure and Narrative Cinema," *Screen* 16/3 (1975): 6–18. On specularity, see John Fiske, *Television Culture* (New York: Methuen, 1987).

18. There are, of course, many factors at work in destroying symbolic distance: the role of citizen monies and PAC monies flowing directly into presidential (vis-à-vis party) coffers; the sheer expansion of political news coverage; the rise of investigative reporting; a press still unhappy about being used by the presidency, especially during the Watergate era; and political campaign strategists willing to use the personal or private side of candidates (families depicted in social settings) for electoral gain. I do not mean to propose a kind of technological determinism in this argument. Rather, I am suggesting that the money, press scrutiny, and campaign exhibitionism are able to have their effects because of electronic mediations between politicians and constituents.

19. The arguments of this paragraph are influenced by the thinking of Harold Garfinkel, "Conditions of Successful Degradation Ceremonies," *American Journal of Sociology* 61 (1955–56): 420–24; Ernest H. Kantorowicz, *The King's Two Bodies: A Study in Mediaeval Political Theology* (Princeton, N.J.: Princeton University Press, 1957); and Murray Edelman, *The Symbolic Uses of Politics* (Urbana: University of Illinois Press, 1964).

20. The roots for these ideas can be found in Georges Balandier, *Political Anthropology,* trans. A. M. Sheridan Smith (New York: Vintage Books, 1970). They are articulated clearly in Kari Palonen, "Introduction: From Policy and Polity to Politicking and Politicization," in *Reading the Political: Exploring the Margins of Politics,* eds. Kari Palonen and Tuija Parvikko (Tampere, Finland: Finnish Political Science Association, 1993), 6–16.

21. Stephen Houlgate, "The 'Hegemony of Vision' from a Hegelian Point of View," in *Modernity and the Hegemony of Vision,* ed. David M. Levin (Berkeley: University of California Press, 1993), pp. 87–123; Jacques Ellul, *The Humiliation of the Word* (Grand Rapids, Mich.: Wm. B. Eerdmans, 1985).

22. On depiction, see Michael Osborn, "Rhetorical Depiction," in *Form, Genre, and the Study of Political Discourse,* eds. Herbert W. Simons and Aram A. Aghazarian (Columbia, S.C.: University of South Carolina Press, 1986), pp. 79–108.

23. The utility of analyzing the Vanderbilt archives is demonstrated in David Woodard's study of coverage of elections on the evening television news, 1972–92. Coding the Abstracts's descriptions of news stories for kind of story and amount of time devoted to each party as well as searching out reaction stories—stories with opposing viewpoints presented within them—allowed Woodard to characterize shifting amounts of TV news coverage in each phase of campaigns over two decades, to chart the growing emphasis on controversy in that coverage, and to theorize changes in voter spectatorship as the century draws to a close. Computer-aided research based on computer-organized archives can add important new facets to rhetorical studies. See J. David Woodard, "Coverage of Elections on Evening Television News Stories: 1972–1992," in Miller and Gronbeck, *Presidential Campaigns and American Self Images,* pp. 109–27.

24. For other works on refashioning our understanding of political rhetoric and on symbolic operations of the presidency, see Edelman, *The Symbolic Uses of Politics;* Robert E. Denton, Jr., *The Symbolic Dimensions of the American Presidency: Description and Analysis* (Prospect Heights, Ill.: Waveland Press, 1982); Kathleen Hall Jamieson, *Eloquence in an Electronic Age: The Transformation of Political Speechmaking* (New York: Oxford University Press, 1988); Kathleen Hall Jamieson, *Dirty Politics: Deception, Distraction, and Democracy* (New York: Oxford University Press, 1992); Bruce E. Gronbeck, "Electric Rhetoric: The Changing Forms of American Political Discourse," *Vichiana,* 3rd series, 1st yr. (Napoli: Loffredo Editore, 1990), pp. 141–61; Bennett, T*he Governing Crisis;* Roderick P. Hart, *Seducing America: How Television Charms the Modern Voter* (New York: Oxford University Press, 1994); Miller and Gronbeck, *Presidential Campaigns and American Self Images.* For an example of right-wing critique, see Robert E. Denton, Jr., "Primetime Politics: The Ethics of Teledemocracy," in *Ethical Dimensions of Political Communication,* ed. Robert E. Denton, Jr. (New York: Praeger, 1991), pp. 91–114. For an example of concern over the deemphasis of the verbal in political process, see Neil Postman, *Amusing Ourselves to Death: Public Discourse in the Age of Show Business* (New York: Viking Penguin, 1985). For examples of French postmodern attitude, see Jean Baudrillard's *In the Shadow of the Silent Majorities,* trans. P. Foss, J. Johnston, and P. Patton (New York: Semiotext[e], 1983), and also Baudrillard's *The Ecstasy of Communication,* trans. B. Schutze and C. Schutze, ed. S. Lotringer (New York: Semiotext[e], 1988). For an example of Marxist commitment, see J. J. Welsh, "Dramaturgy and Political Mystification: Political Life in the United States," in *Life as Theatre: A Dramaturgical Source Book,* ed. David Brisset and Charles Edgley, 2nd ed. (1985; rpt. New York: Aldine de Gruyter, 1990), p. 399.

25. Iranian television is discussed in Annabelle Sreberny-Mohammadi, "Media Integration in the Third World: An Ongian Look at Iran," in *Media, Consciousness, and Culture: Explorations of Walter Ong's Thought,* ed. Bruce E. Gronbeck, Thomas Farrell, and Paul Soukup (Newbury Park, Calif.: Sage, 1991), pp. 113–146. For Dayan and Katz's arguments, refer to *Media Events.*

26. These ideas are discussed at greater length in Bruce E. Gronbeck, "Rhetoric, Ethics, and Telespectacles in the Post-Everything Age," in *Postmodern Representations: Truth, Power, and Mimesis in the Human Sciences and Public Culture,* ed. Richard Harvey Brown (Urbana: University of Illinois Press, 1995), 216–38.

27. This is the thesis of his *Presidential Power: The Politics of Leadership from FDR to Carter* (1960; rev. New York: John Wiley and Sons, 1980).

28. See the analysis of Edwin Black in *Rhetorical Questions: Studies of Public Discourse* (Chicago: University of Chicago Press, 1992).

29. Edelman, *Constructing the Political Spectacle,* pp. 3, 6.

30. See the arguments of Palonen, "Introduction."

31. My thanks to the University of Iowa's Project on Rhetoric of Inquiry for providing me with an office and other support during 1994-95. The care and goodwill of its administrative director, Kate Neckerman, have been much appreciated.

Chapter 4: *Desktop* Demos

1. The literature on public sphere and on civil society is vast; both areas are currently the subject of intense scholarly attention. From the point of view of this chapter, useful entry works on the public sphere are: Thomas McCarthy, *The Critical Theory of Jürgen Habermas* (Cambridge: MIT Press, 1978); Bruce Robbins, ed., *The Phantom*

Public Sphere (Minneapolis: University of Minnesota Press, 1993); Gerard A. Hauser, "Administrative Rhetoric and Public Opinion: Discussing the Iranian Hostages in the Public Sphere," in *American Rhetoric: Context and Criticism,* ed. Thomas W. Benson (Carbondale: Southern Illinois University Press, 1989), pp. 323–83; Charles Ess, "The Political Computer: Hypertext, Democracy, and Habermas," in *Hyper/Text/Theory,* ed. George P. Landow, (Baltimore: Johns Hopkins University Press, 1994), pp. 225–67. On civil society, see Jean Bethke Elshtain, *Democracy on Trial* (New York: Basic Books, 1995); Robert D. Putnam, *Making Democracy Work: Civic Traditions in Modern Italy* (Princeton, N.J.: Princeton University Press, 1993); J. G. A. Pocock, *The Machiavellian Moment: Florentine Political Thought and the Atlantic Republican Tradition* (Princeton, N.J.: Princeton University Press, 1975); Christopher Lasch, *The Revolt of the Elites and the Betrayal of Democracy* (New York: W. W. Norton, 1995); Philip Selznick, *The Moral Commonwealth: Social Theory and the Promise of Community* (Berkeley: University of California Press, 1992); Amitai Etzioni, *The Spirit of Community: Rights, Responsibilities, and the Communitarian Agenda* (New York: Crown Publishers, 1993).

2. Thomas E. Patterson, *Out of Order* (New York: Vintage Books, 1994), p. 245. On press coverage of Whitewater, see also Gene Lyons, "Fool for Scandal: How the Times Got Whitewater Wrong," *Harper's* (Oct., 1994), pp. 55–63. For another harshly critical analysis of the media that explicitly proposes to remedy poor press performance with the participatory democracy of the Internet, see Patrick Garry, *Scrambling for Protection: The New Media and the First Amendment* (Pittsburgh, Penn.: University of Pittsburgh Press, 1994). I have commented in more detail on Garry's book in "Permanence and Change in the Global Village," *Postmodern Culture* 5.1 (Sept., 1994). See also Thomas W. Benson, "Implicit Communication Theory in Campaign Coverage," in *Television Coverage of the 1980 Presidential Campaign,* ed. William C. Adams (Norwood, N.J.: Ablex, 1983); Kathleen Hall Jamieson, *Dirty Politics: Deception, Distraction, and Democracy* (New York: Oxford University Press, 1992); Larry Sabato, *Feeding Frenzy: How Attack Journalism Has Transformed American Politics* (New York: Free Press, 1991); Richard Ben Kramer, *What It Takes: The Way to the White House* (New York: Random House, 1992).

3. John Anthony Maltese, *Spin Control: The White House Office of Communications and the Management of Presidential News* (Chapel Hill: University of North Carolina Press, 1992), p. 16.

4. Ibid., p. 44.

5. See Howard Rheingold, *The Virtual Community* (New York: HarperPerennial, 1994); Steven G. Jones, ed., *CyberSociety: Computer-Mediated Communication and Community* (Thousand Oaks, Calif.: Sage, 1995); Jeffrey B. Abramson, F. Christopher Arterton, and Gary R. Orren, *The Electronic Commonwealth* (New York: Basic Books, 1988); Richard A. Lanham, *The Electronic Word: Democracy, Technology, and the Arts* (Chicago: University of Chicago Press, 1993); Starr Roxanne Hiltz and Murray Turoff, *The Network Nation,* rev ed. (Cambridge: MIT Press, 1993); Slavko Splichal and Janet Wasko, eds., *Communication and Democracy* (Norwood, N.J.: Ablex, 1993).

6. "The Future of the Telephone," *Scientific American,* January 10, 1880, p. 16, quoted in Carolyn Marvin, *When Old Technologies Were New* (New York: Oxford University Press, 1988), p. 65.

7. Marvin, *When Old Technologies Were New,* p. 65.

8. For further discussion of the social adaptation to new technologies, see James

W. Carey, *Communication as Culture* (Boston: Unwin Hyman, 1989); Timothy Detwiler, "The Technotheological Rhetoric of the Local Catalysts of Public Access Cable Television in Grand Rapids, Michigan" (Ph.D. diss., Pennsylvania State University, 1991); Elizabeth Eisenstein, *The Printing Press as an Agent of Change* (Cambridge: Cambridge University Press, 1980); Mary Mander, "Utopian Dimensions in the Public Debate on Broadcasting in the Twenties," *Journal of Communication Inquiry* 12 (1988): 71–88; Henri-Jean Martin, *The History and Power of Writing*, trans. Lydia G. Cochrane (Chicago: University of Chicago Press, 1994); Brian Winston, *Misunderstanding Media* (Cambridge: Harvard University Press, 1986); Ithiel de Sola Pool, ed., *The Social Impact of the Telephone* (Cambridge: The MIT Press, 1977).

9. For a description of the Clinton e-mail campaign, see Thomas W. Benson, "The First E-Mail Election: Electronic Networking and the Clinton Campaign," in *Bill Clinton on Stump, State, and Stage: The Rhetorical Road to the White House,* ed. Stephen Smith (Fayetteville: University of Arkansas Press, 1994), pp. 315–40.

10. The e-mail address for Newt Gingrich, Speaker of the House, is Georgia6@hr.house.gov. For general descriptions of the Internet and special services such as Gopher, electronic mail, FTP, Telnet, and the World Wide Web, consult an up-to-date guide to the Internet. A sample of such guides would include Tony Abbott, ed., *On Internet 94* (Westport, Conn.: Mecklermedia, 1994); M. Gibbs and R. Smith, *Navigating the Internet* (Carmel, Ind.: Sams, 1993); P. Gilster, *The Internet Navigator* (New York: Wiley, 1993); Harley Hahn and Rick Stout, *The Internet Complete Reference* (Berkeley: Osborne McGraw-Hill, 1994); Ed Krol, *The Whole Internet* (Sebastopol, Calif.: O'Reilly, 1992); T. LaQuey and J. C. Ryer, *The Internet Companion* (Reading, Mass.: Addison-Wesley, 1993). For additional information on accessing government data bases, see also Susan M. Ryan, "Uncle Sam Online: Government Information on the Internet," *Communication Education* 43 (1994): pp. 151–58.

11. Howard Rheingold, *The Virtual Community: Homesteading on the Electronic Frontier* (1993; rpt. New York: HarperPerennial, 1994), p. 8.

12. Robert Kolker, "The Moving Image Reclaimed," *Postmodern Culture* 5.1 (Sept., 1994).

13. Roderick P. Hart, *The Sound of Leadership: Presidential Communication in the Modern Age* (Chicago: University of Chicago Press, 1987).

14. See Jean Baudrillard, *Simulacra and Simulation,* trans. Sheila Faria Glaser (Ann Arbor: University of Michigan Press, 1994). Cf. William Gibson's description of cyberpunk in *Neuromancer* (New York: Ace Books, 1984); the protagonist, Case, "lived for the bodiless exultation of cyberspace. . . . The body was meat" (6).

15. The Senate gopher is at gopher.senate.gov; the House gopher is at gopher.house.gov. House documents are on the World Wide Web at Thomas.loc.gov in the Library of Congress web pages.

16. Newt Gingrich, interviewed on National Public Radio, Jan. 5, 1995.

17. "White House Electronic Publications and Public Access Email: Frequently Asked Questions," updated November 14, 1994, version 2.2. The latest version of this document may be obtained through electronic mail by sending a note to faq@whitehouse.gov. No subject line is necessary and the contents section of the note should be left blank; the document will be sent automatically.

18. Automatically generated electronic mail message to author from Stephen K. Horn, director, Presidential E-Mail, Jan. 15, 1995.

19. Nicholas Negroponte, *Being Digital* (New York: Knopf, 1995), 228–30.

20. Electronic mail to author from Robert Walker (PA16@hr.house.gov), Jan. 30, 1995.

21. Jeffrey K. Tulis, *The Rhetorical Presidency* (Princeton, N.J.: Princeton University Press, 1987). See also Hart, *The Sound of Leadership*. (Chicago: University of Chicago Press, 1987).

22. Three early books on the Clinton administration's decision-making style variously address the view that deliberation equals indecision or lack of convictions; see Elizabeth Drew, *On the Edge: The Clinton Presidency* (New York: Simon and Schuster, 1994); John Brummett, *High Wire* (New York: Hyperion, 1994); Bob Woodward, *The Agenda* (New York: Simon and Schuster, 1994).

23. See Richard Dyer MacCann, *The People's Films: A Political History of U.S. Government Motion Pictures* (New York: Hastings House, 1973).

24. See, for example, Joseph Schmitz, Everett M. Rogers, Ken Phillips, and Donald Paschal, "The Public Electronic Network (PEN) and the Homeless in Santa Monica," *Journal of Applied Communication Research* 23 (1995): 26–43; Patrick B. O'Sullivan, "Computer Networks and Political Participation: Santa Monica's Teledemocracy Project," *Journal of Applied Communication Research* 23 (1995): 93–107.

25. By 1994, the Lyndon Baines Johnson Library in Austin, Texas, was making some of its reference materials accessible by Gopher through sunsite.unc.edu. All of the presidential libraries have home pages on the World Wide Web, with at least preliminary information about how to conduct research. The Gerald R. Ford Library has partly computerized its data bases to permit keyword searches for relevant folders of documents. According to David E. Alsobrook, acting director of the Bush Presidential Materials Project, the Bush library will have CTRAK, an on-line data base that tracks 250,000 incoming and outgoing White House documents; and "BVAX (Presidential Statements) [which] includes all the public statements made by the President as well as most of the White House press releases. This database can be searched through the full text, and it is our hope that it will be a valuable tool to researchers and will be available on line in the future." In addition, the Bush project will track museum objects by computer and plans to make its finding aids available "on-line and through the internet" (letter from David E. Alsobrook to the author, Apr. 28, 1995).

26. Data reported in "Top 25 Submitters by User by Kbytes for the Last 2 Weeks," (Netnews newsgroup: news.lists) (From: newsstats@uunet.UU.NET, July 25, 1994).

27. Baudrillard, *Simulacra and Simulation,* p. 1. A rhetorical critic cannot resist noting that even in the radical, referential nihilism of Baudrillard's postmodern theorizing, there is an appeal to a stable underlying linearity in Western thought from the project of Enlightenment rationality through the nineteenth-century replacement of appearances with meaning and then the twentieth-century replacement of referential meaning with postmodernist nonreferentiality. It is not always clear whether Baudrillard is describing postmodernism as a historical stage; as an empirical condition, a sensibility created by the forces of mass production of illusions; or as a philosophical principle. Tania Modleski describes a similar mode of theorizing in a gesture by Frederic Jameson to replace organicist aesthetics with a theory of postmodern fragmentation, arguing that it is essentially a rhetorical gesture: "What is made possible by this move . . . is a replacement of the older notion of the artist as master with one of the theorist as master: the man who is able to situate the fragmented, partial, decentered aspects of art and daily life into a historical totality" (Tania Modleski, *Women Who Knew Too*

Much [New York: Routledge, 1988], p. 120). But none of these observations about post-modernist theorizing prove that it is wrong. On nonreferential rhetorical action, see also Thomas W. Benson and Gerard A. Hauser, "Ideals, Superlatives, and the Decline of Hypocrisy," *Quarterly Journal of Speech* 59 (1973): pp. 99–105; Thomas W. Benson, "Another Shooting in Cowtown," *Quarterly Journal of Speech* 67 (1981): 347–406.

28. Lanham, *The Electronic Word,* p. 147.

Chapter 5: *Lyndon Johnson and the Problem of Politics*

1. Doris Kearns recounts how central oral conversation became to Lyndon Johnson during his life: "When urged by his mother, who taught elocution and de-bate, to participate in public speaking classes, he was dismissed for mumbling too much. Yet over time, he did develop an extraordinary facility in conversation; he became perhaps the greatest storyteller of his age." See *Lyndon Johnson and the American Dream* (New York: New American Library, 1976), p. 370.

2. "No Longer a 'Problem' But a Revolution," *New York Times,* June 16, 1963.

3. Ibid., "Races," June 7, 1963; "Races," June 21, 1963.

4. For a discussion of observers' arguments about Kennedy's recalcitrance, see James C. Harvey, *Civil Rights during the Kennedy Administration* (Jackson: University and College Press of Mississippi, 1971), p. 65. Roy Wilkins is quoted in Robert D. Loevy, "'To Write in the Book of Law': President Lyndon B. Johnson and the Civil Rights Act of 1964," in *Lyndon Baines Johnson and the Uses of Power,* eds. Bernard J. Firestone and Robert C. Vogt (New York: Greenwood Press, 1988), p. 124.

5. Roland Evans and Robert Novak, *Lyndon B. Johnson: The Exercise of Power* (New York: New American Library, 1966), p. 328.

6. As quoted in James C. Harvey, *Black Civil Rights during the Johnson Administration* (Jackson: University and College Press of Mississippi, 1973), p. 5. As Mark Stern has observed, Johnson's early reluctance to press for civil rights legislation haunted him and probably motivated his attempt to right that wrong when he became chief executive. See his "Lyndon Johnson and the Democrats' Civil Rights Strategy," paper presented at the annual convention of the American Political Science Association, September, 1989, 10.

7. These are the remarks of Louis Martin, one-time deputy chairman of the Democratic National Committee. See Loevy, "'To Write in the Book of Law,'" p. 107.

8. See, for example, the sudden flurry of activities reported in Mr. Johnson's "Daily Diary," *Papers of Vice President Lyndon B. Johnson, 1961–1963,* Lyndon Baines Johnson Presidential Library, Austin, Texas.

9. Paul Conkin, *Big Daddy from the Pedernales: Lyndon Baines Johnson* (Boston: Twayne, 1986), p. 166.

10. James David Barber, *The Presidential Character: Predicting Performance in the White House* (Englewood Cliffs, N.J.: Prentice-Hall, 1972), p. 87.

11. Kearns, *Lyndon Johnson and the American Dream,* p. 143.

12. A complete, retranscribed copy of the conversation may be obtained from the authors.

13. See James Reston's comments in "No Longer a 'Problem' But a Revolution," *New York Times,* June 16, 1963, sec. 4; praise for Kennedy's bipartisan efforts in "Capi-tal Girds for Battle over Civil Rights Program," *New York Times,* June 23, 1963, sec. 4; quotation on shift in Kennedy administration in *Time,* June 21, 1963, pp. 16–17; An-

thony Lewis's comments in "Campaign for Desegregation Gains Momentum on Two Fronts," *New York Times,* June 23, 1963, sec. 4.

14. Some of the specifics in Mr. Johnson's conversation may not have originated with him. A confidential, untitled memo dated May 24, 1963, appears in Johnson's presidential archives and outlines in detail many of the arguments and strategies he shared with Sorensen in the June 3 conversation. The memo appears in the files of George Reedy, one-time aide to Lyndon Johnson, suggesting either that Reedy had been briefing the vice president on civil rights matters or, equally likely, that he had been working collaboratively with Mr. Johnson on these issues. See *Papers of Vice President Lyndon B. Johnson, 1961–1963,* Lyndon Baines Johnson Presidential Library, Austin, Texas, "Civil Rights," Box 6, 6 pp.

15. For an unusually rich discussion of modernism and its discontents see Joli Jensen, *Redeeming Modernity: Contradictions in Media Criticism* (Newbury Park, Calif.: Sage, 1990). Also see Carl Schorske, *Fin-de-Siecle Vienna* (New York: Vintage, 1981), p. 117; and David Harvey, *The Condition of Postmodernity: An Enquiry into the Origins of Cultural Change* (Oxford: Blackwell, 1989), p. 12.

16. Albert Borgmann, *Crossing the Postmodern Divide* (Chicago: University of Chicago Press, 1990), p. 47.

17. Nowhere was this fateful aspect of Johnson's thinking more in evidence than during Vietnam, a case that has been soundly made in Kathleen Turner's *Lyndon Johnson's Dual War: Vietnam and the Press* (Chicago: University of Chicago Press, 1985).

18. Bruce Miroff convincingly argues that although Lyndon Johnson was unquestionably committed to enlightened social policies as president, he also felt a strong need to control the intensity and direction of civil rights organizations lest they interfere with his own political agenda. See his "Presidential Leverage over Social Movements: The Johnson White House and Civil Rights," *Journal of Politics* 43 (1981): 2–23.

19. See, for example, Erving Goffman, *Interaction Ritual: Essays in Face-to-Face Behavior* (Chicago: Aldine, 1967).

20. Doris Kearns indicates how thoroughly modernist LBJ's understanding of the collective was when she observes that he put his faith in the "bargaining among organized groups, which are far less likely than individuals to act on the basis of transient impulses or irrational decisions." See Kearns, *Lyndon Johnson and the American Dream,* 161. Theodore White makes the same point more directly: "When he thought of his America, he thought of it either in primitive terms of Fourth-of-July patriotism or else as groups of people, forces, individuals, leaders, bosses, lobbies, pressures that he had spent his life in intermeshing" (White, *The Making of the President—1964* (New York: Atheneum, 1965), pp. 60–61.

21. Arendt develops this concept throughout her classic book, *The Human Condition* (Garden City, N.Y.: Doubleday, 1959).

22. For an extended discussion of Johnson's attitudes toward speech, see Barber, *The Presidential Character,* pp. 78–87.

23. Yet another way of interpreting Johnson's use of visual metaphors is to treat them as evidence of his inordinate need to control others by maintaining surveillance over them. Michel Foucault outlines this "panoptic" view of power in his book *Discipline and Punish: The Birth of the Prison,* trans. A. Sheridan (New York: Vintage, 1979).

24. Kenneth Burke, *Language as Symbolic Action: Essays on Life, Literature, and Method* (Berkeley: University of California Press, 1966).

25. J. L. Austin, *How to Do Things with Words,* 2nd ed. (Cambridge: Harvard University Press, 1975).

26. As it turns out, John Kennedy developed this very rhetorical theme during his televised address to the nation on June 11, 1963. See *Public Papers of the President— 1963* (Washington, D.C.: U.S. Government Printing Office, 1964), p. 468.

27. Over the years, Mr. Johnson became even more specific about such matters. He once told Dick Russell that "New Orleans is the place to make a real civil rights speech." Nobody, to date, has yet explained LBJ's complete theory of rhetorical geography, but it is discussed briefly in David Zarefsky's "Subordinating the Civil Rights Issue: Lyndon Johnson in 1964," *Southern Speech Communication Journal* 48 (1983): 103–18. For an illuminating analysis of how Johnson's sometimes fatefully strategic mind undid some of the social programs he most prized, see also Zarefsky's *President Johnson's War on Poverty: Rhetoric and History* (University: University of Alabama Press, 1986).

28. Jim Heath, *Decade of Disillusionment: The Kennedy-Johnson Years* (Bloomington: Indiana University Press, 1975), p. 37.

29. Ralph Lane, *Political Ideology: Why the American Common Man Believes as He Does* (New York: Free Press, 1962).

Chapter 6: Invention of Nixon

1. Comment about Charles de Gaulle in *Richard Nixon, Leaders* (New York: Touchstone, 1990), p. 43; comment about Nixon in Stephen E. Ambrose, *Nixon* (New York: Simon and Schuster, 1987–91), 3: 590.

2. First quotation about the "Silent Majority Speech" is in Richard Nixon, *RN: The Memoirs of Richard Nixon* (New York: Grosset and Dunlap, 1978), p. 410; second quotation about the same speech is in Nixon's *In the Arena: A Memoir of Victory, Defeat, and Renewal* (New York: Simon and Schuster, 1990), p. 216.

3. Critiques of the speech have been assembled by James R. Andrews in *The Practice of Rhetorical Criticism,* 2nd ed. (New York: Longman, 1990), pp. 100–10. Stelzner's essay, "The Quest Story and Nixon's November 3, 1969 Address," is included in the Andrews collection, pp. 111–20.

4. "In 1968, Richard recalled of his mother, '. . . we dreaded far more than my father's hand, her tongue. It was never sharp, but she would just sit you down and she would talk very quietly and then when you got through you had been through an emotional experience.' So, Nixon declared, 'In our family we would always prefer spanking'" (Ambrose, *Nixon,* 1: 24). About his father, Nixon said: "When I was in college, my father accompanied me whenever he could to debates. On the way home, he would dissect the arguments of our opponents and take a few shots at the judges who had voted against us. His encouragement and advice were the primary factor that led me to develop any talents I may later have had as a debater" (Nixon, *In the Arena,* p. 81).

5. Nixon's accounts of the last words of his mother and father are in Nixon, *In the Arena,* pp. 83 and 86, respectively. Italics in the original.

6. In Richard M. Nixon, *Six Crises* (Garden City, N.Y.: Doubleday and Co., 1962), for example, the battle metaphor appears, by my count, fourteen times. Nixon recorded in his memoirs an epiphany concerning the battle metaphor. On December

22, 1967, he was alone in his study thinking about whether to be a candidate for the presidential nomination. Then, as he recollected it, inspiration struck, and he recorded his insight: "I wrote 'Combat is the essence of politics'" (Nixon, *RN*, p. 291).

7. Richard Gardner, "Fighting Quaker: The Story of Richard Nixon," Richard Nixon Collection, Whittier College Library, Whittier, California, p. 44.

8. Julie Nixon Eisenhower, *Pat Nixon: The Untold Story* (New York: Simon and Schuster, 1986).

9. Christopher Lasch, *The Culture of Narcissism: American Life in an Age of Diminishing Expectations* (New York: W. W. Norton and Co., 1978), pp. 79–80.

10. Indignant denials that he is ever a "quitter" occur in Nixon's works throughout his career, including his speech of resignation from the presidency. Perhaps his most poignant comment on the issue occurs in his *RN*, p. 1080, in which he recounts his final days in the White House: "I turned to Ziegler and said, 'How can you support a quitter? You know, when I was a kid I loved sports. I remember running the mile in track once. By the time we reached the last fifty yards, there were only two of us straggling in for next to last place. Still, I sprinted those last yards just as hard as if I were trying for the first-place ribbon. I have never quit before in my life. Maybe that is what none of you had understood this whole time. You don't quit.'"

11. *Nomination of Robert H. Bork to Be Associate Justice of the Supreme Court of the United States: Hearings before the Senate Committee on the Judiciary*, 100th Cong., 1st sess. (1987): 854.

12. David Lilienthal responded eloquently to a question from Senator Kenneth MacKellar during Lilienthal's confirmation hearing as head of the Atomic Energy Commission. The event is an example of the sort of opportunity that Bork botched. See David E. Lilienthal, *The Journals of David E. Lilienthal, 1945-1950* (New York: Harper and Row, 1964), 2: 646–48. The circumstances surrounding Lilienthal's testimony are discussed in David McCullough, *Truman* (New York: Simon and Schuster, 1992), pp. 537–39.

13. Nixon's last memoir contains an inventory of his antipathies (Nixon, *Arena*, p. 133). In scope, character, and implication, his indictment is reminiscent of the betrayal-from-within *topos* that had been quiescent in the country since the era of Joe McCarthy:

> America's leadership class will be remembered for the role it played in helping lose two wars: the war in Vietnam and, at least so far, the war on drugs. The leadership class is made up of highly educated and influential people in the arts, the media, the academic community, the government bureaucracies, and even business. They are characterized by intellectual arrogance, an obsession with style, fashion, and class, and a permissive attitude on drugs. In Vietnam, they felt more comfortable criticizing the United States for trying to save South Vietnam than criticizing the Communists for trying to conquer it. In the drug war, they simply went over to the other side. For years, the enemy was them.

14. Nixon, *In the Arena*, pp. 75–76.

15. Platitudes are, of course, the stock-in-trade of politicians and diplomats, and Nixon's books contain them in profusion. My personal favorite is in his first memoir: "If a man comes out of college with only the narrow and thin background of the highly trained political specialist . . . he will be a sitting duck for every . . . time-worn cliché that comes along" (Nixon, *Six Crises*, p. 297).

16. Roger Morris, *Richard Milhous Nixon: The Rise of an American Politician* (New York: Henry Holt and Co., 1990), p. 72.

17. Fawn M. Brodie, *Richard Nixon: The Shaping of His Character* (New York: W. W. Norton and Co., 1981), p. 77.

18. Isaiah Berlin, *The Hedgehog and the Fox: An Essay on Tolstoy's View of History* (London: Weidenfeld and Nicolson, 1954).

19. In Lincoln this was not a matter of modesty, but of discipline and detachment. "John Hay, who was Lincoln's secretary and observed him at close range all the time he was in the White House, insisted that it was 'absurd to call him a modest man. No great man is ever modest. It was his intellectual arrogance and unconscious assumption of superiority that men like Chase and Sumner could never forgive'" (Edmund Wilson, *Patriotic Gore: Studies in the Literature of the American Civil War* [New York: Oxford University Press, 1966], pp. 118–19.)

Chapter 7: Reagan, Vietnam, and Central America

1. For a discussion of how various influences weakened American institutions of governance, see Jonathan Marshall, Peter D. Scott, and Jane Hunter, *The Iran Contra Connection: Secret Teams and Covert Operations in the Reagan Era* (Boston: South End Press, 1987), p. 1; quotation in William M. LeoGrande, "From Reagan to Bush: the Transition in Policy Towards Central America," *Journal of Latin American Studies* 22 (Oct., 1990): 596.

2. Mark Danner, "How the Foreign Policy Machine Broke Down," *New York Times Magazine,* Mar. 7, 1993, sec. 6, p. 32.

3. Quotation on shared power as an issue of contention in Norman J. Ornstein, "The Constitution and the Sharing of Foreign Policy Responsibility," in *The President, the Congress and Foreign Policy,* eds. Edmund S. Muskie, Kenneth Rush, and Kenneth W. Thompson (Lanham, Md.: University Press of America, 1986), p. 35; quotation on the struggle between Congress and the president in Stephen E. Ambrose, "The Presidency and Foreign Policy," *Foreign Affairs* 70 (Winter, 1991–92): 136; quotation on founding fathers' ambivalence in Ornstein, "The Constitution," p. 35; Krauss's conclusion in his "Every New President Gets a Rematch," *New York Times,* Sept. 26, 1993, sec. 4, p. 3.

4. Adrian Kuzminski, "Archetypes and Paradigms: History, Politics, and Persons," *History and Theory* 25 (1986): 227.

5. Ibid.

6. Chaim Perelman and L. Olbrechts Tyteca, *The New Rhetoric: A Treatise on Argumentation,* eds. John Wilkinson and Purcell Weaver (Notre Dame, Ind.: Notre Dame University Press, 1969).

7. See Robert A. Pastor, *Condemned to Repetition: The United States and Nicaragua* (Princeton, N.J.: Princeton University Press, 1987), pp. 216–27. Pastor argues that Castro's Cuba provides the relevant historical analogy in a policy context to explain the intervention. While Cuba figured prominently in the discussion, this chapter examines the link between policy argument and the broader, defining historical contexts that linked policy and public discussion.

8. This chapter proceeds from the assumption that presidential rhetoric emerges, in part, as a dialogue with other state actors, namely, members of the administration with their own respective institutional obligations and members of other branches of

government. Quotation about Reagan's determination to save Nicaragua from Soviet-Cuban expansionism in Thomas M. Leonard, "Search for Security: The United States and Central America in the Twentieth Century," *The Americas: A Quarterly Review of Inter-American Cultural History* 47 (Apr., 1991): 489. See the influential essay by Jeane Kirkpatrick, "Dictatorships and Double Standards," *Commentary,* Nov., 1979, pp. 34–35. Quotation about Central America as the most important place in the world in Saul Landau, "Remember Central America?" *Tikkun* 4 (Nov./Dec., 1989): 53.

9. Quotation from State Department White Paper cited in Fred I. Greenstein, ed., *The Reagan Presidency: An Early Assessment* (Baltimore: Johns Hopkins University Press, 1983), p. 138; Reagan's press conference response in Ronald Reagan, "Remarks during a White House Briefing on the Program for Economic Recovery," *Public Papers of the Presidents of the United States, Ronald Reagan, 1981,* January 20–December 31, 1981 (Washington, D.C.: U.S.Government Printing Office, 1982), p. 153.

10. White's and Long's quotations are from Jack Kemp, *American Foreign Policy, Current Documents, 1981* (Washington, D.C.: U.S. Government Printing Office, 1984), p. 1258, 1259. See also *Hearings before the Subcommittee on Foreign Operations and Related Agencies of the Committee on Appropriations, House of Representatives, 97th Congress, 1st Session* (Washington, D.C.: U.S. Government Printing Office, 1981), pp. 253–80.

11. Ronald Reagan's comments are from "Excerpts from an Interview with Walter Cronkite of CBS News," *Public Papers of the President of the United States—Ronald Reagan, 1981: January 20, 1981–December 31, 1981* (Washington, D.C.: U.S. Government Printing Office, 1982), p. 191. Al Haig's comment is from *American Foreign Policy, Current Documents, 1981* (Washington, D.C.: U.S. Government Printing Office, 1984), p. 1289. U.S. military reaction in James A. Nathan and James K. Oliver, eds., *Foreign Policy Making and the American Political System* (Baltimore: Johns Hopkins University Press, 1984), p. 136.

12. Authorization of CIA covert action cited in "Congress Curtails Aid to the Nicaraguan Rebels," *Congressional Quarterly Almanac* 40 (1984): 86. For a history of United States involvement see Morris H. Morley, *Washington, Somoza, and the Sandinistas: State and Regime in United States Foreign Policy toward Nicaragua, 1969–1981* (Cambridge: Cambridge University Press, 1994).

13. Ronald Reagan, "Remarks on the Caribbean Basin Initiative to the Permanent Council of the Organization of American States," *Public Papers of the Presidents of the United States, Book I, January 1–June 2, 1982* (Washington, D.C.: U.S. Government Printing Office, 1983), p. 214.

14. Cynthia J. Arnson, *Crossroads: Congress, the President, and Central America, 1976–1993* (University Park: Pennsylvania State University Press, 1993), p. 64.

15. "Central America: Fears of War Along the Border," *Time,* Dec. 6, 1982, p. 37.

16. All debate comments are in *Congressional Record,* 97th Cong., 2nd sess., Dec. 8, 1982, 128: H9148, H9149 (Harkin), 128: H9149 (Leach), 128: H9152 (Mikulski).

17. Ibid., 128: H9152.

18. Ibid., 128: H9154.

19. Ronald Reagan, "Interview with USA Today," *Public Papers of the Presidents of the United States—Ronald Reagan, 1983, Book I, January 1–July 1, 1983* (Washington, D.C.: U.S. Government Printing Office, 1986), p. 587; and Ronald Reagan, "Remarks and a Question-and-Answer Session with Reporters on Domestic and Foreign Policy

Issues," *Public Papers of the Presidents of the United States—Ronald Reagan, 1983, Book I, January 1–July 1, 1983* (Washington, D.C.: U.S. Government Printing Office, 1983), p. 540.

20. Ronald Reagan, "Address before a Joint Session of the Congress on Central America," *Book I, 1983*, pp. 601, 605.

21. *Congressional Record,* 98th Cong., 1st sess., July 27, 1983, 129: H5728.

22. Ibid., 129: H5733.

23. Ibid., 129: H5760.

24. George Bush discovered this rhetorical problem. Bush's strongest argument for fighting Iraq was fashioned in his personal demonization of Sadam Hussein as the incarnation of Adolf Hitler. The U.S.–Iraq war was not about Hitler, of course, but about oil and the balance of power in the Middle East. When the war was over and regional stability required that Hussein be left in power, the American public was left without its sacrificial victim—Saddam. The result was that the Bush administration received generous dollops of blame for being soft in foreign policy and little credit for pursuing a successfully executed policy.

25. Don Ritter's comments are in *Congressional Record,* 98th Cong., 1st sess., July 27, 1983, 129: H5760. Failure to increase public support is discussed in Arnson, *Crossroads,* p. 146.

26. "Congress Curtails Aid to the Nicaraguan Rebels," *Congressional Quarterly Almanac* 40 (1984): 7.

27. Administrative denials are cited in Ronald Reagan, "Written Responses to Questions Submitted by Le Monde of France," *Public Papers of the Presidents of the United States—Ronald Reagan, Book I, 1984* (Washington, D.C.: U.S. Government Printing Office, 1986), pp. 384–85; instances of the use of "covering terms" cited in Robert A. Pastor, *Condemned to Repetition: The U.S. and Nicaragua* (Princeton, N.J.: Princeton University Press, 1987), p. 216.

28. *Congressional Record,* 98th Cong., 2nd sess., Mar. 29, 1984, 130: S3398.

29. *Congressional Record,* 98th Cong., 2nd sess., Apr. 10, 1984, 130: S4200.

30. Ronald Reagan, "Address to the Nation on United States Policy in Central America," *Public Papers of the Presidents of the United States—Ronald Reagan, Book I, January 1–June 29, 1984* (Washington, D.C.: U.S. Government Printing Office, 1986), p. 665.

31. *Congressional Record,* 98th Cong., 2nd sess., June 18, 1984, 130: S7485-7486.

32. *Congressional Record,* 98th Cong., 2nd sess., Aug. 2, 1984, 130: H8269.

33. *Congressional Record,* 98th Cong., 2nd sess., June 18, 1984, 130: S7490–91 (Biden), 130: S7494 (Dodd).

34. Ibid., 130: S7498.

35. Stephen A. Flanders and Carl N. Flanders, *Dictionary of American Foreign Affairs* (New York: MacMillan Inc., 1993), p. 304.

36. "Congress Votes to Resume Nicaraguan Rebel Aid," *Congressional Quarterly Almanac* 41 (1985): 73.

37. Ronald Reagan, "Remarks and a Question-and-Answer Session with Regional Editors and Broadcasters," *Public Papers of the Presidents of the United States—Ronald Reagan, Book I, January 1–June 28, 1985* (Washington, D.C.: U.S. Government Printing Office, 1988), p. 472.

38. *Congressional Record,* 99th Cong., 1st sess., June 7, 1985, 131: S7756.

39. Flanders and Flanders, *Dictionary of American Foreign Affairs,* p. 504.

40. *Congressional Record,* 99th Cong., 1st sess., June 12, 1985, 131: H4188 (Courter), 131: H4190 (Tauzin).

41. Michel quoted in Arnson, *Crossroads,* p. 203; Nicaraguan aid as a litmus test cited in Kenneth Roberts, "Bullying and Bargaining: the United States, Nicaragua, and Conflict Resolution in Central America," *International Security* 15 (Sept., 1990): 67–103; Abrams quoted in Barbara Epstein, "The Reagan Doctrine and Right-Wing Democracy," *Socialist Review* 19 (Jan., 1989): 32.

42. Epstein, "The Reagan Doctrine," p. 32.

43. Ronald Reagan, "Remarks at the Annual Dinner of the Conservative Political Action Conference," *Public Papers of the Presidents of the United States—Ronald Reagan, 1985, Book I, January 1–June 28, 1985* (Washington, D.C.: U.S. Government Printing Office, 1988), p. 229.

44. *Congressional Record,* 99th Cong., 1st sess., June 6, 1985, 131: S7634.

45. Ibid.

46. Reagan's comments in "Radio Address to the Nation on United States Assistance for the Nicaraguan Democratic Resistance," *Public Papers of the Presidents of the United States—Ronald Reagan, 1986, Book I, January 1–June 27, 1986* (Washington, D.C.: U.S. Government Printing Office, 1988), pp. 384–85; Sasser's comments in "Democratic Response to Reagan's Address," *Congressional Quarterly Weekly Report,* Mar. 22, 1986, p. 672.

47. *Congressional Record,* 99th Cong., 2nd sess., August 11, 1986, 132: S11232 (Leahy); ibid., Mar. 20, 1986, 132: H1452 (Murphy); ibid., Aug. 12, 1986, 132: S11337 (Hatfield).

48. *Congressional Record,* 99th Cong., 2nd sess., Mar. 12, 1986, 132: H1088 (Mrazek); ibid. (Ritter); ibid., June 25, 1986, 132: H4216 (Robinson).

49. Ibid., Mar. 20, 1986, 132: H1491.

50. Ibid., Aug. 13, 1986, 132: S11537 (Wilson); ibid., Aug. 12, 1986, 132: S11366 (Domenici).

51. Ibid., March 20, 1986, 132: H1444 (Bloomfield); ibid., Aug. 11, 1986, 132: S11202 (Kerrey).

52. *Congressional Record,* 99th Cong., 2nd sess., August 11, 1986, 132: S11191 (Sen. Thomas Harkin). Vietnam provided a narrative for interpreting administration activities or motives early on in the Central American debate. What appeared to change over time was a growing emphasis on the textualization of Vietnam and Central America. Administration arguments were displayed as parts of a transparent and discredited script for public persuasion. The echo effect of rhetoric involves a doubling of address so that arguments take on the interdefining aspect of both historical and contemporary context.

53. *Congressional Record,* 99th Cong., 2nd sess., March 20, 1986, 132: H1448 (Oakar).

54. *Congressional Record,* 99th Cong., 2nd sess., Aug. 12, 1986, 132: S11219 (Kennedy); S11348 (Matsunaga); ibid., 132: S11367 (Metzenbaum); ibid., March 20, 1986, 132: H1456 (Downey).

55. Tower Commission report in John Felton, "Tower Panel Lays Out Reagan Policy Failures," *Congressional Quarterly Weekly Report,* Feb. 28, 1987, p. 339; Gingrich quotation in ibid.; Dole quotation in Steven Pressman, "Job for Capitol Hill: Select Committees Will Try to Fill in Remaining Gaps," *Congressional Quarterly Weekly Report,* Feb. 28, 1987, p. 343; Trible quotation in ibid., p. 343.

56. Ronald Reagan, "Address to the Nation on the Iran Arms and Contra Aid,"

Public Papers of the Presidents of the United States—Ronald Reagan, 1987, Book I, January 1–July 3, 1987 (Washington, D.C.: U.S. Government Printing Office, 1989), p. 209.

57. "Ship of Fools," *Progressive* 53 (Mar., 1989): 7.

58. Rhetorically, foreign policy episodes may be formed into master narratives whose unfolding patterns still cast a shadow on present events. The power of archetype is the power to define and to move to completion without variation. Alternatively, episodes may be forwarded as examples which inform general principles of prudent action. In the former case, the rhetorical form defines a policy alternative within a single horizon of historical experience. In the later case, the argument compares similarities and differences in the interests of specifying particular principles of action.

Chapter 8: *Tragic Fear and the Rhetorical Presidency*

1. Stephen R. Graubard, *Mr. Bush's War: Adventures in the Politics of Illusion* (New York: Hill and Wang, 1992).

2. Ibid., p. xvi.

3. Ibid., pp. xi–xii.

4. Ibid., pp. 3, 8, 10.

5. Ibid., pp. 20-21, 22, 27, 28, 29, 35, 60.

6. Ibid., pp. 66, 91, 92, 94, 101, 124, 140, 166–67.

7. Landmark essay by James W. Ceaser, Glen E. Thurow, Jeffrey Tulis, and Joseph M. Bessette, "The Rise of the Rhetorical Presidency," *Presidential Studies Quarterly* 11 (1981): 158–71; reprinted in Theodore Windt, ed. *Essays in Presidential Rhetoric* (Dubuque: Kendall/Hunt, 1983), pp. 3–22. Tulis's key themes are in Jeffrey K. Tulis, *The Rhetorical Presidency* (Princeton, New Jersey: Princeton University Press, 1987). Neustadt's claims on the powers of the presidency to persuade are in Richard Neustadt, *Presidential Power* (New York: John Wiley and Sons, 1960). Quotation is in Ceaser et al., "The Rise in the Rhetorical Presidency," p. 7.

8. Ceaser et al., "The Rise in the Rhetorical Presidency," p. 7; Tulis, *The Rhetorical Presidency*, pp. 27–28.

9. Tulis, *The Rhetorical Presidency*, pp. 112, 114.

10. Ibid., p. 128.

11. Ibid., pp. 130–36.

12. Quotation in Ceaser et al., "The Rise in the Rhetorical Presidency," p. 19; discussion of the corruption of deliberative discourse in Tulis, *The Rhetorical Presidency*, pp. 147, 172.

13. David Henry, "Ronald Reagan and Aid to the *Contras:* An Analysis of the Rhetorical Presidency," in *Rhetorical Dimensions in Media: A Critical Casebook*, ed. Martin J. Medhurst and Thomas W. Benson, 2nd ed. (Dubuque: Kendall/Hunt, 1991), p. 74.

14. Kurt Ritter, "Reassessing Reagan's Oratory: The Rhetorical Presidency from a Classical Perspective," Working Paper No. 4, Center for Presidential Studies, Texas A&M University, Nov., 1994, pp. 2, 20–21.

15. Karlyn Kohrs Campbell and Kathleen Hall Jamieson, *Deeds Done in Words: Presidential Rhetoric and the Genres of Governance* (Chicago: University of Chicago Press, 1990), pp. 5–6, 213–19.

16. Tulis, *The Rhetorical Presidency*, pp. 173, 146–47, 152, 157–59.

17. Ibid., pp. 164–65.

18. Ibid., pp. 167–68.

19. David Zarefsky's study of LBJ's poverty campaign is *President Johnson's War on Poverty: Rhetoric and History* (University: University of Alabama Press, 1986); Tulis, citing Zarefsky, is in Tulis's *The Rhetorical Presidency*, p. 172.

20. My comments on Zarefsky's book are taken from Robert L. Ivie, "The Complete Criticism of Political Rhetoric," *Quarterly Journal of Speech* 73 (1987): 104–105; quotations by Zarefsky are in his *President Johnson's War on Poverty*, pp. 1, 6–7.

21. Zarefsky, *President Johnson's War on Poverty*, pp. 11, 13, 14, 16.

22. Ibid., p. 20.

23. Ibid., p. 202.

24. Leroy G. Dorsey, "Theodore Roosevelt and the Birth of the Rhetorical Presidency," Working Paper No. 3, Center for Presidential Studies, Texas A&M University, May, 1994, pp. 16–18; for the published version of the paper, see Leroy G. Dorsey, "The Frontier Myth in Presidential Rhetoric: Theodore Roosevelt's Campaign for Conservation," *Western Journal of Communication* 59 (1995): 1–19.

25. Frederick M. Dolan and Thomas L. Dumm, eds., *Rhetorical Republic: Governing Representations in American Politics* (Amherst: The University of Massachusetts, 1993), pp. 1, 2, 6. The term "governing representations" was originated by Anne Norton. For a detailed treatment of her perspective, see Anne Norton, *Republic of Signs: Liberal Theory and American Popular Culture* (Chicago: University of Chicago Press, 1993).

26. Avital Ronell, "Support Our Tropes: Reading Desert Storm," in Dolan and Dumm, *Rhetorical Republic*, pp. 13–16.

27. See Campbell's analysis of the rhetorical republic in David Campbell, "Cold Wars: Securing Identity, Identifying Danger," in Dolan and Dumm, *Rhetorical Republic*, pp. 39–60; quotation about national identity always at risk is in Dolan and Dumm, *Rhetorical Republic*, p. 11; quotation about the consequences of using the interpretative practices of the Soviet Union threat in the war against Iraq is in Campbell, "Cold Wars," pp. 40–43.

28. See Campbell's comments in Campbell, "Cold Wars," pp. 43–46, 58–59. See Wicker's comments in Tom Wicker, introduction to *The Liberal Tradition in America: An Interpretation of American Political Thought Since the Revolution*, by Louis Hartz, 2nd ed. (San Diego: Harcourt Brace Jovanovich, 1991), pp. xi–xii.

29. Karen Rasmussen and Sharon D. Downey, "The Rhetoric of the Gulf War: Restoring American Dominance and Control," paper presented at the annual meeting of the Speech Communication Association, November, 1994, New Orleans, La; see quotations on pp. 30–31.

30. Mark A. Pollock, "The Battle for the Past: Bush and the Gulf Crisis," in *The Modern Presidency and Crisis Rhetoric*, ed. Amos Kiewe (Westport, Conn.: Praeger, 1994), pp. 203–204, 208–209, 210, 220.

31. See, for instance, Judith Miller and Laurie Mylroie, *Saddam Hussein and the Crisis in the Gulf* (New York: Times Books, 1990).

32. Many of the details of Saddam Hussein's atrocities and the Reagan and Bush administration's economic and military support of his regime as well as my quotations from U.N. and Amnesty International reports are taken from Murray Wass, "What Washington Gave Saddam for Christmas," originally published in the December 18, 1990, issue of *Village Voice* and subsequently reprinted in *The Gulf War Reader: His-*

tory, Documents, Opinions, eds. Micah L. Sifry and Christopher Cerf (New York: Times Books, 1991), pp. 85–95.

33. "A Return to Cold War Thinking (Speech of January 10, 1991)," reprinted in Sifry and Cerf, *The Gulf War Reader,* p. 286.

34. Doug Bandow, "The Myth of Iraq's Oil Stranglehold," originally published on the *New York Times* op-ed page on Sept. 17, 1990, reprinted in Sifry and Cerf, *The Gulf War Reader,* 219–20.

35. For one discussion of this problem of American identity, see Marcy Darnovsky, L. A. Kauffman, and Billy Robinson, "What Will This War Mean?" in Sifry and Cerf, *The Gulf War Reader,* 483–86. Also see Theodore Draper, "American Hubris," originally published in *New York Review of Books,* July 16, 1987, and reprinted in Sifry and Cerf, *The Gulf War Reader,* pp. 40–56; Draper's quotations can be found in "American Hubris," pp. 40–43.

36. Bush's comments on what was at stake quoted in Micah L. Sifry, "U.S. Intervention in the Middle East: A Case Study," in Sifry and Cerf, *The Gulf War Reader,* p. 27. Bush's comments on Iraq's brutality quoted from his speech of Nov. 8, 1990, in Sifry and Cerf, *The Gulf War Reader,* 229.

37. For Bush's various comments about the war, see his speeches of Nov. 8, 1990, Aug. 8, 1990, and Jan. 16, 1991, all in Sifry and Cerf, *The Gulf War Reader,* pp. 228 and 229, 197, and 312, respectively. For a deconstruction of the metaphorical system operating in the Bush administration's Persian Gulf War rhetoric generally and, specifically, the metaphoric treatment of the Iraqi state as a person, and metonymic reduction of Iraq to its ruler, Saddam Hussein, see George Lakoff, "Metaphor and War: The Metaphor System Used to Justify War in the Gulf," in *Engulfed in War: Just War and the Persian Gulf,* ed. Brien Hallett (Honolulu: Spark M. Matsunaga Institute for Peace, 1991), pp. 95–111. A complementary rhetorical analysis of the administration's themes and strategies is provided by George Cheney, "We're Talking War: Symbols, Strategies and Images," in *Desert Storm and the Mass Media,* ed. Bradley S. Greenberg and Walter Gantz (Cresskill, N.J.: Hampton Press, 1993), pp. 61–73.

38. Edward W. Said, "On Linkage, Language, and Identity," in Sifry and Cerf, *The Gulf War Reader,* pp. 439, 442. See also Edward W. Said, *Culture and Imperialism* (New York: Vintage Books, 1993), pp. 282–303. For an analysis of how Bush's "terrorist narrative" discouraged a balanced assessment of Iraq's motives, means, and culpability, see Carol K. Winkler, "Narrative Reframing of Public Argument: George Bush's Handling of the Persian Gulf Conflict," in *Warranting Assent: Case Studies in Argument Evaluation,* ed. Edward Schiappa (Albany: State University of New York Press, 1995), pp. 33–55. For a related discussion of rhetoric-limiting options in the Persian Gulf crisis, see John Louis Lucaites and Charles A. Taylor, "Theorizing the Grounds of Rhetorical Judgment," *Informal Logic* 15 (1993): 29–40.

39. Quotation on Iraqi's claims against Kuwait is in Walid Khalidi, "Why Some Arabs Support Saddam," in Sifry and Cerf, *The Gulf War Reader,* p. 170. See Frankel's comments in Glenn Frankel, "Lines in the Sand," reprinted in Sifry and Cerf, *The Gulf War Reader,* p. 17. Sir Anthony Parson's comment reported by Frankel, "Lines in the Sand," p. 17.

40. Avi Shlaim has observed, for example, that America fought a "neat war . . . followed by a messy peace." The war's aftermath reminds us, he argues, "that military force, when used to tackle complex political problems, is merely a blunt instrument. The war also demonstrated that Americans are better at short, sharp bursts of military

intervention designed to restore the status quo than at sustained political engagement to resolve the underlying origins of instability in the Middle East" (Shlaim, *War and Peace in the Middle East: A Critique of American Policy* [New York: Whittle Books, 1994], p. 103).

41. For an example of the tropological dynamics of such secret deliberations about the Vietnam War within the Johnson administration, see Robert L. Ivie, "Metaphor and Motive in the Johnson Administration's Vietnam War Rhetoric," *Texts in Context: Critical Dialogues on Significant Episodes in American Political Rhetoric,* eds. Michael C. Leff and Fred J. Kauffeld (Davis, Calif.: Hermagoras Press, 1989), pp. 121–41.

42. Draper, "American Hubris," pp. 55–56.

43. Ibid., p. 42.

44. Kenneth Burke develops his notion of the comic frame in a number of places, but most extensively and directly in his *Attitudes Toward History,* 3rd ed. (1937; Berkeley: University of California Press, 1984). For a useful summary of his views and an example of their application in rhetorical criticism, see A. Cheree Carlson, "Gandhi and the Comic Frame: 'Ad Bellum Purificandum,'" *Quarterly Journal of Speech* 72 (1986): 446–55. Also note that a number of writers have pointed to alternatives short of war available to the administration had it been motivated to achieve justice as peacefully as possible. Even Michael Walzer, who has argued that the war satisfied the criteria of the just-war doctrine, observes that it would have been "possible to seek alternative resolutions of the conflict. The blockade was merely one of many alternatives, which included United Nations condemnation of Iraq, its diplomatic and political isolation, various degrees of economic sanction, and a negotiated settlement involving small or large concessions to the aggressor. The actual blockade might have taken different forms, adapted to different ends; the coalition might, for example, have aimed at the containment rather than the reversal of Iraqi aggression." See his "Justice and Injustice in the Gulf War," in *But Was It Just? Reflections on the Morality of the Persian Gulf War,* ed. David E. Decosse (New York: Doubleday, 1992), p. 5. The crusading spirit of the administration's war rhetoric made the pursuit of peace by means short of war difficult to envision, as noted by Jean Bethke Elshtain, "Just War as Politics: What the Gulf War Told Us about Contemporary American Life," in Decosse, *But Was It Just?,* p. 49. Motivated by the right intention of avoiding war (rather than by inordinate fear of the other), even by the dictates of the just-war doctrine, which entails a presumption against the use of force, the United States could have employed tactics more in proportion to the circumstances faced in the Middle East. The coalition forces, for example, might have "agreed upon Iraqi withdrawal from Kuwait to deal with the manifest injustices and the situation, potentially strangling to Iraq, of the Rumaila oil field and the islands of Bubiyan and Warba," as suggested by Kenneth L. Vaux, *Ethics and the Gulf War: Religion, Rhetoric, and Righteousness* (Boulder, Colo.: Westview Press, 1992), p. 26. For a discussion of the need to develop a more comprehensive and complex view of international relations, see Francis A. Beer, "Reflections on Collective Consciousness: The Persian Gulf Debate," *Modern Science and Vedic Science* 5 (1992): 37–43.

Chapter 9: Rhetorical Presidency

1. Betty Boyd Caroli, *First Ladies* (New York: Oxford University Press, 1987), p. xxi.

2. Hanna Papanek, "Men, Women, and Work: Reflections on a Two-Person Career," *American Journal of Sociology* 78 (Jan., 1973): 852–72. Cited material on pp.

862, 863. Specific application of this concept to the First Lady is made on pp. 872–73.

3. When interviewed on *Good Morning, America,* October 21, 1992, Perot's wife explained that a president's wife cannot go to Washington and live a private life. Earlier when questioned about what project she might pursue, she asked the reporter to suggest one (Garry Wills, "A Doll's House," *New York Review of Books,* Oct. 22, 1992, p. 10). Stockdale's wife indicated an interest in helping single parents and fighting AIDS (Jane Meredith Adams, "No Shrinking Violet, She," *Boston Globe,* Nov. 2, 1992, p. 10, and "'In Love and War'—and Now in Politics," *Chicago Tribune,* Oct. 30, 1992, sec. 5.1).

4. Comparison of First Ladyship duties to royal family obligations in Abigail Q. McCarthy, "ER As First Lady," in *Without Precedent: Eleanor Roosevelt,* eds. Joan Hoff-Wilson and Marjorie Lightman (Bloomington: Indiana University Press, 1989), p. 215. Marital partnership ties with the presidency have been exemplified historically— e.g., when the president has been widowed or unmarried, or when his wife has been unable to perform these duties, a surrogate has always been found to perform them.

5. Richard Schickel, *Intimate Strangers: The Culture of Celebrity* (Garden City, N.Y.: Doubleday, 1985).

6. Barbara Welter, *Dimity Convictions: The American Woman in the Nineteenth Century* (Athens: Ohio University Press, 1966), p. 21.

7. Martha Washington's comments are from a letter dated Oct. 22, 1789, Martha Washington Papers, Mount Vernon, cited in Carl Sferrazza Anthony, *First Ladies: The Saga of the Presidents' Wives and Their Power, 1789–1961* (New York: William Morrow, 1990), p. 48. Reaction to Martha Washington's levées are also reported in Anthony, *First Ladies,* p. 48. For a complete study of presidential wives, see also Anthony's *First Ladies: Volume II: The Saga of the Presidents' Wives and Their Power, 1961-1990* (New York: William Morrow, 1991).

8. *Ecce Homo,* trans. Walter Kauffman, pp. 266–67, quoted in Ellen Kennedy, "Nietzsche: Women as Untermensch," *Women in Western Political Philosophy: Kant to Nietzsche,* eds. Ellen Kennedy and Susan Mendus (New York: St. Martin's Press, 1987), p. 187.

9. Kitty Kelley, *Nancy Reagan: The Unauthorized Biography* (New York: Simon and Schuster, 1991) offers extensive evidence of the key role that Reagan's wife played in all these areas, including her impact on the INF Treaty with the Soviet Union and her importance in the drafting of presidential addresses (e.g., pp. 341, 451, 488). That is also demonstrated by other books by members of Reagan's staff and cabinet. See also *My Turn: The Memoirs of Nancy Reagan with William Novak* (New York: Dell, 1989), pp. 159, 347–49. The roles that other First Ladies played are cited in the following: Caroli, *First Ladies,* pp. xix, 266–71 (Rosalynn Carter); pp. 58–67 (Julia Tyler and Sarah Polk); p. 134 (Ellen Wilson); p. xix (Dolley Madison and Julia Grant). Bess Truman cited in David McCullough, *Truman* (New York: Simon and Schuster, 1992), p. 579, and Anthony, *First Ladies,* 1: 529.

10. She was a partner in Val-Kill, a furniture factory, and in Todhunter School, where she taught. Subsequently, during FDR's presidency, she continued to write and speak, earning such large sums of money that a congressional investigation ensued, which ended only when it was revealed that all her earnings had gone to charity. She served on the platform committee at the New York state 1926 Democratic convention, and she was active in the Women's Trade Union League and other women's

political groups (Blanche Wiesen Cook, *Eleanor Roosevelt: Volume 1, 1884–1933* [New York: Viking, 1992]).

11. Quotation about Eleanor Roosevelt as "center of controversy" in McCarthy, "ER As First Lady," p. 214. Eleanor's press conference comments are in *The White House Press Conferences of Eleanor Roosevelt*, ed. Maurine Beasley (New York: Garland Publishing, Inc., 1983), p. 128, quoted in Caroli, *First Ladies*, p. 192. Eleanor's letter is from Joseph Lash, *Eleanor and Franklin* (New York, Norton, 1971), p. 471, quoted in Caroli, *First Ladies*, p. 192.

12. Stanley G. Hilton, *Bob Dole: American Political Phoenix* (Chicago: Contemporary Books, 1988), p. 127; Bob and Elizabeth Dole with Richard Norton Smith, *The Doles: Unlimited Partners* (New York, Simon and Schuster, 1988), pp. ix–xii; Ann Grimes, *Running Mates: The Making of a First Lady* (New York: William Morrow, 1990), pp. 73–74; Grimes, *Running Mates*, p. 89; quoted in Grimes, *Running Mates*, p. 91; italics in original; ibid., p. 92.

13. Clinton's comments to CNN interviewer and during fund-raiser are in Marjorie Williams, "First Ladies," *Washington Post Magazine*, Nov. 1, 1992, p. 24. Hillary's definition of First Lady's role is in Patricia O'Brien, "The First Lady with a Career?" *Working Woman*, Aug., 1992, p. 72. Sheehy's reaction to Hillary Clinton's comments are in Gail Sheehy, "What Hillary Wants," *Vanity Fair*, May, 1992, pp. 142–47, 212–17. O'Brien's comments are in her article "The First Lady with a Career?," p. 47; see also Deirdre McMurdy, "The Political Wife: Hillary Clinton Redefines Her Role," *Maclean's*, July, 1992, p. 34. Related to Governor Brown's charges during the Illinois primary: Two days before the primary the *Washington Post* published a story noting that Hillary Rodham Clinton's law firm did significant work for the Arkansas state government, though she did not share profits from the firm's state business. In a debate among the Democratic candidates in Chicago, Jerry Brown made the charge and Clinton exploded angrily saying Brown wasn't fit to "be on the same platform with my wife" (see Special Election Issue, *Newsweek*, November–December, 1992, p. 39). Rodham Clinton's famous cookies-and-tea comment quoted on NBC's *Dateline* with Jane Pauley. Rodham Clinton's comments on women having choices is quoted in Margaret Carlson, "All Eyes on Hillary," *Time*, Sept. 14, 1992, p. 30.

14. Poll results cited in Jeffrey Schmalz, "A Spouse Who Grabs the Stage," *New York Times*, Apr. 28, 1992, p. A9. A *Newsweek* poll in July found 55 percent favorable; cited in Doug Grow, "Hillary Clinton Seen as Radical and Inspirational," [Mpls.] *Star Tribune*, July 28, 1992, p. 3B. News story quotation is from Carol Byrne and Robert Whereatt, "Stopping In and Speaking Out," [Mpls.] *Star Tribune*, July 29, 1992, p. A1. August poll results reported in *New York Times*, Oct. 8, 1992, p. A31. In October her approval ratings were 32 percent.

15. Quayle's first quote is in Ellen Goodman, "Call Off GOP Attack-Hillary Dogs," (*Boston Globe*) [Mpls.] *Star Tribune*, Aug. 23, 1992, p. A30; second quote is in Larry Rohter, "Unrepentant, Marilyn Quayle Stresses Family and Values," *New York Times*, Oct. 28, 1992, p. A10.

16. Elizabeth Kolbert, "Test Marketing a President," *New York Times Magazine*, Aug. 30, 1992, p. 68.

17. Mimi Hall, "No Last Word on the New First Lady," *USA Today*, Nov. 13, 1992. Overall ratings were 49 percent favorable, 30 percent unfavorable. Of men, 44 percent were favorable, 31 percent unfavorable; of women 52 percent were favorable,

30 percent unfavorable. Favorable-unfavorable ratings among those age 18–29 were 43 to 42 percent, age 30–49 were 51 to 30 percent, age 50–64 were 43 to 30 percent, and age 65 and over were 56 to 17 percent. Those "most likely to identify with her: Easterners, college graduates, urbanites. Least likely: Midwesterners, suburbanites, high school dropouts, and baby boomers."

18. See Felicity Barringer, "Hillary Clinton's New Role: A Spouse or a Policy Leader?" *New York Times*, Nov. 16, 1992, p. A1, A14; all quoted material appears on p. A14.

19. "Women in the Race," *Washington Post*, April, 1987, quoted in Grimes, *Running Mates*, p. 40.

20. Caroli, *First Ladies*, p. 63.

21. Susan Riley, *Political Wives: The Lives of the Saints* (Toronto: Deneau, 1987), p. 47.

22. Jane Reilly's comment is in "Hers," *New York Times*, Sept. 11, 1987, p. 2C, quoted in Grimes, p. 110. Susan Riley's comment is quoted in Grimes, *First Ladies*, p. 318. See also Riley, *Political Wives*, pp. 3–4.

23. Lewis L. Gould, "First Ladies," *American Scholar* (Autumn, 1986): 528–35; quotation cited on p. 535.

24. Hagen's comments are in Charles Hagen, "Reading the Candidates Family Portraits," *New York Times*, Oct. 25, 1992, p. 28H. Riley's comments on the importance of family photographs is in Riley, *Political Wives*, pp. 186–87.

25. Deborah Tannen, *You Just Don't Understand: Women and Men in Conversation* (New York: Ballantine Books, 1990), p. 243.

26. Gould's comment is in Gould, "First Ladies," p. 535. Quindlen's comment is in Anna Quindlen, "Hillary at Midterm," *New York Times*, Oct. 12, 1994, p. A19.

27. Caroli's quotation about Sarah Polk in Caroli, *First Ladies*, p. 65. Sellers's quotation about Sarah Polk's role in Charles Sellers, "Sarah Childress Polk," in *Notable American Women*, eds. Edward T. James, Janet Wilson James, and Paul S. Boyer, (Cambridge: Harvard University Press, 1971), 3: 82. Polk's refusal to lend her support at Seneca Falls is documented in Anthony, *First Ladies*, 1: 144. Sarah Polk's response about making butter is documented in Anson Nelson and Fanny Nelson, *Memorials of Sarah Childress Polk: Wife of the Eleventh President of the United States* (New York: Anson D. F. Randolph and Co., 1892), p. 80. She followed traditional norms in dress, entertainment, and religious piety, however.

28. Caroli, *First Ladies*, pp. 291–92.

29. Reaction to Rosalynn Carter's attendance at Cabinet meetings is in *Rosalynn Carter, First Lady From Plains* (New York: Fawcett Gold Medal, 1984), pp. 165–66. The AK-47 incident is reported in Donnie Radcliffe, *Simply Barbara Bush: A Portrait of America's Candid First Lady* (New York: Warner Books, 1989), p. 44. News norms dictating close observation of Rodham Clinton's activities is from Patricia O'Brien, personal interview with the author, Nov. 11, 1992.

30. For a full account of press coverage and its fallout, see Kathleen Hall Jamieson, *Beyond the Double Bind: Women and Leadership* (New York: Oxford University Press, 1995), pp. 25–34. NBC's Andrea Mitchell was the reporter who recognized the news value of Rodham Clinton's statement. Patricia O'Brien's comment is from her personal interview with the author.

31. Randolph's complaint is in Mary Randolph, *Presidents and First Ladies* (New York: Appleton Century, 1936), p. 124. Charles Black's comment is in *Star Tribune*, Aug. 27, 1992, p. 7A. MacIvor's comment is quoted in Deirdre McMurdy, "The Political Wife: Hillary Clinton Redefines Her Role," *Maclean's*, July, 1992, p. 34.

32. The Clinton campaign was salvaged by a second-place finish behind Paul Tsongas. Because Clinton survived, with 25 percent of the vote, he was widely perceived as winning in New Hampshire because Paul Tsongas, from neighboring Massachusetts, was favored to win. Rodham Clinton's comments on *60 Minutes* are quoted in *USA Today,* Oct. 9, 1992, p. 8A.

33. Quotation about the Republican strategy to represent Rodham Clinton's views as Mr. Clinton's is in Michael Kelly, "Contest of Two Generations Has Risks for Both Nominees," *New York Times,* Aug. 30, 1992, p. A15. Daniel Wattenberg's essay appears in *American Spectator* 25 (Aug., 1992): 25–32.

34. Toner's comment appears in Robin Toner, "Backlash for Hillary Clinton Puts Negative Image to Rout," *New York Times,* Sept. 24, 1992, p. A1; see, for example, Elizabeth Kolbert, "Test Marketing a President," *New York Times Magazine,* Aug. 30, 1992, p. 24. Various epithets and terms applied to Rodham Clinton are discussed in Ellen Goodman, (*Boston Globe*) [Mpls.] *Star Tribune,* Aug. 23, 1992, p. A30; and Catherine Manegold, "Women Get into Political Football—as the Ball," *New York Times,* Aug. 23, 1992, p. E1.

35. Bond's and Quayle's comments appear in Gwen Ifill, "G.O.P. Makes Hillary Clinton Issue of the Day," *New York Times,* Aug. 13, 1992, p. A11.

36. Comments appear in *New York Times,* Aug. 20, 1992, p. A6 (Buchanan), p. A20 (Pat Robertson).

37. Flashpoint's views are analyzed in Anna Quindlen, "The Cost of Free Speech," *New York Times,* Feb. 9, 1994, p. A15. Gritz's community and views are documented in Timothy Egan, "Idaho Community Built on Hatred and Fear," *New York Times,* Oct. 5, 1994, p. A10. Anti-Hillary activities are documented in the following sources: Anna Quindlen, "Don't Ditch Dee Dee," *New York Times,* Sept. 24, 1994, p. 15Y (tobacco farmers); Martin Walker, *Star Tribune,* Aug. 19, 1994, p. A22 (health care rally); "30 Arrested in Protest at a Clinic in Arkansas," *New York Times,* July 9, 1994, p. 9Y (Arkansas clinic); letter to the editor, [Mpls.] *Star Tribune,* June 10, 1993 (Playboy bunny). Regarding Rodham Clinton's conservative views on abortion, an interview published in *Newsweek* (Oct. 31, 1994) reveals that she considers abortion "wrong" and is "not comfortable" with the school distribution of condoms (cited in David Walsh, "Out On A Spiritual Limb," *Star Tribune,* Nov. 28, 1994, p. 6A).

38. "What Happened to Bill Clinton?" PBS, January 31, 1995. This information was provided by David Maraniss, a *Washington Post* reporter and author of *First In His Class: A Biography of Bill Clinton* (New York: Simon and Schuster, 1995).

39. Reaction to the *Vogue* photo is documented in a letter to the editor, *New York Times,* Dec. 25, 1993, p. 14Y; and also in Maureen Dowd, "Hillary Rodham Clinton Strikes a New Pose and Multiplies Her Images," *New York Times,* Dec. 12, 1993, p. E3. Photo of Rodham Clinton in white suit and accompanying article appear in Michael Kelly, "Saint Hillary, *New York Times Magazine,* May 23, 1993, pp. 22–25, 63–66. Photographs of Rodham Clinton's ten hairdos are in an Associated Press story in the *Star Tribune,* Dec. 2, 1994, p. 3B.

40. Karlyn Kohrs Campbell, "Shadowboxing with Stereotypes: The Press, the Public, and the Candidates' Wives," Joan Shorenstein Barone Center on Press, Politics, and Public Policy, John F. Kennedy School of Government, Harvard University, Research Paper R-9, July, 1993.

Chapter 10: *Presidential Rhetoric*

1. David Zarefsky, *Lincoln, Douglas, and Slavery: In the Crucible of Public Debate* (Chicago: University of Chicago Press, 1990), p. xi.

2. Ibid., pp. 103, 110.

3. Zarefsky's arguments are in ibid., pp. 137–38, 165, 196–97, 223, 228–29.

4. Effects of the debate are in ibid., pp. 204, 218; reference to the *American Almanac* is on p. x; audience reaction is on p. 233.

5. Ibid., pp. 222, 236–38, 245 (quotation).

6. The limits to presidential rhetoric is discussed in Jeffrey K. Tulis, *The Rhetorical Presidency* (Princeton, NJ: Princeton University Press, 1987), p. 146, for example. Woodrow Wilson's League of Nations campaign is on pp. 146–47, 148–61. Presidential rhetoric as an influence is on p. 178. Reagan's rhetorical skills are discussed on pp. 189–202; see also pp. 145 and 178, and p. 203 (quotation).

7. Ibid., pp. 102, 106.

8. Ibid., pp. 161–72.

9. Quotations are in Roderick P. Hart, *The Sound of Leadership: Presidential Communication in the Modern Age* (Chicago: University of Chicago Press, 1987), pp. 14, 79, 110, respectively. Effects of presidential speeches are discussed on pp. 75–76; see also pp. 92–93.

10. Hart's assessments are in ibid., pp. 208, 213.

11. Ibid., p. 75.

12. Quotations are in ibid., pp. 79, 103, respectively.

13. See Martin J. Medhurst, *Dwight D. Eisenhower: Strategic Communicator* (Westport, Conn.: Greenwood Press, 1993), p. 86 (Eisenhower's ability to inspire); pp. 72–73, 91 (his use of rhetoric to influence others); p. 5 (his ability to inspire others); see also pp. 17–18 on the 1952 presidential election; and p. 18 (his charisma).

14. Ibid., pp. 60, 62 (quotation), 63, 67–68, 80.

15. The president's ability to establish the terms of discourse is discussed in Theodore Otto Windt, Jr., *Presidents and Protestors: Political Rhetoric in the 1960s* (Tuscaloosa, Ala.; University of Alabama Press, 1990), pp. 3–4. The author cites himself as the source of this conclusion. See also "Presidential Rhetoric: Definition of a Discipline of Study," 2nd ed., in *Essays in Presidential Rhetoric*, eds. Theodore Windt and Beth Ingold (Dubuque: Kendall/Hunt, 1987), pp. xv–xliii; see also p. 4. The president's ability to define a crisis is discussed in Windt, *Presidents and Protestors*, p. 5; see also pp. 6–9.

16. Kennedy's speeches on the Berlin crisis, the Soviet Union, and civil rights are discussed in Windt, *Presidents and Protestors*, p. 44, 76, and 84, respectively.

17. George C. Edwards III, *Presidential Approval* (Baltimore: Johns Hopkins University Press, 1990), pp. 143–52.

18. Craig Allen Smith and Kathy B. Smith, *The White House Speaks: Presidential Leadership as Persuasion* (Westport, Conn.; Praeger, 1994), p. 20; see also p. 235.

19. Ibid., p. 127.

20. Reagan's, Carter's, and Kennedy's rhetoric is discussed in ibid., pp. 147, 157, and 148–51, respectively.

21. Reagan's storytelling is discussed in ibid., p. 233; Reagan as a polarizing influence is discussed in Edwards, *Presidential Approval*, pp. 175–79.

22. Karlyn Kohrs Campbell and Kathleen Hall Jamieson, *Deeds Done in Words:*

Presidential Rhetoric and the Genres of Governance (Chicago: University of Chicago Press, 1990), p. 3; see also p. 5.

23. Ibid., p. 12.

24. Ibid., pp. 12–13.

25. Ibid., p. 190.

26. Inaugural addresses, in general, and Lincoln's first inaugural are in ibid., chap. 2 and p. 33, respectively. State of the Union messages are discussed in chap. 3, pp. 63, 74, 75, and 215; see also p. 163. The effects of presidential ceremonial functions is on p. 73.

27. War rhetoric is discussed in ibid., pp. 111, 126, 215; Reagan's response is on p. 132; and rhetoric to forestall impeachment is on pp. pp. 143, 164.

28. Reagan's speech is quoted in "Reagan Bids Nation Farewell: 'We've Made a Difference,'" *Congressional Quarterly Weekly Report*, Jan. 14, 1989, p. 95. Johnson's comment is in Haynes Johnson, *Sleepwalking Through History* (New York: Norton, 1991), p. 167.

29. George C. Edwards III, *At the Margins: Presidential Leadership of Congress* (New Haven, Conn.: Yale University Press, 1989).

30. Both Anderson quotations are in Martin Anderson, *Revolution: The Reagan Legacy* (Stanford: Hoover Institution Press, 1990), p. 7 and pp. xviii–xix, respectively. Johnson's quotation is in Haynes Johnson, *Sleepwalking Through History*, p. 49. Johnson, p. 79, also argues that Reagan's election as governor of California in 1966, during the period of discord over the war in Vietnam, civil rights, and campus unrest, occurred because "through Reagan the public had a vehicle to express resentment at both national disorder and political leadership."

31. William A. Niskanen, *Reaganomics* (New York: Oxford University Press, 1988), p. 22.

32. Ibid., p. 22.

33. See James A. Stimson, *Public Opinion in America: Moods, Cycles, and Swings* (Boulder: Westview, 1991), pp. 64, 126–27; Benjamin I. Page and Robert Y. Shapiro, *The Rational Public* (Chicago: University of Chicago Press, 1992), pp. 127, 136; James A. Davis, "Changeable Weather in a Cooling Climate," *Public Opinion Quarterly* 56 (Fall, 1992): 261–306; William G. Mayer, *The Changing American Mind* (Ann Arbor: University of Michigan Press, 1992), p. 123; and Tom W. Smith, "Liberal and Conservative Trends in the United States Since World War II," *Public Opinion Quarterly* 54 (Winter, 1990): 479–507.

34. Martin P. Wattenberg, *The Rise of Candidate-Centered Politics* (Cambridge: Harvard University Press, 1991), chap. 4.

35. Ronald Reagan, *An American Life* (New York: Simon and Schuster, 1990), p. 471–79.

36. Reports of surveys of public opinion can be found in the following sources: Seymour Martin Lipset, "Beyond 1984: The Anomalies of American Politics," *PS* 19 (1986): 228–29; Mayer, *The Changing American Mind*, chaps 5 and 6; Page and Shapiro, *The Rational Public*, pp. 133, 136, 159; William Schneider, "The Voters' Mood 1986: The Six-Year Itch," *National Journal*, Dec. 7, 1985, p. 2758. See also "Supporting a Greater Federal Role," *National Journal*, Apr. 18, 1987, p. 924; "Opinion Outlook," *National Journal*, Apr. 18, 1987, p. 964; "Federal Budget Deficit," *Gallup Report*, Aug., 1987, pp. 25, 27; "Changeable Weather in a Cooling Climate," *Public Opinion Quarterly* 56 (Fall, 1992): 261–306. See also CBS News/*New York Times* Poll (news release),

Oct. 27, 1987, tables 16, 20. A change in support for increased defense expenditures is documented in Larry M. Bartels, "The American Public's Defense Spending Preferences in the Post–Cold War Era," *Public Opinion Quarterly* 58 (Winter, 1994): 479–508; Lipset, "Beyond 1984," p. 229; Mayer, *The Changing American Mind*, pp. 51, 62, 133. See also "Defense," *Gallup Report*, May, 1987, pp. 2–3; "Opinion Outlook," *National Journal*, June 13, 1987, p. 1550; CBS News/*New York Times* Poll (news release), Oct. 27, 1987, table 15.

37. Reagan's frustration in gaining support for aid to the Contras is cited in Reagan, *An American Life*, pp. 471, 479; Page and Shapiro, *The Rational Public*, p. 276. See also CBS News/*New York Times* Poll (news release), Dec. 1, 1986, table 5; CBS News/*New York Times* Poll (news release), Oct. 27, 1987, table 17; "Americans on Contra Aid: Broad Opposition," *New York Times*, Jan. 31, 1988, sec. 4. The shift in public opinion is cited in Page and Shapiro, *The Rational Public*, pp. 271–81; John E. Reilly, ed., *American Public Opinion and U.S. Foreign Policy, 1987* (Chicago: Chicago Council on Foreign Relations, 1987), chaps. 5 and 6; and Mayer, *The Changing American Mind*, chaps. 4 and 6.

38. For evidence that Americans did not move to the Right, see, for example, John A. Fleishman, "Trends in Self-Identified Ideology from 1972 to 1982: No Support for the Salience Hypothesis," *American Journal of Political Science* 30 (1986): 517–41; Martin P. Wattenberg, "From a Partisan to a Candidate-Centered Electorate," in *The New American Political System*, ed. Anthony King (Washington, D.C.: American Enterprise Institute, 1990), pp. 169–71; Wattenberg, *The Rise of Candidate-Centered Politics*, pp. 95–101. Movement away from conservative views is discussed in Stimson, *Public Opinion in America*, pp. 64, 127. See Mayer, *The Changing American Mind*, p. 127 (quotation).

39. R. W. Apple, "Bush Sure-Footed on Trail of Money," *New York Times*, Sept. 29, 1990, p. 8.

40. Crewe's conclusions are discussed in Ivor Crewe, "Values: The Crusade that Failed," in *The Thatcher Effect: A Decade of Change*, eds. Dennis Kavanagh and Anthony Seldon (Oxford: Oxford University Press, 1989), p. 241. See also Ivor Crewe, "Has the Electorate Become Thatcherite?" in *Thatcherism*, ed. Robert Skidelsky (London: Chatto and Windus, 1988); Ivor Crewe and Donald Searing, "Ideological Change in the British Conservative Party," *American Political Science Review* 82 (June, 1988): 361–84. The lack of increase in Conservative partisanship, vote, or party members is documented in Ivor Crewe and Donald Searing, "Mrs. Thatcher's Crusade: Conservatism in Britain, 1972–1986," in *The Resurgence of Conservatism in Anglo-American Democracies*, eds. B. Cooper, Allan Kornberg, and William Mishler (Durham, N.C.: Duke University Press, 1988). See studies by John Rentoul, *Me and Mine: The Triumph of the New Individualism* (London: Unwin Hyman, 1989), p. 158; and by John Curtice, "Interim Report: Party Politics," in *British Social Attitudes: The 1987 Report*, eds. Roger Jowell, Sharon Witherspoon, and Lindsay Brook (Aldershot Hants: SCPR\Gower, 1986), chap. 8 and pp. 171–82. See also John Curtice, "Political Partisanship," in *British Social Attitudes: The 1986 Report*, eds. Roger Jowell, Sharon Witherspoon, and Lindsay Brook (Aldershot Hants: SCPR\Gower, 1986), chap. 3 and pp. 39–53.

41. Tulis, *The Rhetorical Presidency*, pp. 179–80; and David Zarefsky, *President Johnson's War on Poverty* (University, Ala.: University of Alabama Press, 1986).

42. See, for example, George C. Edwards III, "Frustration and Folly: Bill Clinton

and the Public Presidency," in *The Clinton Presidency: First Appraisals,* eds. Colin Campbell and Bert A. Rockman (Chatham, N.J.: Chatham House, 1995); and Edwards, *At the Margins,* pp. 206–209.

Afterword: The Ways of Rhetoric

1. James W. Ceaser, Glen E. Thurow, Jeffrey Tulis, and Joseph M. Bessette, "The Rise of the Rhetorical Presidency," *Presidential Studies Quarterly* 11 (1981): 158–71.

2. For an overview of rhetoric as a field of study, see Thomas W. Benson, ed., *Speech Communication in the 20th Century* (Carbondale: Southern Illinois University Press, 1985), pp. 3–62; Lloyd F. Bitzer and Edwin Black, eds., *The Prospect of Rhetoric* (Englewood Cliffs, N.J.: Prentice-Hall, 1971). On presidential rhetoric specifically, see Karlyn Kohrs Campbell and Kathleen Hall Jamieson, *Deeds Done in Words: Presidential Rhetoric and the Genres of Governance* (Chicago: University of Chicago Press, 1990); Denise M. Bostdorff, *The Presidency and the Rhetoric of Foreign Crisis* (Columbia: University of South Carolina Press, 1994); Roderick P. Hart, *The Sound of Leadership: Presidential Communication in the Modern Age* (Chicago: University of Chicago Press, 1987); and Halford Ryan, ed., *U.S. Presidents as Orators: A Bio-Critical Sourcebook* (Westport, Conn.: Greenwood Press, 1995).

3. The quoted material is part of a Protagorean fragment known as "Concerning the Gods." See Edward Schiappa, *Protagoras and Logos: A Study in Greek Philosophy and Rhetoric* (Columbia: University of South Carolina Press, 1991), p. 142.

4. See Isocrates, trans. George Norlin, Loeb Classical Library (1928–29); *Cicero De Oratore,* trans. E. W. Sutton and H. Rackham, Loeb Classical Library (1942). For an explanation of rhetoric as an ideal of culture see Thomas W. Benson and Gerard A. Hauser, "Ideals, Superlatives, and the Decline of Hypocrisy," *Quarterly Journal of Speech* 59 (1973): 99–105.

5. For the original formulation of this way of configuring rhetoric, see Thomas W. Benson, "Rhetoric and Autobiography: The Case of Malcolm X," *Quarterly Journal of Speech* 60 (1974): 1–13. Also see Thomas W. Benson, "Rhetoric as a Way of Being," in *American Rhetoric: Context and Criticism,* ed. Thomas W. Benson (Carbondale: Southern Illinois University Press, 1989), pp. 293–322.

6. Contemporary rhetorical theorist Kenneth Burke traces the reflexive nature of language to the "invention" of the negative—the linguistic turn by which humans can articulate what things are not. The dramatistic negative is hortatory—"Thou shalt not"—and becomes the basis for distinguishing good from bad, moral from immoral. Since it is by virtue of the negative that mankind becomes "moralized," Burke holds that "we could not properly say that man 'invented' the negative unless we can also say that man is the 'inventor' of language itself. As far as sheerly empirical development is concerned, it might be more accurate to say that language and the negative 'invented' man." See Kenneth Burke, *Language as Symbolic Action: Essays on Life, Literature, and Method* (Berkeley: University of California Press, 1966), p. 9.

7. Contemporary rhetorical theorist Richard M. Weaver holds that "rhetoric at its truest seeks to perfect men by showing them better versions of themselves, links in that chain extending up toward the ideal, which only the intellect can apprehend and only the soul have affection for." See Richard M. Weaver, *The Ethics of Rhetoric* (Chicago: Henry Regnery Company, 1953), p. 25.

8. Debate over the nature and requirements for a public sphere remains open. For representative examples of positions, see Lloyd F. Bitzer, "Rhetoric and Public

Knowledge," in *Rhetoric, Philosophy, and Literature: An Exploration,* ed. Don M. Burks (West Lafayette: Purdue University Press, 1978), pp. 67–95; Gerard A. Hauser and Carole Blair, "Rhetorical Antecedents to the Public," *Pre/Text* 3 (1982): 139–67; G. Thomas Goodnight, "The Personal, Technical, and Public Spheres of Argument: A Speculative Inquiry into the Art of Public Deliberation," *Journal of the American Forensic Association* 18 (1982): 214–27; and Gerard A. Hauser, "Administrative Rhetoric and Public Opinion: Discussing the Iranian Hostages in the Public Sphere," in *American Rhetoric,* pp. 323–83.

9. For an overview of the different perspectives on and approaches to rhetorical criticism, see Carroll C. Arnold, *Criticism of Oral Rhetoric* (Columbus: Charles E. Merrill, 1974); James R. Andrews, *The Practice of Rhetorical Criticism,* 2nd ed. (New York: Longman, 1990); Bernard L. Brock, Robert L. Scott, and James W. Chesebro, eds., *Methods of Rhetorical Criticism: A Twentieth-Century Perspective* 3rd ed., rev. (Detroit: Wayne State University Press, 1990); Malcolm O. Sillars, *Messages, Meanings, and Culture: Approaches to Communication Criticism* (New York: HarperCollins, 1991); Martin J. Medhurst and Thomas W. Benson, eds., *Rhetorical Dimensions in Media: A Critical Casebook,* 2nd ed. (Dubuque: Kendall/Hunt, 1991); Thomas W. Benson, ed., *Landmark Essays on Rhetorical Criticism* (Davis, Calif.: Hermagoras Press, 1993). On the idea of "audience effectivity" see John Fiske, *Television Culture* (London and New York: Routledge, 1987), pp. 19–20.

10. The idea that rhetorical critics are engaged in an enterprise that is "pre-scientific" and, therefore, problematic is set forth in its classic form in John Waite Bowers, "The Pre-Scientific Function of Rhetorical Criticism," in *Essays on Rhetorical Criticism,* ed. Thomas R. Nilsen (New York: Random House, 1968), pp. 126–45. Bowers, a communication theorist, also misconceived the essential nature of rhetorical inquiry.

11. On the current "rhetorical turn" in the human sciences, see John S. Nelson, Allan Megill, and Donald N. McCloskey, eds., *The Rhetoric of the Human Sciences: Language and Argument in Scholarship and Public Affairs* (Madison: University of Wisconsin Press, 1987); Herbert W. Simons, ed., *Rhetoric in the Human Sciences* (London and Newbury Park: Sage Publishers, 1989); Herbert W. Simons, ed., *The Rhetorical Turn: Invention and Persuasion in the Conduct of Inquiry* (Chicago: University of Chicago Press, 1990); and Francis A. Beer and Robert Hariman, eds., *Post-Realism: The Rhetorical Turn in International Relations* (East Lansing: Michigan State University Press, 1996).

Contributors

THOMAS W. BENSON, the Edwin Erle Sparks professor of rhetoric at Penn State University, is a former editor of *Communication Quarterly* and the *Quarterly Journal of Speech*. Benson is the author or editor of nine books, including *Rhetoric and Political Culture in Nineteenth-Century America*.

EDWIN BLACK, professor emeritus of communication arts at the University of Wisconsin-Madison, has published numerous essays and books in rhetorical criticism. His most recent book is *Rhetorical Questions: Studies of Public Discourse*.

KARLYN KOHRS CAMPBELL, professor and chair of the Department of Speech-Communication at the University of Minnesota, is the author or editor of numerous books, including *Deeds Done in Words: Presidential Rhetoric and the Genres of Governance* and *Man Cannot Speak for Her*.

259

GEORGE C. EDWARDS III, distinguished professor of political science at Texas A&M University and director of the Center for Presidential Studies, holds the Jordan Professorship in liberal arts. Edwards is the author or editor of fifteen books, including *At the Margins: Presidential Leadership of Congress* and *Presidential Approval.*

G. THOMAS GOODNIGHT, professor of communication studies at Northwestern University, has written extensively on the recovery of a contemporary public sphere. His work on presidential public address focuses on foreign policy in the nuclear age.

BRUCE E. GRONBECK, the A. Craig Baird professor of public address at the University of Iowa, is the author or editor of numerous books, including *Media, Consciousness, and Culture* and *Presidential Campaigning and American Self Images.*

RODERICK P. HART, the F. A. Liddell professor of communication, professor of government at the University of Texas at Austin, and former Woodrow Wilson Fellow, is the author of numerous books on presidential communication, including *The Sound Leadership* and *Seducing America: How Television Charms the Modern Voter.*

ROBERT L. IVIE, professor and chair of Speech Communication at Indiana University, has published widely on presidential rhetoric and the rhetoric of war, including *Congress Declares War* and *Cold War Rhetoric: Strategy, Metaphor, and Ideology.*

KATHLEEN E. KENDALL, associate professor of communication at the University of Albany, State University of New York, is the author of *Presidential Campaign Discourse: Strategic Communication Problems.*

MARTIN J. MEDHURST, professor of speech communication and coordinator of the Program in Presidential Rhetoric at Texas A&M University, is the author or editor of seven books, including *Dwight D. Eisenhower: Strategic Communicator* and *Eisenhower's War of Words: Rhetoric and Leadership.*

GLEN E. THUROW, provost and dean of the College, as well as professor of politics at the University of Dallas, is the author of *Abraham Lincoln and American Political Religion* and the co-editor of *Rhetoric and American Statesmanship.*

JEFFREY K. TULIS, associate professor of government at the University of Texas at Austin, is the author of *The Rhetorical Presidency* and coauthor of *The Presidency in the Constitutional Order.*

Index

Atwater, Lee, 6
Austin, J. L., 97

Baathists, 170, 174
Baldrige, Letitia, 186
Baldwin, James, 78, 84, 95, 100
Barber, James David, xv, 28, 29, 81, 117, 161
Barthes, Roland, 188
Baudrillard, Jean, 73
Bay of Pigs, 137
Begin-Sadat peace accord, 34, 46
Bennett, William, 6
Benson, Thomas, xix, xx, xxi, 218, 223
Berlin, Isaiah, 119, 120
Bermudez, Enrique, 143
Bessette, Joseph M., x, 4, 157, 218
Biden, Joe, 138
Big Stick, 126
Bill of Rights, 19
BITNET, 55
Bitzer, Lloyd F., xiii
Black, Charles, 192
Black, Edwin, x, xxii, 222
Boggs, Hale, 99
Boland, Edward P., 131
Boland amendment, 131, 134, 138, 139, 143
Boland resolution. See Boland amendment
Bond, Richard N., 193
Boren, David, 136, 138
Borgmann, Albert, 85
Bork, Robert, 113, 114
Bormann, Ernest, 164
Brezhnev, Leonid, 150
Brezhnev doctrine, 142
Brinkley, David, 39
British Election Surveys, 214
British Labor Party, 189
Broder, David, 187
Brodie, Fawn M., 117, 118
Broomfield, William, 147
Brown, Edmund G. (Jerry), 185
Buchanan, Patrick, 193
bully pulpit, 10, 159, 212
Burke, Kenneth, xv, 97, 177
Burton, John L., 130, 133
Bush, Barbara Pierce, 180, 186, 191
Bush, George H. W., xxii, 5–7, 9, 28, 36, 40, 45, 150, 154–57, 162, 167, 169–73,
175, 177, 186, 192, 204, 221; inaugural address of, 25; State of the Union address of, 6

Cambodia, 108, 137
Campbell, David, 167, 168
Campbell, Karlyn Kohrs, xvii, xxii, 161, 162, 207, 222, 223
Capra, Frank, 34
Caroli, Betty Boyd, 190, 195
carrot-and-the-stick, 142, 143, 147
Carter, James Earl (Jimmy), 24–28, 40, 42, 48, 126–28, 180, 206, 207, 210
Carter, Rosalynn Smith, 180, 183, 187, 190
Cartice, John, 214
Carville, James, 36
cause-and-effect relationship, xvi
CBS, 34, 185, 192
Ceaser, James W., x, 4, 157, 158, 161, 218
Central Intelligence Agency (CIA), 128, 135
Challenger, 34
Chamberlain, Neville, 133
character, presidential, xv, xix, 15–18, 22, 24, 26, 44, 192. See also rhetoric; ethos
Chiang Kai-Shek, Madame, 193
Churchill, Sir Winston, 32, 133, 154, 155
Cicero, Marcus Tullius, 219, 222
civic space. See public sphere
civic virtue, 101, 114, 120
civil rights, 77–82, 84, 86, 90, 93, 96–102, 183, 206, 207
Civil Rights Act of 1963, 79
Clark, Joe (Canadian prime minister), 195
Clark, Kenneth, 79
Clausewitz, Carl Von, 153
Clinton, Bill, xxii, 5–10, 34, 36, 37, 39, 40, 42–45, 47, 50, 51, 55, 56, 62, 67, 68, 71, 74, 180, 183, 185, 192–95; inaugural address of, 28; State of the Union address of, 12
Clinton, Chelsea, 45
Clinton, Hilary Rodham, xxii, 180, 185–87, 189, 191–95, 223
CNN, 46, 185
Cold War, 126, 129, 132, 146, 149, 151, 154, 156, 157, 162, 167–69, 172, 175, 176, 178
collaborative communities, 55
Commission on Mental Health, 187

performance, XVI, 4, 32, 44, 97, 112, 156, 180

Perón, Eva (Evita), 192

Perot, Margot Birmingham, 180

Persian Gulf, 36, 38, 43, 44, 45, 153–55, 162, 174, 175, 177, 203, 220, 221; and rhetorical republic, 166, 167–69, 171, 172

Personality and Politics (Greenstein), xv

Pierce, Jane Appleton, 183

Plato, 41, 78

Plow That Broke the Plains, The (Lorenz), 34

policy agenda, 11

polis, xx, 40, 96

political broadcasting, 30

political distance, 39

political drama, 33

Political Science Quarterly, 226

Politics (Aristotle), x

politics, American, 31, 35, 37

politics of illusion, 153, 154

Polk, James, 188, 190

Polk, Sarah Childress, 183, 190

Pollock, Mark, 169, 170

poll tax, 80

popular leadership, x, XIX, 5–7, 8, 23, 159, 162

Populist Party, 194

Postmodern Culture, 57

postmodern dislocation, 73

postmodernism, 46

postmodern mélange, 99

presidency, XI, 23, 66, 159, 162, 166; as constitutional office, 6; as hybrid, 5; as institution, 49, 106, 158, 179, 180, 208; as rhetorical office, 61; roles of, XIX, 7, 12, 24, 28, 29, 52, 68, 164, 175, 188, 210

Presidential Character, The (Barber), xv, 28, 29

presidential election, 16, 18

presidential leadership, 5, 10, 11, 31, 51, 203

presidential responsibility, 11

presidential rhetoric, IX, X, XII, XVII, XVIII, XXI–XXIII, 17, 18, 22, 29, 41, 42, 49, 51, 59, 62, 72, 161, 165, 199, 202, 206, 207, 208, 210, 214–17; and farewell address, 166; and fireside chat, 61; and Saturday morning radio address, 52, 60; and

State of the Union address, 12; and television address, 52; and veto messages, 11; and war rhetoric, 154, 169

principled rhetoric, 6

principles of the Union, 20

private sphere, 27, 28, 108, 182

Prodigy, 54, 71

Profiles in Courage, 120

Protagoras, 218

public action, 38

public memory, 69, 124, 125, 132, 135, 145, 146, 149, 152, 221, 222

public opinion, 32–36, 206, 213–14

public opinion polling, XVI, XXIII, 36, 40, 42, 107, 129, 185, 186, 208, 214–16

Public Papers of the President, 45, 57

public sentiment, 23

public sphere, XXI, 27, 28, 35, 43, 44, 57, 54, 61, 70, 73, 108, 158, 181, 182, 223, 224

Publius, 16

quadrivium, 225

Quakerism, 109

qualitative research, 217

quantitative research, 217

Quarterly Journal of Speech, 226

Quassim, Abdul Karim, 170, 174

Quayle, Dan, 44, 193

Quayle, Marilyn Tucker, 186

Quindlen, Anna, 189, 194

Randolph, Mary, 191

Rasmussen, Karen, 168, 169

Rauh, Joseph, 79

Rawls, John, 78

Rayburn, Sam, 101

Reagan, Nancy Davis, 180, 183, 186, 187, 193

Reagan, Ronald, XXII, 4–7, 34, 40, 42, 45, 101, 113, 129, 131–33, 135, 138, 140–42, 148–52, 154, 156, 160, 161, 170, 186, 202, 206, 209–14; and Caribbean Basin speech, 128; first inaugural address of, 24; State of the Union address (1985) of, 141

Reagan doctrine, 141–44

Reagan Revolution, 210, 211

Stalin, Josef, 150
Stalinist, 69
Star Wars. *See* Strategic Defense Initiative
Steenburgen, Mary, 193
Stelzner, Hermann G., 107
Stennis, John, 130
Stevenson, Adlai, 33, 205
Stimson, Henry, 212
Stockdale, Sybil Bailey, 180
Strategic Defense Initiative (Star Wars), 4, 202
Student Nonviolent Coordinating Committee, 95
style, forms of, xv, 87, 89–91, 93, 96, 110, 141, 152, 160, 162, 163, 165, 177, 220
subject positioning, 38
Supreme Court, 13
symbolic action, xx, xxii
symbolic interaction, 163

Tannen, Deborah, 189
Tate, Sheila, 186, 187
Tauzin, W. J. 142
Taylor, Robert, 88
technological changes, 13, 51
Tennessee Valley Authority, 34
textual meaning, 60
Thatcher, Margaret, 214
Thomason, Harry, 34
Thomason, Linda Bloodworth, 34
Thucydides, 125
Thurow, Glen E., x, xi, xix, xx, xxi, 4, 157, 218, 220
Time magazine, 64, 79, 84
Tolstoy, Leo, 119
Toner, Robin, 193
topoi, 225
Tower, John, 138
Tower Commission, 148, 149
town hall, 67
Townsend, Francis, 32
tragic fear, 172, 173, 175–78
Trible, Paul S., 149
trivium, 225
Truman, Bess Wallace, 183
Truman, Harry S., 33, 48
Truman Doctrine, 32, 172, 176
Tulis, Jeffrey K., x, xviii, xx, xxi, 30, 31,

66, 67, 157–59, 161, 162, 166, 215, 218, 220; and *Rhetorical Presidency, The,* xi, 3, 13, 202, 203
Tyler, Julia Gardiner, 183

Union Party, 32
United Nations Human Rights Commission, 170
United States Constitution, xi, xviii, xix, 5, 6, 9–13, 16, 18–21, 23, 29, 123, 124, 157, 158, 187, 220
United States Department of Defense (DOD), 54
Univac, 33
USA Today, 131, 186
USENET, 54, 71, 72
US News and World Report, 186

Vandenberg, Arthur H., 32
Vietnam, 34, 83, 107, 108, 122–32, 134–41, 143–46, 150, 151, 155, 204
Vietnam analogy, 130, 139, 141, 142, 145, 146, 150, 151, 221
Vietnam syndrome, 127, 169
virtue, xix, xxi, 17–25, 27–29, 121, 156, 220
Vogue, 195
Voice of America, 137

Walker, Robert, 64, 65
Wallace, George, 78, 89, 92, 94
Wallin, Jeffrey, xi
War on Poverty, 4, 162, 201, 202
Washington, Fanny Bassett (niece), 182
Washington, George xix, 12, 18–23, 25–28, 147
Washington, Martha Dandridge, 182
Washington Post, 36
Watergate, 34, 42, 108, 112, 115, 149, 209
Wattenberg, Daniel, 192, 193
Weaver, Richard, xv
web page, 57, 58
Weekly Compilation of Presidential Documents, 57
Weidenfeld, Sheila Rabb, 187
White, Theodore, 80, 127
White House Coordinating Council on Women, 184

White House Office of Public Liaison, 184

White House Speaks, The (Smith and Smith), 206

White Man's Burden, 126

Why We Fight (Capra), 34

Wicker, Tom, 168

Wilkins, Roy, 79

Wilson, Ellen Axson, 183

Wilson, Pete, 146

Wilson, Woodrow, 4, 11, 17, 22–24, 27, 61, 66, 108, 158–60, 162, 202

Windt, Theodore, 205

Wirthlin, Richard, 42

Wohl, Richard, 35

women's rights movement, 190

World Court, 135, 148

World Wide Web, 57, 58, 62, 63

Wright, Jim, 150

Zarefsky, David, 163–66, 201, 215